Nick Duffell has curated a series of interlocking works that, together, form a devastating indictment of the enormous harm that boarding schools have inflicted, for far too long, on far too many.

Charles Spencer, 9th Earl Spencer, historian
and author of *A Very Private School*

A first-class anthology that digs deep into the psychological harm done by boarding schools. For the first time, there is a serious attempt to identify and understand the abuse suffered by girls who fall prey to older boys at co-educational boarding schools where staff are incapable of protecting them.

Robert Verkaik, author of *Posh Boys: How English*
Public Schools Ruin Britain

A timely and useful summary of therapeutic approaches, with original contributions of particular interest and importance about women ex-boarders and co-educational boarding.

Richard Beard, author of *Sad Little Men*

An important additional enquiry that broadens out from Nick Duffell's pioneering work on identifying the psycho-social fall-out from boarding. It explores the widespread harm resulting from this pernicious way of raising children, and describes a range of treatment approaches for this difficult client group. All clinicians who want to be up to date must read this.

Professor Andrew Samuels, former chair of UKCP,
author of *A New Therapy for Politics*

This book is a welcome contribution to the growing literature on the boarding school experience. Offering a range of essays by different authors, it highlights the relatively neglected topic of the female experience of boarding school as well as issues that arise for female psychotherapists who are themselves ex-boarders. Using vivid examples from clinical practice, we are reminded of the complex impact of ruptured attachment relationships on adult emotional life.

Sue Gerhardt, author of *Why Love Matters*

Nick Duffell's work has illuminated my life ever since I first started to address the traumas that arose from my 'privileged' schooling. He has helped me immeasurably, and that has helped me to help others. His latest book brings together a fascinating range of thinkers and practitioners in the field of boarding school and associated syndromes – a force to ensure that children in institutions, state and private, are understood and protected better than we were. Let's listen to them.

Alex Renton, writer and broadcaster, author of *Stiff Upper Lip*

To what extent has Britain's class system been dependent on traumatising children? This is the wonderfully uncomfortable question that opens Duffell's newest book on 'boarding school survivors'. Although aimed at therapists helping those grown-up children to recover, the book's core concerns are relevant to all of us. If modern life is governed by the ruthless economics of neoliberalism, then guess where the global elite are choosing to send their children for education? Duffell and colleagues ask us to pay attention to distress. We should listen.

Dr Suzanne Zeedyk, developmental psychologist, University of Dundee

Duffell presents a brand new collection of essays by experienced therapists working with adults who were, as children, sent to boarding school. The lasting impact of the traumatic losses are vividly conveyed by practitioners from diverse counselling and psychotherapy modalities, many of them boarding school survivors themselves. The deeply moving and rich collection of narratives will inform and inspire. A timely addition to the literature, this book will be a vital resource for therapists and ex-boarders alike.

Professor Joy Schaverien, PhD, Jungian psychoanalyst and author of *Boarding School Syndrome: The Psychological Trauma of the 'Privileged' Child*

A bold and pioneering contribution to human psychology.

Professor Brett Kahr, senior fellow at the Tavistock Institute of Medical Psychology; author of 20 books, including *Forensic Psychoanalysis: From Sub-Clinical Psychopaths to Serial Killers*

With extensive knowledge of the challenges faced by those who experienced this unique form of trauma, psychotherapist Nick Duffell has curated a comprehensive selection of clinically focused chapters. Each of these is written by an author with understanding of the complexities of healing from abuse and neglect masked as privilege. This book needs to be read by anyone supporting boarding school survivors on their journey to recovery.

Dr Naomi Murphy, consultant clinical & forensic psychologist, honorary professor of psychology, Nottingham Trent University

The Un-Making of Them

Ex-boarders can be among the most challenging clients for therapists, with many clinicians struggling to address their unique needs. This book presents a ground-breaking collection of chapters sharing insights and reflections on clinical work with ex-boarders in different settings and circumstances with the aim of expanding the body of knowledge for therapeutic work with such clients.

The contributors reveal that the fall-out from boarding is much wider than pre-viously thought and also report on innovative treatment methods that may help therapists address these consequences with ex-boarders in treatment.

Featuring the experience and insights of some 16 different clinicians, many of whom are ex-boarders themselves, this new collection offers contributions from a wide range of theoretical backgrounds, including psychodynamic, Jungian, trans-actional analysis and 'energy psychology'. It tells how the understanding of the 'boarding school syndrome' has been enlarged by recent advances in attachment therapy, trauma studies, neuroscience, including pastoral, and safeguarding aware-ness within education. Topics covered include the effects of boarding on girls, on both intimate and sibling relationships, on military family boarders and on ex-boarder therapists, as well as how both careful, patient attention and dynamic EMDR may be used to alleviate boarding school trauma.

The reader will gain a wider understanding about how individuals and society are impacted by this way of raising children and what evidence-based pathways to recovery are being evolved.

This book is written in an accessible jargon-free style and will appeal to psycho-therapists, psychologists, psychoanalysts and counsellors, as well as ex-boarders and parents interested in the impact of boarding schools from a professional or personal perspective.

Nick Duffell, MA, Dip Psych IP, was trained in Systemic Family Therapy and Psychosynthesis before pursuing extensive studies in psychoanalysis and post-Jungian theory and training in developmental somatic therapy. He pioneered the understanding of boarding school syndrome and his work has been featured on TV and radio since the early 1990s. A psycho-historian and trainer, he is the author of several books on boarding as well as on couple-relations and political psychology.

The Un-Making of Them

Clinical Reflections on Boarding
School Syndrome

Edited by Nick Duffell

R Routledge
Taylor & Francis Group

LONDON AND NEW YORK

Designed cover image: Getty Images

First published 2025
by Routledge
4 Park Square, Milton Park, Abingdon, Oxon OX14 4RN

and by Routledge
605 Third Avenue, New York, NY 10158

Routledge is an imprint of the Taylor & Francis Group, an informa business

British Library Cataloguing-in-Publication Data
A catalogue record for this book is available from the British Library

ISBN: 9781032848969 (hbk)
ISBN: 9781032848945 (pbk)
ISBN: 9781003515517 (ebk)

DOI: 10.4324/9781003515517

Typeset in Times New Roman
by Newgen Publishing UK

Contents

Acknowledgements

I would like to thank all staff and students involved in the 'The Un-Making of Them' postgraduate training programme, where the impetus for this book was born. On the final module of one these training sessions, many questions about the wider impact of boarding were asked. My response was to say: Why not look to your own clinical experience, do some research and write a paper? The idea for a collection of chapters then arose and this book began to take shape, primarily driven by the contributors' choice of topics.

Further thanks are due to Tracy Carter and John Andrew Miller for reading parts of the manuscript, to Grace McDonnell and Manon Berset of Routledge for their caring guidance on the project and to Susan Leaper of Florence Production for timely and skilful editing, and to Tracey Warr for the index.

I would also like to thank HEPI News, Private Education Policy Forum, Springer Nature, Colin Luke and Mosaic Pictures, the *Journal of Child & Adolescent Trauma*, Professor Bob Johnson and Honey Bee TV for permission to use quotations in Chapter 1; also Taylor and Francis (Books) Ltd, UK, for the use of quotations in Chapter 2, Andrew Waddington for kind permission to reproduce his engraving and thanks to Gus Cwik for the quotations in Chapter 9; thanks again to Professor Bob Johnson and Honey Bee TV for the use of quotations in Chapter 14. The helpful cooperation and speedy response from all these copyright owners has been much appreciated.

Contributors

Editor

Nick Duffell is a psychotherapist, trainer, author and psycho-historian who pioneered the psychological understanding of boarding, beginning with the 'Boarding School Survivors' workshops, which continue to be popular today. Since 1990, his work has been featured on film, TV and radio. Prior to editing this volume, his books on boarding are: *The Making of Them: The British Attitude to Children and the Boarding School System* (2000), *Wounded Leaders: British Elitism and the Entitlement Illusion – A Psychohistory* (2014), and, with Thurstine Basset, *Trauma, Abandonment and Privilege* (2016). As a child he attended European and English boarding schools and as a young man taught in one in India. Today, he provides specialist training to therapists working with former boarders and couples.

Contributors

Eric Blencowe is a counsellor who has been working in private practice with ex-boarders for a number of years. His practice includes clients from military backgrounds who were sent to boarding school from an early age. An ex-boarder himself, he has extensive clinical experience of the unique challenges that such clients face and has attended several workshops and specialist training in working with ex-boarders, including 'The Unmaking of Them' in 2023.

Elizabeth Carter is an integrative psychotherapist in private practice, working with adults and children in West Sussex. She previously worked in education, having trained in Montessori pedagogy, focusing on child development and psychology and specialising in supporting young people with special educational needs, including within boarding schools. As a child, she boarded from the ages of 8 to 18 years. She completed 'The Un-Making of Them' training in 2023, while working with and supporting individuals who have experienced the psychological impact of boarding school. She continues to develop her understanding of mental health in young people and graduated from Stanford University in working with addiction.

Stephanie Collins previously worked with adults and children in the charity sector, prisons and the NHS. She studied at University College London, London South Bank and Portsmouth universities. She qualified as an HCPC registered forensic psychologist in 2012 and is author of a published article on therapists' experiences facilitating sex-offender treatment programmes. Born in Malaysia to expatriate parents, she attended an all-girls boarding school in England from the ages of 9 to 18 years during the 1970s and 1980s. She completed 'The Un-Making of Them' training in working with ex-boarders in 2023. She works as a trauma-informed therapist in private practice, including working with ex-boarders.

Susannah Cornish previously worked as a litigation solicitor in the City of London for over 20 years. She is now a BACP accredited, UKCP registered integrative psychotherapist and an EMDR Europe accredited practitioner. An ex-boarder herself, she completed 'The Un-Making of Them' training in 2023. In her London practice she works with individuals and also uses Eye Movement Desensitisation and Reprocessing (EMDR) for trauma. She finds this a useful tool for dealing with abandonment issues and historical bullying. Issues around the emotional repercussions of dyslexia, both diagnosed and undiagnosed, are a particular interest.

Pippa Foster has worked exclusively in private practice since 1990 and for several years facilitated 'Boarding School Survivors' workshops for women. As a child, she travelled from India to her boarding school in England. She graduated in psychology from Durham University before training in clinical psychology and later in adult psychotherapy at the Tavistock Clinic, London. She ran a psychology department in a psychiatric unit before returning to the Tavistock teaching staff. She has worked as a consultant advisor to industry, GP surgeries and the Church, and has trained senior managers in twelve different countries. She is a mother and a grandmother and lives with her husband in Sussex, enjoying walking, gardening and sculpting.

Dawn Grundy is a person-centred psychotherapist who works with adults in private practice in Cheshire. At the age of 11, she boarded in an all-girls convent school, before joining an all-boys boarding school in the sixth form. It was there that she noticed pertinent similarities and differences between the genders in their boarding experiences, which fuelled her curiosity to study the impact of boarding school on adulthood. This interest led to specialist training in working with ex-boarders, and she completed 'The Un-Making of Them' training in 2023.

Professor Brett Kahr is senior fellow at the Tavistock Institute of Medical Psychology in London, as well as visiting professor of psychoanalysis and mental health at Regent's University, London, He also serves as honorary director of research and as honorary fellow at the Freud Museum, London. Additionally, he is chair of the Scholars Committee of the British Psychoanalytic Council and consultant psychotherapist at The Balint Consultancy. Kahr is the author of 20 books including, most recently, *Forensic Psychoanalysis: From Sub-Clinical Psychopaths to Serial Killers*. He practises full-time in Central London, working with individuals and with couples and families.

Dr Rosemary Lodge is a counselling psychologist working in private practice and an academic. She has a particular interest in existential approaches to teaching and practice. She was not herself a boarder, but her partner was a boarder from a military family. In 2023 she completed 'The Unmaking of Them' training to support her clinical work with ex-boarders.

Karen Macmillan is a transactional analysis counsellor working in private practice, after a first career as a chartered accountant. She spent her early childhood in Malaysia and attended an all-girls boarding school in England from the age of 11 years. She completed 'The Un-Making of Them' training in working with ex-boarders in 2018 and specialises in working with ex-boarders in Hove and online.

Sally McLaren is a Jungian analyst and psychoanalytic psychotherapist, registered with the International Association for Analytical Psychology (IAAP) and with the British Psychoanalytic Council (BPC). She has 30 years' clinical experience and works in private practice in Sussex. Her paper, 'Birds, Beasts and Babies – Notes from an Infant Observation', won the Rozsika Parker Essay Prize and was published in the *British Journal of Psychotherapy* in 2014. Her interest in the long-term emotional and psychological impact of boarding school began when a male patient presented a photograph of himself on his first day at school, aged 7 years. Not an ex-boarder herself, she completed 'The Un-Making of Them' training in 2023.

John Andrew Miller, PhD, has a long career in innovative teaching, interdisciplinary learning, and an in-depth knowledge of different approaches to psychotherapy. He created and directed the first UK Master's degree course in psychotherapy, has organised numerous training courses and conferences and has served as an external moderator for several training institutions and as a trustee for one of them. This background has allowed him, although a non-boarder, to work with Nick Duffell as both supervisor and academic consultant on the specialist training programme since its beginning. After more than 45 years as a body-oriented and attachment-based psychotherapist, he is now retired from clinical practice but continues to provide supervision on boarding school issues.

Nicola Miller was born into a military family with generations of early separation including boarding and had a childhood of many moves. She apparently adapted 'well' to boarding school, but her adult life has been spent unravelling these adaptations in order to feel more joyfully alive and visible. She has practised as a body-psychotherapist over 30 years and facilitated the 'Boarding School Survivors' workshops for women with Pippa Foster and then Ruth Tudor. From 2016 to 2021 she taught on the 'Un-Making of Them' training courses.

Dr Virginia Sherborne initially trained as a chartered accountant in the City of London, before spending 30 years teaching classics in UK independent schools, including an elite girls' boarding school. In 2010 she qualified as a counsellor, completing an MA in Trauma Studies in 2017 and, in 2022, a PhD for research on the psychological effects of mesothelioma, a terminal asbestos-related cancer. Although not an ex-boarder, she completed 'The Un-Making of Them' training in working with ex-boarders in 2016 and is now a counsellor in private practice in Sheffield. specialising in trauma, bereavement and parenting.

Ruth Tudor grew up on a farm in Eryri, Snowdonia, with Welsh as her first language. At the age of 11 years she was sent away to boarding school. Although outwardly successful as an adult, she needed to engage in a long process of recovering her birthright to live her full expression as a woman and to re-inhabit her sexuality as a vulnerable, lively, connected being. She has facilitated the 'Boarding School Survivors' workshops and taught on the 'The Un-Making of Them' training.

Amelia White is a BACP accredited therapist and tutor who has worked for many charities and organisations, including the NHS and Brighton University. She attended a co-educational boarding school herself in Sussex from the ages of 11 to 16. After acknowledging the impact that her own experience had on her development as a child – and subsequent behaviour as an adult – she went on to attend a specialist psychotherapy training with ex-boarders, completing 'The Un-Making of Them' training in 2017. From her Brighton practice, she offers individual therapy, courses and workshops for ex-boarders and therapists.

Foreword
Professor Brett Kahr

When I first entered the field of psychology, back in the late 1970s and early 1980s, virtually no one spoke at all about child abuse. From a contemporary twenty-first-century perspective, when all forms of child abuse have at last become much studied and, indeed, truly illegalised, it might seem rather shocking that back then people had not examined abuse more seriously. But nearly half a century ago, few people – even mental health professionals – rarely ever considered the consequences of cruelty towards youngsters with sufficient concern.

Professor Sigmund Freud had, of course, underscored the potentially devastating role of early infantile and childhood traumata on the development of the human personality, but apart from fellow Freudian psychoanalysts, very few members of the psychiatric profession had studied the impact of sexual assault, physical abuse or, indeed, abandonment. Fortunately, as the 1940s and 1950s unfolded, a small number of noted British clinicians – in particular the eminent child psychiatrist and psychoanalyst Dr John Bowlby – began to examine the impact of parental separation and loss upon youngsters in a truly groundbreaking manner. But even so, virtually no one had investigated the consequences of sending children away to boarding schools.

Some of the most esteemed psychiatrists and psychoanalysts, such as Bowlby and, also, Dr Donald Winnicott, had in fact spent years at boarding school during childhood, then considered quite normal for individuals from even moderately privileged backgrounds. Bowlby's father, a distinguished physician, and Winnicott's father, a long-standing Mayor of Plymouth, would eventually receive knighthoods. Indeed, back in the 'good old days', people would have regarded the failure of such royally sponsored men to send their children to such schools as inconceivable.

Many would have felt shamed and embarrassed at *not* having attended an elite boarding school. Unsurprisingly, most British leaders left their homes for years at a time to study at such institutions during childhood. Robert Walpole, our very first prime minister, attended Eton College; Winston Churchill became a pupil at Harrow School; and, in more recent years, Tony Blair, David Cameron, Boris Johnson and Rishi Sunak had all studied at prestigious boarding school institutions.

Many years ago, I facilitated a psychotherapy session with a male patient who burst into tears, confessing that, although he had grown up in a wealthy family home with lots of money in the bank, he had failed to obtain a place at Eton and felt extremely ashamed to have attended Harrow instead. During a discussion with this patient about why he felt so devastated, despite having become a student at the famous old school of Sir Winston Churchill, he confessed:

> Well, Harrow was only founded in 1572, and it is not nearly as old or as pioneering as Eton, which, I believe, first accepted students back in 1440.

Nowadays, the world has begun to question the elitism of such ancient institutions, while still respecting the skills and capacities of the members of staff. But whatever one's views about expensive, fifteenth-century or sixteenth-century educational establishments, we must consider not only the academic expertise but also the psychological consequences of spending so much time away from one's family. These schools unquestionably offer their pupils tremendous advantages, but few ever dared to question the emotional impact upon the attachment style of the attendees, all of whom will have endured lengthy separations from their mothers, fathers, brothers and sisters.

Over the years, I have worked psychotherapeutically with many adult male patients who had boarded in childhood. I can report that a large majority of those men struggled to maintain loyal marriages and would often engage in extra-marital affairs, more frequently than those who lived consistently in their homes, unaffected by significant separations. But boarding schools cannot simply be dismissed as destructive institutions. I have also encountered many patients – mostly males – who grew up in horrifically abusive parental homes, and who ultimately experienced comfort, relief and safety at their boarding schools. Many of those same individuals unquestionably suffered from parental and familial separations, nonetheless. As mental health practitioners, we must hold in mind the potential consequences of such early broken attachments.

As a young psychologist, I worked intensively with patients who suffered from quite severe forms of schizophrenia, and I discovered that many of them had experienced grotesque forms of sexual abuse and other traumata. Few of my colleagues at that time considered trauma as a potential aetiological factor in the development of schizophrenic psychoses. Thus, as an initiative to expand our understanding of childhood abuse, in 1990, I launched a three-year series of monthly lectures in Hampstead, London, entitled 'Aspects of Child Abuse: Psycho-Analytical and Historical Perspectives'.

At that time, a colleague of mine introduced me to Nick Duffell – then a newcomer to the profession – who had already begun to examine the psychological impact of sending young children to boarding schools. I remain very grateful that Duffell accepted my invitation to deliver a talk in the new lecture series. I can still recall the impressive presentation that he offered to our audience, having shared his original approach to the previously unquestioned British concept of public school education. It pleases me that, over the last 30 years and more, he has persevered with his careful examination of the 'boarding school syndrome' and has lectured about and written about this topic widely, so much so that many other colleagues have studied his contributions carefully and have begun to examine the consequences of such early separations.

Happily, Duffell has now compiled this wonderful, edited book, in which he has offered insights and wisdom not only from his personal research but, also, from the discoveries of no fewer than 13 additional colleagues. Each of these authors has blessed us with a rich chapter, exploring not only the impact of boarding schools upon *boys* but also upon *girls*, across the lifecycle. In his conclusion, Duffell remarks with great clarity and boldness:

I suggest that we, as a nation, have to embrace recovery from boarding.

No doubt many graduates of notable boarding schools may disagree with his assessment, and some may well champion the rich, educational benefits of attending such long-standing, esteemed institutions. But, in view of the new clinical research that has emerged through the groundbreaking work of Duffell and his colleagues, we now have the opportunity to reconsider the impact of raising our babies at home and then discharging them to faraway educational institutions at a young age without sufficient attention to how this might affect psychological intimacy and emotional safety in the years to come.

This new book on the boarding school syndrome deserves our deepest attention. I regard it as a bold and pioneering contribution to human psychology. I remain grateful to have first encountered Duffell's work back in the early 1990s, and I look forward to further investigations into this vital subject of modern mental health.

About this Book

Within the covers of this book the reader will find a collection of essays by working psychotherapists from different theoretical orientations who, for the first time, describe their work with adult ex-boarders – and sometimes their partners and therapists – elucidating the nature and effect of 'boarding school syndrome'.

Such a book could not have existed 35 years ago. It breaks new ground, partly because it highlights girls' experience of boarding as well as boys', but primarily because it bears witness to a clinical understanding that is relatively recent. In fact, when I began researching the psychology of boarding in the late 1980s I could not fathom why the subject seemed of no interest to the therapy profession. I imagined, perhaps because I was a beginner at psychotherapy, that it was not a suitable subject for enquiry or that perhaps I was still taking my own schooling way too seriously.

But it bothered me that there was absolutely nothing at all about boarding in the psychological literature. All I could find was a book of extraordinary anonymous interviews with children at boarding schools in the mid-1960s written by a sociologist.[1] It had resulted in multiple disclosures of sexual abuse by teaching staff, but in order, apparently, not to compromise the science and to respect confidentiality, no action was taken. This is still shocking, but only since the Jimmy Savile affair have the British public begun to think seriously about child abuse. Getting to grips with the normalised neglect that makes boarding children so vulnerable and liable to abuse is a further challenge still.

Nevertheless, both the intellectual climate as well as attitudes to child protection are finally changing, and there is now a growing body of literature about the psychology of boarding. So, I am really delighted to introduce this new book about psychotherapy with ex-boarders and observations on the sent-away children that they were. It is extremely gratifying that these clinicians have put together such a diverse and creative volume.

Some readers may find what they encounter within these pages shocking, and some of the stories are clearly heartbreaking. Some readers may want to point out that the intense hothousing of children cannot but confer a competitive advantage in the world of work to the adults that these children become; some will want to note how useful it may be to have a respite from a difficult family situation. These views have their merit, but the clinical perspective offered in these pages provides a different focus.

Young children sent away early from home must accomplish a creative but costly mental manoeuvre in order to manage being on their own at boarding school without parental guidance or protection. Fear, loneliness, vulnerability, shame and loss all get detached from a sense of social privilege and sometimes entitlement. The children are unaware of having made this split, and later in life it may come back to haunt them. These chapters show how bewildering getting through boarding can be and in how many different areas of their lives adult ex-boarders are affected.

A further groundbreaking aspect of this book is the focus on the clinical reflections of practitioners with considerable experience of a specific client group, rather than a case made through classic interview-based research. The former approach is often classed as 'anecdotal', while the latter tends to be thought of as rigorous science. Psychotherapists may consider such a classification unfair, given the time and energy they put into their work. Besides, my time as an honorary research assistant at University College London taught me that, in understanding the backdrop to psychological research at universities, the old adage 'follow the money' is useful, because it all requires funding. In psychotherapy, the client funds the enquiry.

I doubt whether qualitative research can ever be purely objective. Besides, boarding school syndrome is notoriously difficult to research since, typically, it begins perhaps around the age of 8 years and does not surface till perhaps around the mid-30s or later. Additionally, as investigative journalist Robert Verkaik revealed, boarding has a powerful financial lobby behind it.[2] And, as the emerging psychology behind boarding school syndrome starts to become more recognised, there will inevitably be some push-back: we have seen some interview-based research concluding that negative aspects of boarding can be mitigated by better parenting.[3] This directly contradicts the experience of those seeing boarding through an attachment therapy lens, since ruptured attachments are the main feature of boarding.

Introducing the chapters

The choices of topic in this book came entirely from the contributors themselves rather than from the editor; so, the attention on the female experience in several of the chapters is important. Generally, when boarding comes up most people usually think about boys, and girls' experiences of boarding draws less attention in media coverage. These new clinical reflections are, I believe, invaluable, and I now have the pleasure of introducing them to the reader.

Following my opening, introductory essay, Chapter 2 starts with Stephanie Collins' survey of the boarding scene in Britain and her endeavour to look beyond a one-size-fits-all approach to boarding. Working alongside her colleague Bella Cranmore, Collins has constructed what she calls a 'clinical framework for nuanced narratives in therapy with ex-boarders'. Collins' grid is a useful tool that practitioners might employ to rank additional factors in a client's boarding school experience; it will be especially helpful to therapists new to the topic to prevent them making assumptions about all ex-boarders. Collins shows how ethnicity, gender and whether the children attended schools funded by local authorities or the military complicate the public's generalised picture of boarding being an elitist phenomenon.

Such a nuanced framework – so not all are tarred with one brush – is becoming increasingly necessary as more professionals begin to recognise boarding as a real problem. I recently heard of a person seeking therapy through an agency being referred to a worker who was known to have studied boarding psychology. The client, however, was extremely displeased at being classified as a 'boarding school survivor' because that was a label she had yet to identify with.

Chapter 3 goes deeply into one of the extra-difficult aspects of boarding, as Pippa Foster reflects on her work with adults who were boarders from an expatriate background. Foster names these 'children in exile'. Drawing on several case studies, she shows how these children had to leave their real homes in far-flung places only to make long journeys (often unaccompanied) to a place called 'home' in a cold country they have never known. Her clients, displaced as children due to their parents' jobs in military, colonial or corporate service, tell heartbreaking stories. It was as if the parental bond and need for home were not even considered in most cases. Foster's patient and empathic attention pays off and demonstrates how ex-boarders who have suffered such trauma may make a new start by becoming at home in themselves, once they have been fully witnessed and heard.

Both Collins' and Foster's work finds a further echo later on, in Chapter 11, where Eric Blencowe and Rosemary Lodge consider whether boarders from military families are ever able to come home again. Boarding for these children does not involve the typical high social privilege; however, their sense of homelessness can reach epic proportions, since their parents' posting means there never is a familiar family home to return to. Blencowe and Lodge share some of the subtleties of treating such clients: for example, military ex-boarders have a particular need to be noticed, rewarded or acknowledged for normal activities around the home. The therapist's presence is crucial in such work by providing, perhaps for the first time, a secure attachment relationship; now these ex-boarders may be able to find a new sense of home within themselves – one that involves a full connection with and articulation of their own inner experience.

The focus on the female experience begins in Chapter 4, 'Beyond the Glass', in which Nicola Miller and Ruth Tudor share their experience of running Boarding School Survivors workshops for women. For me, this is an important document because it is the first written feedback from these therapeutic groups for women, which first ran in 1994, a few years after the men's workshops had started. At that time, practitioners were only at the beginning of trying to understand how a public school experience impacted on girls, brought up in schools historically designed for boys from a blend of military and monastic influences. Miller and Tudor delicately tease out some of the ineffable ways girls are affected by being raised in institutions that are not conducive for mirroring the emerging womanhood that these girls are trying to embody. Through the facilitators' careful listening approach, many subtleties of the women's stories about their lives at school and subsequently as uncertain adult women are illuminated.

Miller and Tudor's reflections give implicit weight to the post-Jungian idea that self-formation frequently takes distinct paths for boys and girls: the former principally building their egos by their 'doing' and the latter by means of their 'being'. The difficulties of meeting the girls' specific but unvoiced requirements in these masculine institutions is starkly revealed in the words of the adult workshop participants. I was left imagining that this chapter will sharpen the attention of many psychotherapists, because such stories are going to need drawing out 'Beyond the Glass'.

Amelia White continues the female theme in Chapter 5 by asking whether co-educational boarding – increasingly available as boarding schools broaden their marketing – is really 'Good for Girls'. She builds on her personal experience alongside the references to her clinical practice, which includes online exploratory groups for ex-boarders. For her chapter, White conducted a specialised survey of women who had attended co-educational boarding schools and the direct words of these ex-boarders are reproduced at length; they bear precise testimony to what a difficult experience this has been for many. Additionally, White puts her material into useful historical, sociological and psychological context.

The third essay specifically looking at women as ex-boarders comes near the end and uses transactional analysis as its chief lens. In Chapter 12, Karen Macmillan tackles the difficult and intriguing question that runs through many of the chapters: how well someone who boarded as a child can work therapeutically with other ex-boarders. Macmillan views the issue as fraught with many traps, but also as one offering advantages. Drawing on her own experience as a boarder, as well as her clinical practice, and, especially illuminatingly, on her mistrust of the therapeutic process during her own counselling training, she asks whether the female ex-boarder therapist can be experienced by the client as a 'collaborator' or an 'ally'. Given our learning from Chapter 4, that ex-boarder women frequently mistrust the company of other women, particularly if they boarded too, this is an important topic.

In Chapter 6, 'Boarding School Syndrome and Intimate Relationships', Elizabeth Carter tackles the most regularly presented problem for ex-boarders: how, after being forced to disown their feelings under duress as children, they can contribute sharing and empathy in a couple situation. Frequently, the challenge amounts to how *not* to see their partners as a threat. Although this is a common, if rarely recognised, symptom of boarding school syndrome, it may take many years for a couple to hit crisis point in a marriage. Carter takes as her starting point an astonishing quotation from John Bowlby, which I had never encountered before, addressing the Royal College of Psychiatrists in the 1970s:

> A man who during childhood was frequently threatened with abandonment can easily attribute such intentions to his wife.[4]

To survive, abandoned children can easily betray themselves and those they love – as it were, abandoning *before* getting abandoned. The survival child who still unwittingly runs the ex-boarder's adult intimate relationships can do this frequently, but unconsciously. Such perverse abandoning does not only apply to boarders: a Swedish TV series, *Deliver Me*, dramatically shows how a traumatised boy from a seemingly 'good' family compulsively destroys the one person he really loves.[5] Ex-boarders can betray their loved ones in a consistent and recognisable way, but a way that may feel incomprehensible to their partner, as Carter shows us.

Boarding, she argues, can be thought of as a 'wound of love' and one that has a bizarre 'ripple effect' on those around an ex-boarder. By closely following the twists and turns in the story of one of her female clients, beset with anxiety, confusion and despair in trying to love an ex-boarder, Carter illustrates how complex and painful the effects of a boarding school survivor's love life can be.

My argument in favour of clinical reflections is not to say that anonymous research does not have a place alongside a treatment programme, as White shows in Chapter 5. And in Chapter 7, Dr Virginia Sherborne reports on a study she conducted asking how counsellors in UK independent schools experience the effects of working with children who attend boarding schools. One of the things that has changed in boarding over the years is that schools are now required to have pastoral care, safeguarding teams, Ofsted inspections and in-school counselling facilities. It is not an easy job for these school counsellors, caught between the school who are their employers and the children who must survive the experience. Moreover, the traditional counselling method of encouraging clients to share their feelings may not be appropriate for these children. Sherborne's chapter reveals that many of the counsellors absorb the disowned feelings from their clients and many suffer vicarious trauma effects. What I found particularly interesting is that, having witnessed what unparented children have to go through, many are also inspired to concentrate harder on parenting their own children.

My own general preference is to fit theory and methodology to the client in therapeutic work with ex-boarders, rather than trying to fit these clients into methods learned in the various training programmes. At the same time, however, I am usually sceptical about mixing up approaches from very diverse disciplines. I tend to recall the warning from one of my former teachers, the late Professor Robert

Young, a Texan intellectual who ran Free Association Books out of his eccentric home in South Islington. 'Nick, you have to pitch your tent somewhere,' he advised.

However, in Chapter 8, Susannah Cornish reports stunning results from combined therapies featuring the use of Eye Movement Desensitisation and Reprocessing Therapy (EMDR). Even though the work of recovering from boarding trauma has shown itself to be very long-term, Cornish's creative experiments on shifting the anxiety state of those who have experienced trauma is really encouraging. As we now know from the neuroscience revolution, those who suffer complex trauma in childhood tend to store their traumatic experiences in the wrong place in the brain, so that they subsequently re-evoke a hypervigilant alertness at inappropriate times. Cornish shows that a session or two of targeted EMDR, employed at the right time and in the right way, can reprogramme a lifetime of habit of recapitulating trauma responses, so that the work of boarding recovery can be addressed in an effective way.

Chapter 9 shifts gear completely and provides an 'archetypal perspective on the ex-boarder'. Sally McLaren's 'English Landscape' is a fascinatingly detailed case study of Jungian psychoanalysis with one ex-boarder patient. Not an ex-boarder herself, McLaren allows her patient to get under her skin; over time, she creatively allows the deep-seated issues to emerge and reveal themselves. The therapy appears haunted by the shadowy presence of a fox. This wily, secretive survivor is featured in many English myths and legends, rooted in landscape; here he becomes a totem animal for the ex-boarder strategic survival personality. After much hunting for her patient's fox, McLaren finds her way, inspired by Donald Kalsched:

> In trauma work … we must learn to speak a soulful language, because it is uniquely the human soul that is threatened with annihilation by early trauma in a child's life.[6]

In Chapter 10, Dawn Grundy considers the effect of boarding school on sibling relationships. The sibling relationship is known for its tendency towards rivalry, envy and sometimes violence, but it can also be a loving relationship, and it comes under new focus when considered on the light of boarding, when children are already experiencing considerable loss and dislocation. This is a neglected but crucial topic, because boarding can create more separations than just from parents and home: many ex-boarders entirely miss their siblings' lives for multiple reasons, as Grundy details. In this chapter, the reader encounters a series of cases studies with quotations from clients, detailing the bewildering effect of boarding. There are some tragic stories, for example when a boarding sibling came home again but no longer felt at home amongst the siblings that had remained, or when siblings were sent to the same school, but the age difference in the social fabric of boarding school meant they could not connect.

I have discussed Chapters 11 and 12 above, and our penultimate chapter, Chapter 13, is a place for Dr John Andrew Miller to share his many years' experience of supervising therapists with clients impacted by boarding school. Miller also tells us about working with supervisees who were themselves ex-boarders – often complicated by the latter bringing ex-boarder clients as well: there are wheels within wheels here. The ex-boarder's familiar tendency to cut off and project is carefully noted. Miller's account is important because, as an American resident in Britain for many years, he brings both an outsider's perspective as well as a close familiarity with British life and especially with the world of psychotherapy, where he has played an important role in setting up and accrediting many training programmes.

In my own concluding short piece, Chapter 14, I introduce the reader to the complex challenges that face the ex-boarder who has recognised that the *solution* to boarding school developed at the time – the strategic survival personality – has now perversely become the pressing *problem*. Given that boarding affects an entire nation, its former colonies as well as the global elite, I hope that my very brief foray into the political implications here will be acceptable to readers, now that interdisciplinary approaches are more common.

Rest assured that I do not advance any partisan political views thereby: it is simply a health warning. The neuro-educational reality here is that public school educated men have had a very precise training, which influences the nervous system and replicates predictable results in poor decision-making. This is because those internal feedback systems, which need generation by emotional intelligence, are not working as they should.[7] People need to be able to *feel* properly to be able to conduct leadership in a healthy way, and, in the complex world we inhabit, perhaps we need good leadership now more than ever.

As the reader turns to begin the chapters, I should mention my own introductory essay. Chapter 1 sets the scene for the British boarding habit in its socio-historical context and world-wide importance. I explain what has changed and what has not over recent years. I tell the story of uncovering this hidden and normalised trauma and the therapy profession's silence and collusion about the fall-out from boarding. Finally, I spell out why 'boarding school survivor' – a phrase I first used in the late 1980s – is still an appropriate – if rather crude – term. I once again emphasise how difficult it has been for ex-boarders to get recognition of a normalised problem that has successfully resisted pathologising (and therefore serious study) until so recently.

Notes

1 Lambert, R. (1968) *The Hothouse Society*. London: Weidenfeld & Nicolson. After its publication, Royston Lambert was offered the headmastership of a well-known 'progressive' boarding school.

2 Verkaik, R. (2018) *Posh Boys: How English Public Schools Ruin Britain*. London & Minneapolis: Oneworld.

3 Cavenagh, P., McPherson, S. and Ogden, J. (eds) (2024) *The Psychological Impact of Boarding School: The Trunk in the Hall*. Abingdon and New York: Routledge.

4 Bowlby, J. (2005) *The Making and Breaking of Affectional Bonds*. London & New York: Routledge.

5 Zackrisson, A. (director) (2024) *Deliver Me* (Swedish: *I dina händer*, 'In Your Hands'). A Swedish drama television mini-series based on the novel of the same name by Malin Persson Giolito, available on Netflix.

6 Kalsched, D. (2013) *Trauma and the Soul: A Psycho-Spiritual Approach to Human Development and its Interruption.* Hove: Routledge, p. 117.

7 See Damasio, A.R. (1994) *Descartes' Error: Emotion, Reason, and the Human Brain.* New York: Avon Books.

Chapter 1

The Survival Imperative

Nick Duffell

Boarding in context

In Britain, private boarding schools (misleadingly called 'public schools') have been shaping the character of elites for nearly two centuries. The impact of the boarding school ethos on all aspects of British society, both at the individual- and macro-level (institutional and political) is only now being fully understood. So, before outlining the psychological issues, I propose to briefly consider the phenomenon of boarding in a socio-historical context.

Originally reserved for the children of the aristocracy, boarding education was redesigned and popularised in the mid-nineteenth century to meet the growing demand for administrators and officers in the rapidly expanding British Empire. It then spread throughout the UK and the British colonial and ex-colonial world – in short, to the whole 'Anglosphere'.

Consider the timescale. In 1857, Thomas Hughes' famous novel, *Tom Brown's School Days*, celebrates Dr Arnold, headmaster of Rugby, who reformed the public school system by instilling prefect-led discipline and revisioning the schools as self-contained 'communities', churning out a generation of boys who 'put the traditions of Rugby … above the laws of God'.[1] The following year, 1858, the British imposed Crown rule upon India. In 1861, the Clarendon Commission made a study of the top nine schools in England, resulting in the 1868 Public Schools Act, which enshrined this elite education method in law and custom. It still applies today.

I have argued elsewhere[2] that the British boarding school system became an industrial process, a stream in the development of modernism in which people began to be thought of as commodities. The deliberate separation of children from their families was the primary tool in a production process of churning out 'gentlemen' to run global Britain. Having assured a production line for the Imperial way of life, boarding education then developed in two further and seemingly contradictory ways: as an international forcing process for the upper classes and as a means of corralling and socialising indigenous children in the colonies. At the current time,

DOI: 10.4324/9781003515517-1

the former branch is going stronger than ever, while the latter has recently come under serious study and critique, especially in Canada.[3]

British boarding methods remained largely unchanged well into the latter half of the twentieth century, when they were already anachronistic. At the same time, being ever responsive to their customer base, boarding schools became increasingly attractive to aspirational families after the Second World War, as Britain's social fabric became more permeable. The neo-liberal economic revolution of the mid-1980s seems to have restored the traditional social structure, and boarding remains a popular means for establishing class status. In recent years, boarding has morphed into a luxury education product designed to serve the emergent *nouveaux riche* in Russia, the Persian Gulf, Southeast Asia and China. There are local franchise offshoots in several locations alongside boarding's traditional home base – wealthy families wanting to advance within the still rigidly codified British class system.

Boarding remains, therefore, a crucial aspect of difference and identity between the Anglophone world and its Western European neighbours, all of whom are now rooted in social-democratic political models, which Britain has been reluctant to develop. I suggest that boarding education is one of the leading drivers of this difference: a carefully engineered elite education system can serve as a crucial component of national identity and a building block in the replication of conservative institutions.

The world-wide relevance of the British version, particularly in terms of leadership candidates, is in little doubt. According to the 2020 report of the Oxford-based Higher Education Policy Institute 'over a quarter of countries (52 out of 195) are led by someone [privately] educated in the UK'.[4] Another think tank, the Private Education Policy Forum, reasons:

> The figure for boarding pupils is ... 0.7 per cent. It points up the disproportionate representation of the privately educated in the leading professions, politics and arts. The over-representation of boarding pupils is blatant. The grip of ex-boarders on British society goes largely unnoticed.[5]

A hidden trauma

The predominance of ex-boarders in leadership positions is a familiar feature of the British social landscape. And yet, rooted in the intentional rupture of parental attachments and a rigid regime of forced socialisation, long-term side effects in boarding school alumni ought to be expected. But it is only relatively recently that the resultant psychological problems have been seriously investigated and analysed. Meanwhile, to the general public, boarding remains a normalised privileged path for the education of children of the wealthy.

The deliberate breaking of parental attachments for the sake of hothousing elites is an effective socialisation technique, but it comes at a cost. Psychiatrist Dr Bob

Johnson commented on the successful, but troubled, pop singer Freddie Mercury (born Farrokh Bulsara):

> Being sent away by his parents at the tender age of 8 inevitably had a devastating impact. At birth, the brain is the most under-developed organ in your body. Any serious trauma, such as a sudden separation from parents causes physical changes in the structure of the developing brain. It damages a child's ability to process emotion. It impairs the feelings of safety and trust in others and it can leave profound scars. This trauma can last a lifetime and its effect on Farrokh cannot be overestimated.[6]

Given the enduring British affection for boarding education, there has been little research on the consequences. University research projects, however, cannot be disconnected from funding, and there is a sizeable financial lobby that supports boarding. Outside of Britain, there has been some enquiry: the following summary of research findings come from a very different socio-economic world, Turkey.

> A subset of boarding schools for adolescents was established in 1993 in the rural sections of Eastern Turkey to provide equity in terms of availability of education. Even though these schools were beneficial in many respects, implementation of this institutional model gave rise to many challenges such as weaker relationships with parents and defiance of authority figures. Failure to develop a mature response to these challenges could lead to the development of psychopathologies such as depression, psychosis, and dissociation.[7]

More surprising, though, is the tardiness of home-grown therapeutic enquiry about boarding. This is especially puzzling since there exists not one single theory of child development or pedagogy that supports the removal of children from home and placing them in institutions. How is this to be understood?

Perhaps therapists, too, have been immersed in a kind of defensive social normalisation, popularly called 'groupthink'. Perhaps there is wilful blindness, since in Britain psychotherapy remains a privatised profession, dominated by middle-class and middle-aged females who may have children who boarded and do not want to feel guilty.

At the time I began investigating the psychology of boarding, in 1989, I felt utterly alone and very nervous about trying to expose the subject. The following year, when I was still tentatively exploring it, I happened – by sheer chance – to be offered the opportunity to write a piece about the downside of boarding for *The Independent* newspaper. The published article had a staggering impact.[8] It generated hundreds of unexpected stories about boarding and its effects, as the paper forwarded bundles of readers' letters addressed to me.

Most correspondents appreciated that someone had finally spoken out about the problems of boarding; many asked for help, for themselves or their spouses; and some raged that I was promoting anti-British 'woolly-thinking' nonsense. Here is a typical example of the sort of letter I received (and still receive, to this day):

> My husband is now 70 and still scarred from being sent away to sink or swim in a public school at age 14. He's basically a good man, but he's still that teenager defending himself from a hostile environment, still wanting mother (or a series of mother substitutes) to atone for abandoning him, and acting out forever because there is no atonement. He dreams nearly every night of packing his trunk in a dormitory, not knowing where he's going to next or where he belongs, just as you describe. We've been married 27 years, and I've been imprisoned in that school with him all that time. We're on the point of divorce because I can't stand any more his want home/hate home, need love/don't need you, bully/or be bullied attitudes. I don't want to leave him, but I'm worn out by that poor boy, forever with his fists up braced for a fight, so busy dealing with his neediness that he can't care for others.[9]

Such unsolicited testimonies convinced me that an acknowledgement of this problem was overdue. They may not count as 'science', but they reveal its hidden domestic cost and illustrate the boarding problem just as well as questionnaire-based research.

Unmasking the fall-out from boarding

Also in 1990, I began offering therapeutic workshops for those I called 'boarding school survivors'.[10] Subsequently, in January 1994, a BBC television documentary followed several young children during their first weeks in boarding school and interviewed me, as the sole 'expert' on this subject, even though I was only just discovering the psychological impact of boarding.

In the documentary, *The Making of Them*, the viewer experiences many heart-breaking scenes of little boys attempting to shed their childhoods and morph into little pseudo-adults who have turned away from missing their mummies. 'Boarding school', begins one 9-year-old,

> ... has changed me, and the one thing I can do now is 'get used', and when I'm older, and when I'm something like twenty, and if I become a *businessman*, I am going to have to be able to *manage* by myself, and so being at boarding school is quite a lot about being able to *manage* and *handle* yourself without help from other people.[11]

In the wake of *The Independent* article and the film, journalists regularly cross-examined me, and this still continues. With returning fascination, the British press seize on any news about boarding school culture, typically in a mid-paper feature complete with old photographs of boys in top hats. Media fascination massively increases when celebrities share their boarding memories, for example the dramatic abuse disclosures by Charles Spencer, brother of Princess Diana, in 2024.[12]

In frequent interviews I have struggled to find a way to explain very complex issues in simple and non-sensationalist ways. The most common misunderstanding is that naming the psychological fall-out implies that '*all* children are *damaged* by boarding'. However, from a psychological perspective, the word 'damage' is misleading: the issue is much more nuanced.

What became clear to me was that all boarding children are compelled to *survive* in a potentially hostile institution, manage the fear that is engendered there and get on without their parents, whose expectations become burdensome due to the investment made in their progeny. This affects children in different ways: some fare better than others; but generally, there is a price to pay. And on top of this, some children get shockingly abused. The survival imperative, however, affects them all. I repeat this in interviews and hope it may be understood.

Happily, I eventually discovered that I was not the only one to have noticed it. In the scholarly *British Journal of Psychotherapy*, in 2011, Professor Joy Schaverien, a Jungian analyst, cited examples of famous psychoanalysts such as John Bowlby, Wilfred Bion and Patrick Casement, whose training analysts had entirely overlooked the significance of their boarding experiences.[13]

Over the years, the renewed popularity of attachment therapy, combined with the findings of neuroscience and traumatology, awakened more practitioners to the conspiracy of silence about boarding in Britain. In 2014, the renowned Dutch-American traumatologist, Bessel Van der Kolk, shared his thoughts on visiting London's famous Tavistock Clinic. Standing beneath the portraits of its founding fathers, Winnicott, Guntrip, Bion and Bowlby, he reflected:

> The scientific study of the vital relationship between infants and their mothers was started by upper-class Englishmen who were torn away from their families as young boys to be sent off to boarding schools, where they were raised in regimented same-sex settings.[14]

And some time before this, with more digging, I discovered some older references to the problem.

The earliest I found was from psychiatrist W.H. Rivers (born 1864) who treated 'shell-shocked' soldiers at Craiglockhart, Edinburgh, during the First World War. The main symptom of 'shell shock' was mutism – the inability to speak. Perhaps, in retrospect, this is understandable, since what they had experienced in the trenches was truly unspeakable. Rivers believed that these somatised 'war neuroses' were due more to the 'attempt to banish distressing memories from the mind' than the *actual* experience.[15] Feminist historian Elaine Showalter explains:

When all signs of physical fear were judged as unmanly weakness, men were silenced and immobilised and forced 'like women' to express their conflicts through the body.[16]

Rivers noted that the officers expressed their trauma differently to the common soldiers; he reasoned that this was because they had already experienced the 'benefit' of public school education, as he explained:

The public schoolboy enters the army with a long course of training behind him which enables him to successfully repress, not only the expression of fear, but also the emotion itself.[17]

Another Scottish psychiatrist, Iain Suttie, argued in his 1936 book, *The Origins of Love and Hate* – ironically published the day he died, at the age of 36 – that Freud was blinded by sexuality and had overlooked 'the taboo on tenderness'.[18] One of his examples was how the British upper classes dispatched their children to boarding schools without questioning their abandonment. Suttie was a mentor to Bowlby, who founded attachment theory in the 1950s, in parallel to Winnicott's work on 'attunement' and Fairbairn's work on 'internal objects'.

Bowlby had boarded as a child, but did not elaborate on the topic, presumably imagining it too subjective a theme for scientific method. Perhaps he had bigger fish to fry, or perhaps he was remembering his mother who, like many of her generation, apparently considered that parental attention and affection led to the dangerous 'spoiling' of children.[19] However, in 1972 Bowlby revealed:

I wouldn't send a dog away to boarding school at age seven.[20]

Normalised neglect

By 2015, my colleagues and I had worked with hundreds of ex-boarders, and we now had Schaverien's name for the problem: 'boarding school syndrome'.[21] Thereafter, practitioners began to have an increasing number of relevant publications at their disposal.

Boarding school syndrome refers to a cluster of symptoms in ex-boarder adults, excluding any effects of additional circumstantial trauma, such as bullying and sexual abuse. It includes difficulties with intimate relationships and parenting, fear of failure, poor self-care, a tendency to overwork and either undervalue or overvalue oneself, a deficit of emotional intelligence and habitual but unconscious hypervigilance, resulting from survival strategies put in place in childhood. Being sent away to board as a child could now be understood as *in itself* a trauma.

Boarding trauma is caused by attachment rupture and subsequent institutionalisation, regardless of whether the experience was remembered as favourable, acceptable or horrific. Indeed, classic reframing, such as 'it's character-building', can now be understood as a survival strategy. Subsequent traumatic events, such as child sexual abuse, are consequent disasters overlaid on the original abandonment trauma – horrific, but predictable under conditions of socially normalised neglect.

Survivors' behaviours cause many problems in families, which are not like institutions, and the need to dissociate breeds a facility for seamless duplicity. This may explain why ex-boarders make good spies but problematic political leaders – both sectors where they tend to dominate in Britain. Existentially, whenever survival is required, there is a price to pay, and the overall cost of boarding in British life has to be considerable.

Even for those in the therapy profession, who seem to have normalised the problem of boarding like the rest of the population, I repeatedly have to spell out the survival imperative. Boarding, I explain, produces a specific and identifiable personality type, which I call the 'strategic survival personality' (SSP).[22] This resembles D.W. Winnicott's idea of the 'false self' – quite a well-known concept within the profession – described here by Jan Abram:

> The false self is a structure that is there to *defend* the true self, even – or especially – at the healthy end.[23]

Winnicott formed his theories during 40 years of service at the Paddington Green Children's Hospital. His other lesser-known specialism was working therapeutically with children separated from their parents due to evacuation from London in the Second World War.[24] The famous British expert on childhood had himself boarded as a child – like Bowlby and most of the British psychoanalytic theorists – but as Schaverien revealed, shockingly, this fact has been universally overlooked within the psychotherapy profession.[25]

Nevertheless, Winnicott's concept of a defensive, survival-oriented 'structure' has helped people to understand what is at play. And boarders need this protection. Boarding children could be said to be 'twice abandoned' – not only by their parents but also by British society, which resists acknowledging that boarding harms children. In 2024, I was gratified to see that Earl Spencer had not just told a tale of abuse but had understood the problem:

> People who went to these schools … simply had to become desensitised in order to survive.[26]

Strategic survival

The strategic survival personality is a defensive psychic structure, formed unconsciously as a means of defending the vulnerable child at the very beginning of his or her privileged abandonment. Such a defence, therefore, is both inevitable and necessary. In the absence of caretaker protection, the SSP is *externally defensive* precisely because it is *internally protective.*

The strategic survival personality seems to have its own life. It resembles a Jungian 'complex', in that it can contain multiple 'sub-personalities' and its own will. It is therefore easy for the boarding school survivor to imagine that this sur-vival structure is indeed his real self, rather than what I hypothesise to be a version of the Winicottian 'false self'. This means that ex-boarders do not easily choose the road of boarding recovery until something goes seriously wrong with the survival behaviour.

The unique nature of the SSP is that, since it is formed to compensate for the rupture of parental attachments, it is seamlessly adopted as both an *ego formation* and as a substitute *internal parent*. In modern psychoanalytic writing, the near-est equivalent theoretical structure to the SSP seems to be the Jungian Donald Kalshed's 'self-care system', a complex trauma response.[27] Created as it is under duress by a child, the SSP is very difficult to jettison as an adult, even though it has pseudo-adult features and naturally becomes maladaptive over time.

The specific qualification of 'strategic' I owe to an early client. A high-flying corporate lawyer sought psychotherapy with me because of unexplained fits of panic when making presentations. One day he described himself as 'strategic' and explained why: despite his outward success, all his life he had been trying to stay out of trouble, something that he had learned as a boarder. It had ruined his personal relationships, because he tended to mistake any approach – even an intimate one – as a potential threat. He had always led what he described as a 'double life'. This man was describing the essence of the SSP.

Living in excessively rule-bound institutions where they are unable to show their feelings, constantly surrounded by their peers who are scared and ready to scape-goat any signs of vulnerability in others first, boarders quickly develop a strategic way of life. They become Machiavellian, trying to stay one step ahead, staying out of trouble, anticipating danger, promoting the false selves they are selling, some-times self-effacing, sometimes bullying. They develop a personality that carries high expectations, but is also duplicitous.

The SSP has many varieties, depending on the child's family history and pro-clivities, but there are sufficient recognisable features that are shared to consider it a discrete psychological category. Central to this is a profound lack of transpar-ency: a sense of external functioning or 'masking' that covers an inner, unknown, secret, guarded self.

I have identified three generalised types of personalities, which I call 'complier', 'rebel' and 'crushed'. In the first, complier, the functioning is central; in the second, rebel, not functioning can become a masochistic defence; in the third, crushed, surviving the trauma consumes all psychic energy. The complier type dominates numerically and follows the social normalisation of boarding. This personality type may even identify with (or feels succoured by) his school or class or patriotic value system, as Bowlby knew:

> A school or college, a work group, a religious group or a political group can come to constitute for many people a subordinate attachment 'figure', and for some people a principal attachment 'figure'.[28]

Let us consider the survival constraints: the need to maintain a brave face without any emotion; to stay out of trouble and not be 'wrong'; a double bind with parents back home who are investing in the success of this expensive education; the trials of going through formative developmental stages in an institution without love or touch. Internalised shame, due to knowing that elite boarding is a social privilege, compounds the problem. It is not difficult to see how evasive secrecy and 'strategicness' turn into a way of life.

The SSP takes control as a way of adjusting behaviour and facing the world: this what is understood as an 'ego structure'. At the same time, it becomes an inner protector – a virtual and compensatory attachment figure. Designed in the first hours or days of boarding, its main behavioural feature is action before reflection, in order to avoid trouble. In later life, the ex-boarder is unaware that his SSP is running the show: it is what he has always done and it works.

The SSP has some aspects – like emotional avoidance – that give it excellent social camouflage, for they are associated with a socially valued British national character, or 'gentlemanliness'. Winnicott, as Jim Anderson acutely points out, had already noted that society supported such a defensive structure, stating:[29]

> In effect, the compliant or false self is a pathological version of that which is called in health the polite, socially adapted aspect of the healthy personality.[30]

How this survival-driven desensitisation affects girls, boys, family members and even those trying to support and treat survivors is the subject of the following chapters. At the close of this book, I consider how the SSP typically responds to recovery stimuli and try to gauge what the cumulative cost of this survival to British society may be.

But first, let us find out how wide the reach of this problem is.

Notes

1 Hughes, T. (1999) *Tom Brown's School Days*. Oxford: Oxford World Classics, first published in 1857. Retrieved from https://www.gutenberg.org/files/1480/1480-h/1480-h.htm, 30 March 2024.
2 *Production-Line Living* (2013) BBC Radio 3. A.L. Kennedy asks whether the introduction of the assembly line is when we stopped being fully human? Free Thinking festival at Sage, available https://www.bbc.co.uk/programmes/b03f86k6.
3 'Honouring the Truth, Reconciling for the Future', Summary of the Final Report of the Truth and Reconciliation Commission of Canada. Available https://irsi.ubc.ca/sites/defa ult/files/inline-files/Executive_Summary_English_Web.pdf.
4 Higher Education Policy Institute Annual Soft-Power Ranking Policy Note 26, August 2020. Retrieved from www.hepi.ac.uk, 30 March 2024.
5 Partridge, S. (30 June 2021) 'The 0.7 Per Cent Problem is Much Worse than the 7 Per Cent Problem', in Private Education Policy Forum, a think tank researching private schools and fee-paying education. Retrieved from https://www.pepf.co.uk/opinion/the-0-7-per-cent-problem-is-much-worse-than-the-7-per-cent-problem/, 30 March 2024.

6 Edwards, R. (2021) *Inside the Mind: Freddie Mercury*, TV documentary, Bristol: Honey Bee TV.

7 Mutluer, T., Fatih, P., Tayakisi, E., et al. (2021) 'Psychopathology and Dissociation Among Boarding School Students in Eastern Turkey', *Journal of Child & Adolescent Trauma*, 14: 201–207. https://doi.org/10.1007/s40653-021-00351-3.

8 Duffell, N. (1 September 1990) 'Turning Little Ones into the Old School: An Edifice that Can Crush the Spirit', *The Independent*, Free speech section.

9 Personal correspondence, permission to quote obtained while remaining anonymous.

10 These group workshops are still available, see www.boardingschoolsurvivors.co.uk.

11 *The Making of Them* (1994) film directed by Colin Luke for Mosaic Pictures, first broadcast BBC *40 Minutes*, 9 January 1994. Available on YouTube http://youtu.be/2uRr 77vju8U.

12 Adams, T. (Sunday 17 March) 'The brother of Diana, princess of Wales, talks about his difficult decision to write about being physically and sexually abused and the resistance he faced from members of his own class', *The Observer*. Retrieved from https://www.theguardian.com/education/2024/mar/17/earl-charles-spencer-a-very-private-school-interview, 22 March 2024.

13 Schaverien, J. (2011) 'Boarding School Syndrome: Broken Attachments – A Hidden Trauma', *British Journal of Psychotherapy*, 27(2): 138–155.

14 Van der Kolk, B. (2014) *The Body Keeps the Score: Brain, Mind and Body in the Healing of Trauma*. New York: Viking.

15 Rivers, W.H. (1918) 'The Repression of War Experience', *Procedures of the Royal Society of Medicine*, 11 (Sect. Psych.), pp. 1–20.

16 Showalter, E. (1987) *The Female Malady: Women, Madness and English Culture 1830–1980*. London: Virago.

17 Rivers, W.H. (1918) 'The Repression of War Experience', *Procedures of the Royal Society of Medicine*, 11 (Sect. Psych.), pp. 1–20.

18 Suttie, I. (1988) *The Origins of Love and Hate*. London: Free Association Books, first published 1935.

19 Bowlby, R. and King, P. (2004) *Fifty Years of Attachment Theory: Recollections of Donald Winnicott and John Bowlby*. London: Karnac Books.

20 Bowlby, J. (1973) *Attachment and Loss. Vol 2: Separation, Anxiety and Anger*. London: Hogarth Press.

21 Schaverien, J. (2015) *Boarding School Syndrome: The Psychological Trauma of the 'Privileged' Child*. Hove: Routledge.

22 Duffell, N. (2000) *The Making of Them: The British Attitude to Children and the Boarding School System*. London: Lone Arrow Press.

23 Abram, J. (1996) *The Language of Winnicott: A Dictionary of Winnicott's Use of Words*. London: Karnac Books, p. 304.

24 Kahr, B. (2011) 'The Biographical Roots of Winnicott's Hate in the Counter-Transference', *American Imago*, 68(2): 173–211, pp. 178–179.

25 Schaverien, J. (2015) *Boarding School Syndrome: The Psychological Trauma of the 'Privileged' Child*. Hove: Routledge.

26 Adams, T. (2024) 'The brother of Diana, princess of Wales, talks about his difficult decision to write about being physically and sexually abused and the resistance he faced from members of his own class', *The Observer*, Sunday 17 March. Retrieved from https://www.theguardian.com/education/2024/mar/17/earl-charles-spencer-a-very-private-school-interview, 22 March 2024.

27 Kalsched, D. (2013) *Trauma and the Soul: A Psycho-Spiritual Approach to Human Development and its Interruption*. Hove: Routledge.

28 Bowlby, J. (1969) *Attachment and Loss. Vol 1: Attachment*. New York: Basic Books, p. 255.

29 Anderson, J.W. (2015) 'Winnicott's Constant Search for the Life that Feels Real' in
    M. Boyle Spelman and F. Thomson-Salo (eds), *The Winnicott Tradition: Lines of
    Development-Evolution of Theory and Practice Over the Decades*. London: Routledge.
30 Winnicott, D.W. (1965) *The Maturational Processes and the Facilitating
    Environment: Studies in the Theory of Emotional Development*. New York: International
    Universities Press, p. 225.

Chapter 2

A Clinical Framework for Nuanced Narratives in Therapy with Ex-Boarders

Stephanie Collins

Introduction

About a million people now living in Britain previously attended boarding school,[1] a formative experience that will have impacted on their lives in adulthood.[2] Recently, there has been an explosion of media interest regarding the imprint on ex-boarders – generally negative. Accounts from those who attended the most exclusive public schools, such as journalist Alex Renton, novelist Richard Beard and Earl Spencer, may need to be balanced against those for whom boarding was reported to be a positive or neutral experience.[3]

However, the assumption of privilege and entitlement still prevails, with boarding schools perceived as educational vehicles for children of the financial elite and upper classes.[4] The UK's most influential individuals are five times more likely to have attended private school, mainly comprising boarding schools.[5] Additionally, the Social Mobility Commission noted in 2019 that 'class privilege remains entrenched', suggesting that our private education system continues to be the aspirational bedrock of our society.[6]

Whilst undoubtedly there are many pupils who conform to the archetypical 'white posh boy' image,[7] there are many pupils who do not fit this stereotype. For example, many girls attend boarding school and there are scholars from lower socio-economic strata who attain bursaries. Boarding schools increasingly attract children from overseas, providing the desired elite status for aspirational non-British parents, while ensuring a welcome source of funding; albeit, many independent boarding schools are registered charities, thus receiving significant tax exemptions.[8]

While boarding school syndrome recognises the common abandonment trauma for children sent away from their home environments,[9] the specific circumstances impacting the individual ex-boarder client may vary significantly. Experienced therapists have acknowledged the challenges of working with ex-boarders, attempting to dismantle the defensive barriers developed as children, which continue to negatively impact in adulthood.[10] Boarding schools promote the ability to cultivate autonomy, self-reliance and confidence among those in their care, but this comes at a cost in terms of emotional expression, intimacy and tenderness.[11]

DOI: 10.4324/9781003515517-2

In order to distinguish discernible levels of social systemic effect in ex-boarders' narratives, I present here a clinical framework for therapists, devised by Bella Cranmore, an ex-boarder psychotherapist, and myself. This framework attempts a nuanced and individual understanding of clients' boarding experiences related to their current presenting difficulties. Selected qualitative experiences from some ex-boarders' accounts illustrate the impact these factors can have in shaping their adult lives. Morgan's 'intersectionality model'[12] and Boyle and Johnstone's 'power threat meaning framework'[13] have been applied to further exemplify the use of the framework.

Demographics

There are approximately 600 boarding schools operating globally, with around 440 based in the UK, including 34 state boarding establishments.[14] In 2023, there were 66,325 UK registered boarders, of whom approximately 40 per cent were non-British and whose parents lived abroad, mainly from China and Hong Kong.[15] There is a considerable choice of boarding arrangements: day boarding, where pupils only return home to sleep; flexi-boarding where students sleep at school a few nights a week; weekly boarding, Monday to Friday or Saturday; and full boarding where pupils remain at school for the whole term, barring authorised exeats. Many schools offer boarding from the age of 11, while preparatory schools, take children from 8 years or younger.

Most boarders' education is privately funded, although there are expatriate children whose fees are funded by the corporation or service for whom their parents work, as well as some 8 per cent who have gained a means-tested bursary.[16] Scholarships are also provided to those who excel academically, creatively or in sports but who would otherwise be precluded due to financial restrictions. Termly fees in the UK average £13,000 for full senior boarders, £5,000 for preparatory boarders, with some schools charging considerably more.

Change

Boarding schools have significantly evolved over time. Notable boarders such as Dahl, Orwell and Kipling wrote about scenes of cruelty, shame and neglect, where only academic or sporting achievement represented success and where pastoral care was non-existent. Corporal punishment was finally abolished in the 1990s, and practices such as 'fagging' have disappeared, although bullying remains a feature in many schools. Recently, a spate of disclosures regarding historic sexual abuse, perpetrated by adults in positions of trust and older peers, has led to custodial sentences. New safeguarding policies, namely the Independent Schools Inspectorate's (ISI) Framework 23, have been introduced to minimise such occurrences.[17]

Most schools are now co-educational, with girls being accepted in the sixth form at boys' schools from the late 1960s and becoming increasingly commonplace during the following decade. Academic achievement for girls used to be secondary to developing attributes to attract husbands.[18] But from the early 1970s, arising predominantly from feminism and changes in the workplace, girls were increasingly encouraged to excel academically in competition with their male counterparts. With no established national standards, teachers were the arbiters of what and how to teach their pupils, which was only ratified into a national curriculum following the 1988 Education Reform Act.[19]

In colonial times, children would routinely start boarding from the age of 4 years upwards, often not seeing their parents for years. Post-1945 and up until the end of the twentieth century, children frequently commenced boarding from the age of 8 years in preparatory schools and continued their schooling in secondary schools, aged 11 or 13 years. Junior boarding numbers have decreased from approximately 6,000 in the year 2000 to fewer than 4,500 in 2022.[20]

With access to mobile phones and email, children can now communicate much more freely with their families: homesickness is not thereby removed, but regular family contact may somewhat offset a sense of abandonment. The desire to meet parental expectations will likely remain, effectively silencing children's ability to express their grief of being sent away from home.

Considerable emphasis has lately been placed on implementing diversity, equity and inclusion safeguards within organisations in the UK.[21] The objective is to promote fairness and inclusion to and for everyone, with particular focus on groups who have historically been underrepresented or discriminated against, such as those with disabilities. School prospectuses promote values such as nurturance and inclusion, arising from directives established by the Department for Education (DfE) National Minimum Standards for boarding schools, effective from September 2022.

It is important to differentiate the underlying assumptions between equality and equity: the former directs that everyone should be treated the same whereas equity will consider an individual's unique circumstances, revising treatment accordingly to attain equality.[22]

Power and privilege

Boarding schools became increasingly popular in the nineteenth century at the zenith of Britain's colonial power. Children of colonial governors and local 'top brass' were sent to elite boarding schools to learn about governance, commerce and military strategy.[23] These traditions remain embedded in our culture: 5 of the last 16 UK prime ministers were educated at Eton, with a further 4 who boarded at other elite schools. Similar statistics are replicated in the law, the military, medicine, the civil service and journalism.[24]

The intersectionality model is a theoretical framework, originating from studies on discrimination developed by black American feminist scholars during the 1970s. They proposed that multiple social identities, incorporating factors such as gender, disability and sexual orientation, intersect at the individual- or micro-level of experience. These are then reflected in larger social-structural inequities experienced at a macro-level and these overlapping social identities may be both empowering and discriminatory at varying levels. In 'Describing the Emperor's New Clothes', Morgan used intersectionality to highlight inequalities in the US education system, specifically focusing on gender and how patriarchal discourses continued to disempower females.[25]

Morgan's model is used here to consider the domains of power, privilege and oppression and applied to the UK boarding schools' cultural experience.

The model depicts the archetypal pinnacle of privilege as being a young, white, Anglophone, European, heterosexual male who is able-bodied, fertile, attractive, educated with recognised credentials from an upper-class or aristocratic ancestry. The stereotypical 'posh boy' attending one of the top Clarendon boarding schools accurately embodies those attributes of privilege.[26]

Conversely, individuals not fitting these characteristics are deemed as oppressed or marginalised. Imagine the experience of a non-European girl, whose second language is English and who has a visible disability; all these factors could ostracise her from her peers both in appearance and cultural background. It is hypothesised that her experience of boarding school would not be experienced as privileged or likely to garner envy from others.

'Third culture' pupils, children of British expatriates, may also experience considerable dislocation. Multinational corporations and the military will routinely relocate their personnel every few years; often the main reason cited for sending children to boarding school is to reduce disruption in their education. This can leave children with little sense of belonging anywhere and nowhere to call home.

Of course, many individuals will embody characteristics straddling both dominations, such as children from lower socio-economic status whose superior academic abilities are embraced within the scholarship streams of elite schools. The deciding factor regarding the impact on individuals appears to be the prevailing culture of the school at that time.

Reported experiences

There have been many reported qualitative experiences of ex-boarders that have depicted various positions of privilege and discrimination, and that illustrate the enduring impact these experiences had on these individuals. Whilst many recall negative experiences, examples of positive outcomes are also included for boarders who did not fulfil the stereotype, indicating that individual experiences need to be fully explored in therapy to avoid drawing inaccurate conclusions.

George Orwell – reportedly an unattractive, sickly, but academic child – boarding for the first time aged 8, found himself surrounded by pupils from much wealthier families, in a threatening and alien environment.[27] He noted that his preparatory school was a place where winning was everything. To attain this, it was necessary to bully and oppress more vulnerable peers and where being bigger, tougher, more

Intersectionality

Privilege

Credentialed

Able-bodied   Young

Heterosexual   Attractive

European heritage   Upper and upper-middle class

White   Anglophones

Male   Light, pale

Male and masculine   Gentile
female and feminine   Non-jew

Pro-natalism   Fertile

Domination ——————————————————————————————— Domination

Infertile

Jews   Gender "deviant"

Dark   Female

English as a second   People of color
language   Non-European origin
Working class, poor

Unattractive   LGBTQ
Old   Nonliterate   Persons with disabilities

Oppression

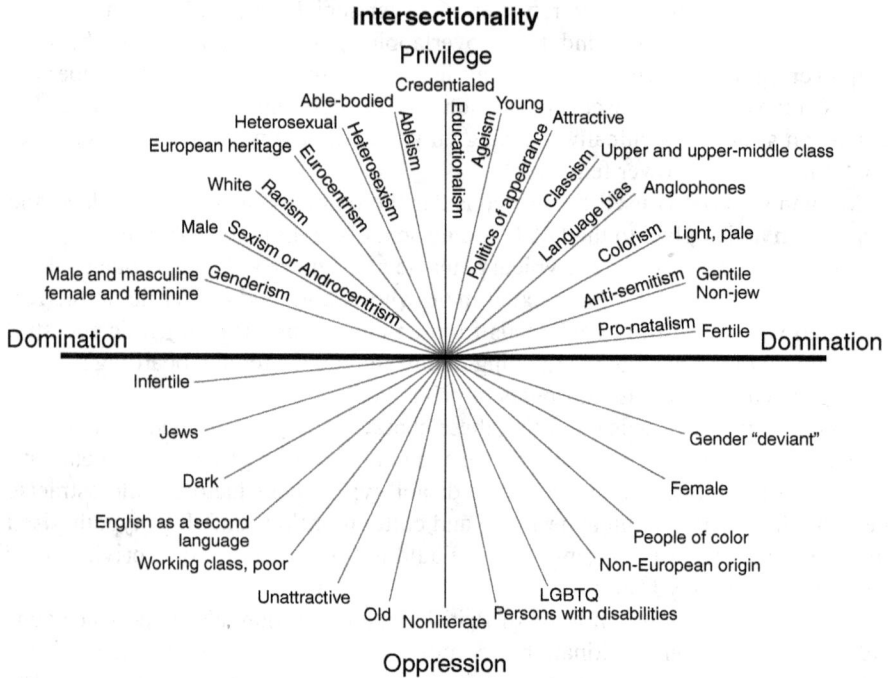

Figure 2.1 Intersectionality in boarding.

attractive, wealthier, more popular, and in many cases more dishonest, paid dividends in terms of climbing the social hierarchy.

Author Frederic Raphael wrote in a letter to his father about his experience at Charterhouse where he felt that he was invisible and powerless.[28] Those he had previously considered to be his allies turned against him because he was Jewish and thus different from the majority, for which he was mercilessly mocked.

In 2021, the BBC reported on black children wrenched from their families in the 1970s. Deemed educationally subnormal, having undertaken culturally biased assessments, they were sent away to boarding schools. Noel, a former pupil sent away when aged 6 years, remembered being racially abused on his first day.[29] He never gained any qualifications, as the school had no academic curriculum. In the same article, it was acknowledged by an education activist that the education system at that time promulgated the belief that black Caribbean children compared unfavourably to their white counterparts in terms of intelligence, a belief that was clearly racist.

Another female ex-boarder writing of her experiences at a famous Scottish co-ed school in the late 1990s, recalled that any vulnerability would be attacked, an inherent aspect of the prevailing culture.[30] Bullying was rife, and the female pupils were overtly evaluated by their male counterparts on their physical attributes, often to their detriment.

Many ex-boarders have reported a sense of otherness, having been disconnected from their families at an early age and having taken on attributes of the school culture. Margaret Laughton, former director of Boarding School Survivors Support, was considered 'posh' by her nursing colleagues for having attended boarding school, and she was consequently excluded from many social events.[31] She experienced this as both irritating and hurtful and wrestled with considerable internal conflict regarding her identity.

Novelist James Scudamore described feeling very dislocated when, aged 10, he started boarding in the UK, having previously lived with his expatriate parents in Japan and Brazil.[32] His understanding of what boarding would be like had been drawn from fictional novels and it came as a great shock when he encountered the brutal forms of discipline meted out to pupils, often for minor infractions of the rules.

Some accounts from those not embodying the traditional privileged status shine a more positive light on boarding. An anonymous contributor wrote in a newspaper article that her seven years at boarding school served as a wonderful release from her mother whom she experienced as cruel and malevolent.[33] This corroborates recent research, highlighting that boarding can represent a positive experience for some children, whose needs had not previously been met by emotionally unavailable or neglectful primary carers.[34]

Novelist Piers Torday, who was reportedly the first openly gay pupil at Eton, described a positive experience in coming out.[35] Aged 15, he unthinkingly disclosed his sexual orientation to a peer, whereupon the news spread around the school. He wrote that he incurred minimal negative reaction from staff or pupils, which was notable given the backdrop of the AIDS epidemic and inequalities in the age of consent at the time, which could have resulted in a very different experience in a homophobic environment.

Therapeutic work with ex-boarders

Psychotherapists acknowledge that working therapeutically with ex-boarders can be a challenging process.[36] E.M. Forster describes one of the problems:

> It is not that the Englishman can't feel – it is that he is afraid to feel. He has been taught at his public school that feeling is bad form, thus adopting the so-called 'stiff upper lip'.[37]

In *Shooting an Elephant*, George Orwell described a white man in Burma as having to adopt a false *persona* to appease expectations of the natives:

He wears a mask, and his face grows to fit it.[38]

It is likely that Orwell drew on his childhood experiences of boarding to aptly describe the loss of his authentic self. The 'strategic survival personality' describes the dissonance between the outwardly confident persona with the vulnerable inner child who has learned to negotiate their survival in the absence of appropriate parental guidance.[39] Shame underpins much of this presentation and the thought of being discovered that one is lacking in any capacity becomes intolerable. In describing boarding school syndrome, Schaverien suggests that the requirement to repress emotions to conceal vulnerabilities may lead to:

> An encapsulation of the self, ... which may be disguised by an armoured and very often socially successful persona.[40]

Reportedly, many ex-boarders will eventually seek therapy, often at the insistence of their partners, to resolve enduring patterns of relational dysfunction and difficulties with intimacy.[41]

Psychotherapist Marcus Evans describes establishing a therapeutic alliance with psychotic clients being susceptible to 'false alliances, enactments, deceptions and denials'.[42] He contends that by developing insight, patients can become traumatised from increased awareness of the 'fragmentation of their minds and their detachment from shared reality'. If triggered, clients may display hypersensitivities that may result in them abruptly ceasing the therapy without explanation or resolution to the issues.[43]

There may be similarities regarding the sensitivity and complexity of the work to be undertaken in dismantling the ex-boarder's mask; research indicates the greater childhood adversity, the higher the risk of mental instability, including psychosis.[44] A survey of female boarders in Turkey were found to be significantly more likely than day pupils to experience trauma symptoms, e.g., depersonalisation and psychoticism.[45]

The difficulties in working with this cohort may not only lie with breaking down the layers of defensive architecture developed over the years. Therapists who are ex-boarders can be significantly challenged when working with this population, and they will need to be acutely aware of their own conditioning to guard against collusion or normalising the shared experience. Therapists with no experience of boarding may be unaware of the subtleties of the presentation and may misinterpret the needs and strategies of this client group.[46]

The clinical framework

The proposed clinical framework highlights areas of exploration with ex-boarder clients, drawing out aspects that may not hitherto have been explicitly discussed. By incorporating the characteristics identified in the intersectionality framework, a more nuanced and personal exploration of an individual's formative boarding

Table 2.1 A clinical framework for therapists to aid exploring ex-boarders' experiences

Theme/circumstance/characteristic	Potential impact on presentation

Boarding school demographics
Age started boarding and how long at boarding
   school – were day pupils there too?
Single sex or co-ed school?
School(s) attended and reputation
Religious orientation (school)
Family home/location and proximity to school
Third culture/expatriate child?
Ethnic diversity

Childhood experience
Experience of the family/growing up
Who were the primary caregiver(s)?
Background of parents (class)
Racial/ethnic background
Religious background (family)
Relationship between parents
Did parents or extended family go to boarding
   school?
Family narrative around why sent to boarding
   school?
Siblings? Were they also sent away to school?
Experience of holidays/exeats

Overall experience at school
Positive/negative/neutral
Academic ability
Good at sports?
Popular or loner – any sense of being 'other'?
Recollection of memories – first day and
   afterwards
Ease of communication with family
Discipline at school
Reaction to authority
Any pastoral care?
Any formal sex education?
Notable teachers/adults in authority
Any bullying or being bullied/or witness to?
Any physical abuse/or witness to?
Any sexual abuse/or witness to attitudes to sex
   at school?
Any emotional abuse/or witness to?
Drugs/alcohol or any other addiction
Mental health – symptoms – what was done
   about it?
Survival strategy:
Male – complier, rebel, crushed? [1]
Female – Henrietta, Eliza, Jane [2]

(Continued)

Table 2.1 (Continued)

Theme/circumstance/characteristic	Potential impact on presentation
Role: clown, bully, crazy rebel, nice guy, victim, swot, hero, complier	
Perception of privilege? (See factors in intersectionality model)	
Perception of oppression/ discrimination? (See intersectionality model)	
Experiences in adulthood	
Highest educational level attained	
Occupation and career history	
Sexual orientation – past and present	
Married/relationship background	
Any enduring relationship difficulties (patterns and trends of relating)	
Own children – current age(s)	
Experience of parenting	
Choice of schooling for children	
Any enduring mental health difficulties or problematic behaviours, e.g. addictions?	
Readiness to seek support from others (previously and now)	
View of boarding school now	
Others' reactions to your education?	
In touch with classmates in adult life?	
Why therapy and why now?	

Notes: (1) Duffell, N. (2000) *The Making of Them: The British Attitude to Children and the Boarding School System.* London: Lone Arrow Press. (2) Miller, N. (2009) 'Some issues that arise for women attending boarding school survivors workshops', retrieved from https://www.boardingrecovery.com/articles.html.

school experience may be enabled. For example, exploring feelings of 'otherness' or a lack of belonging may resonate less with a white male client, primed to attend boarding school as a normal aspect of his education than with a female or transgender client from an ethnic minority, who may have always experienced difference or disconnection from their peers. Additionally, clinicians will be guided in creating a meaningful account of the client's experience in a structured, systematic manner, to clarify the issues needing to be resolved.

The core principles of the power threat meaning framework may also be usefully applied with clients here.[47] This focuses on what happened to clients and the potential distress experienced, rather than centring on what is wrong with them, specifically while considering the impact of power and threat on their experience. The authors suggest employing the following questions:

- What has happened to you? How is power operating in your life?
- How did this impact on you? What types of threats did this bring up for you?

- What sense did you make of it? What meanings did you draw from events and experiences?
- What did you have to do to ensure your survival? What threat responses are you employing?
- What are your strengths? What power resources do you have access to?

To integrate these, it is necessary to elicit the meaning clients make of their experiences: the proposed clinical framework can provide structure to enable a full and detailed line of enquiry. Themes include recollections of the childhood prior to boarding, reasons for boarding, the experience of boarding, and how that experience has impacted on life in adulthood. The framework is not definitive, but it is designed to cover the central topics identified in previous research as being important to recovery. It is hoped that the level of enquiry suggested will not be overwhelming to therapists new to working with ex-boarders.

Not every characteristic will be relevant and there may be others relevant to specific individuals that are omitted – it is a dynamic framework to be used flexibly and creatively. The sequencing of questions requires careful consideration as it is neither appropriate nor helpful therapeutically to expect a new client to talk openly about past abuse. Trust needs to have been established for clients to talk about triggering emotive and frequently distressing memories. Having elicited an ex-boarder's story, the therapist can support them to move from 'surviving to living' a meaningful life, employing Duffell and Basset's recommended staged protocol of recognition, acceptance and commitment to change.[48]

Conclusion

The experiences of boarding for those who were educated in the early to mid-twentieth century may be very different to the experiences of those who were educated in the 1990s onwards. A temporal and cultural understanding of the boarding experience is important, as this will impact on the issues that clients present with, or that arise, during therapy.

By applying the tenets of intersectionality to boarding school education, it is clear how the stereotypical image of the 'posh boy' still prevails in our cultural narrative. Commentary on social media platforms implies that boarding schools are only available for the rich or for children of parents stationed in far-flung parts of the Commonwealth.

Despite the changing demographics of boarding schools, it is hypothesised that for many boarders the same pressures continue to be relevant today. From the lens of the power threat meaning framework, we can examine these demands from a social constructionist perspective, situating the presenting difficulties of clients as a direct consequence of societal demands and expectations, rather than as perceived individual failures.

The difficulties a therapist may encounter when working with an ex-boarder have been recognised. The ruptured attachment experienced by children sent to boarding school is acknowledged by therapists experienced in attachment theory, although this may be less recognised by their clients.[49] This generalisation is notwithstanding that escaping abusive family circumstances may provide a welcome relief for an unfortunate minority.

Enabling clients to first acknowledge and then assist the dissolution of their well-established personas takes specialist knowledge and skills. Ex-boarder therapists need to be vigilant in respect of their own conditioning to avoid normalising or colluding with their client's experience. Non-boarder psychotherapists will need to recognise the vulnerabilities behind the confident, dismissive or overly compliant personas exhibited.

The clinical framework has been developed to incorporate themes deemed relevant to explore therapeutically with ex-boarders, assisting in creating a robust formulation of factors underpinning a client's presenting issues. This will lead to improved treatment outcomes, as well as providing structure for session notes and supervision presentation.

Notes

1   Renton, A. (2017) *Stiff Upper Lip: Secrets, Crimes and the Schooling of a Ruling Class*. London: Weidenfeld & Nicolson.
2   Duffell, N. (2000) *The Making of Them: The British Attitude to Children and the Boarding School System*. London: Lone Arrow Press. Schaverien, J. (2015) *Boarding School Syndrome: The Psychological Trauma of the 'Privileged' Child*. London & New York: Routledge.
3   McPherson, S. Emerson-Smith, M. and Cavenagh, P. (2024) 'British Boarding Schools on Trial: Making the Case for New Evidence' in P. Cavenagh, S. McPherson and J. Ogden (eds), *The Psychological Impact of Boarding School: The Trunk in the Hall*. Oxford & New York: Routledge.
4   Duffell, N. (2000) *The Making of Them: The British Attitude to Children and the Boarding School System*. London: Lone Arrow Press.
5   Sutton Trust and the Social Mobility Commission (2019) *Elitist Britain 2019: The Educational Backgrounds of Britain's Leading People*. Sutton Trust & Crown Copyright 2019. Retrieved from https://www.suttontrust.com/wp-content/uploads/2019/12/Elitist-Britain-2019.pdf.
6   Social Mobility Commission (30 April 2019) Report: 'Class Privilege Remains Entrenched as Social Mobility Stagnates'. Retrieved from https://www.gov.uk/governm ent/news/class-privilege-remains-entrenched-as-social-mobility-stagnates.
7   Verkaik, R. (2018) *Posh Boys: How English Public Schools Ruin Britain*. London: Oneworld Publications. Beard, R. (2021) *Sad Little Men: The Revealing Book About the World That Shaped Boris Johnson*. London: Harvill Secker.
8   Fairbairn, C. and Roberts, N. (14 June 2023) *Charitable Status and Independent Schools*. House of Commons Library, Research briefing. Retrieved from https://resear chbriefings.files.parliament.uk/documents/SN05222/SN05222.pdf.
9   Schaverien, J. (2015) *Boarding School Syndrome: The Psychological Trauma of the 'Privileged' Child*. London & New York: Routledge.
10 Duffell, N. and Bassett, T. (2016) *Trauma, Abandonment and Privilege. A Guide to Therapeutic Work with Boarding School Survivors*. Abingdon & New York: Routledge. Schaverien, J. (2015) *Boarding School Syndrome: The Psychological Trauma of the 'Privileged' Child*. London & New York: Routledge.

11 Bruton Lloyd Educational Consultants (15 December 2021) 'A Fusion of Tradition and Modernity: The British Boarding School'. https://www.brutonlloyd.com/blog/a-fusion-of-tradition-and-modernity-the-british-boarding-school.

12 Morgan, K.P. (1996) 'Describing the Emperor's New Clothes: Three Myths of Educational (In)-Equity' in A. Diller, B. Houston, K.P. Morgan and M. Ayim (eds), *The Gender Question in Education: Theory, Pedagogy, and Politics*. Boulder, CO: Westview Press.

13 Boyle, M. and Johnstone, L. (2020) *A Straight Talking Introduction to the Power Threat Meaning Framework: An Alternative to Psychiatric Diagnosis*. Monmouth, UK: PCCS Books.

14 Boarding School Association. Retrieved from https://www.boarding.org.uk/member_type/full-uk/.

15 Independent Schools Council (2023). Retrieved from https://www.isc.co.uk/media/9316/isc_census_2023_final.pdf.

16 Independent Schools Council (2023). Retrieved from https://www.isc.co.uk/media/9316/isc_census_2023_final.pdf.

17 Independent Schools Inspectorate (2023) 'Framework for the Inspection of Association Independent Schools, Including Residential (Boarding) Schools and Registered Early Years Settings'. Retrieved from https://www.isi.net/inspection-explained/inspection-framework/downloadable-version.

18 Maxtone Graham, Y. (2017) *Terms & Conditions: Life in Girls' Boarding Schools, 1939–1979*. London: Abacus Books.

19 James, M. (2018) *National Curriculum in England: The First 30 years. Part One*. British Educational Research Association. Retrieved from https://www.researchgate.net/publication/328738196_National_Curriculum_in_England_-_the_first_30_years.

20 Independent Schools Council (2022) Retrieved from https://www.isc.co.uk/media/9316/isc_census_2022_final.pdf.

21 CIPD (2022) 'Equality, Diversity and Inclusion (EDI) in the Workplace', Factsheet. Retrieved from https://www.cipd.org/uk/knowledge/factsheets/diversity-factsheet/.

22 McKinsey (17 August 2022). 'What Are the Differences Between Diversity, Equity and Inclusion?'. Retrieved from https://www.mckinsey.com/featured-insights/mckinsey-explainers/what-is-diversity-equity-and-inclusion.

23 Bruton Lloyd Educational Consultants (15 December 2021) *A Fusion of Tradition and Modernity: The British Boarding School*. Retrieved from https://www.brutonlloyd.com/blog/a-fusion-of-tradition-and-modernity-the-british-boarding-school.

24 Kirby, P. (2016) *Leading People 2016: The Educational Backgrounds of the UK Professional Elite*. The Sutton Trust. Retrieved from https://www.suttontrust.com/wp-content/uploads/2020/01/Leading-People_Feb16.pdf.

25 Morgan, K.P. (1996) 'Describing the Emperor's New Clothes: Three Myths of Educational (In)-Equity', in A. Diller, B. Houston, K.P. Morgan and M. Ayim (eds), *The Gender Question in Education: Theory, Pedagogy, and Politics*. Boulder, CO: Westview Press.

26 Green, F. and Kynaston, D. (2019) *Engines of Privilege: Britain's Private School Problem*. London: Bloomsbury Publishing.

27 Orwell, G. (1952) *Such, Such Were the Joys*. New York: The Partisan Review.

28 Raphael, F. (2003) *A Spoilt Boy: A Memoir of a Childhood*. London: Orion.

29 John-Baptiste, A. (2021) 'The Black Children Wrongly Sent to "Special" Schools in the 1970s'. Retrieved from https://www.bbc.co.uk/news/uk-57099654 20 May 2021.

30 Mackay, N. and Mumme, K. (2021) 'Boarding School Survivors Reveal Their Horrific Stories of Childhood Abuse in "Me Too" Moment', in Neil McKay's Big Read, *The Herald*. Retrieved from https://www.heraldscotland.com/news/19529579.neil-mackays-big-read-boarding-school-survivors-reveal-horrific-stories-childhood-abuse-metoo-moment.

31   Laughton, M. (2019). 'The Trunk', in N. Simpson, N. (ed.), *Finding Our Way Home*. London & New York: Routledge, p. 114.

32   Scudamore, J. (2020) *English Monsters*. London: Jonathan Cape.

33   *The Guardian* (22 March 2024) 'For Many of Us, Boarding School Was No Gilded Life', Letters. Retrieved from https://amp.theguardian.com/education/2024/mar/22/for-many-of-us-boarding-school-was-no-gilded-life.

34   Lee, J., Wardman-Browne, J., Hopkins, E., McPherson, S. and Cavenagh, P (2024) 'It's Not All Down to Boarding: Early Family and Peer Relationships Among Boarders', in P. Cavenagh, S. McPherson and J. Ogden (eds), *The Psychological Impact of Boarding School: The Trunk in the Hall*. Oxon & New York: Routledge.

35   Sykes, T. (2015) 'I Was Eton's Only Out Schoolboy', *Daily Beast*. Retrieved from https://www.thedailybeast.com/i-was-etons-only-out-schoolboy.

36   Duffell, N. and Bassett, T. (2016) *Trauma, Abandonment and Privilege. A Guide to Therapeutic Work with Boarding School Survivors*. Abingdon & New York: Routledge. Schaverien, J. (2015) *Boarding School Syndrome: The Psychological Trauma of the 'Privileged' Child*. London & New York: Routledge. Gottlieb, M. (2005) 'Working with Gay Boarding School Survivors', *Self & Society*, 33(3): November 2005–January 2006.

37   Forster, E.M. (1936) *Abinger Harvest. Notes on English Character*. London: Edward Arnold.

38   Orwell, G. (1936) *Shooting the Elephant*. The Literature Network. Retrieved from https://www.online-literature.com/orwell/887/.

39   Duffell, N. (2000) *The Making of Them: The British Attitude to Children and the Boarding School System*. London: Lone Arrow Press.

40   Schaverien, J. (2004) 'Boarding School: The Trauma of the "Privileged" Child', *Journal of Analytical Psychology*, *49*(5): 683–705.

41   Duffell, N. and Bassett, T. (2016) *Trauma, Abandonment and Privilege. A Guide to Therapeutic Work with Boarding School Survivors*. Abingdon & New York: Routledge.

42   Evans, M. (2021) *Psychoanalytic Thinking in Mental Health Settings*, Abingdon & New York: Routledge, p. 35.

43   Schaverien, J. (2015) *Boarding School Syndrome: The Psychological Trauma of the 'Privileged' Child*. London & New York: Routledge.

44   Mate, G. (2022) *The Myth of Normal: Trauma, Illness & Healing in a Toxic Culture*, London: Vermillion, p. 248.

45   Mutluer, T., Fatih, P., Tayakisi, E., et al. (2021) 'Psychopathology and Dissociation Among Boarding School Students in Eastern Turkey,' *Journal of Child & Adolescent Trauma*, 14(1): 201–207.

46   Duffell, N. and Bassett, T. (2016) *Trauma, Abandonment and Privilege. A Guide to Therapeutic Work with Boarding School Survivors*. Abingdon & New York: Routledge.

47   Boyle, M. and Johnstone, L. (2020) *A Straight Talking Introduction to the Power Threat Meaning Framework: An Alternative to Psychiatric Diagnosis*, Monmouth, UK: PCCS Books.

48   Duffell, N. and Bassett, T. (2016) *Trauma, Abandonment and Privilege. A Guide to Therapeutic Work with Boarding School Survivors*. Abingdon & New York: Routledge.

49   Bowlby, J. (1988) *A Secure Base: Clinical Applications of Attachment Theory*. London: Routledge.

Chapter 3

The Child in Exile

Reflections on work with adult expatriate ex-boarders

Pippa Foster

Prologue

I was in a park near to where I live, when I heard an argument brewing between a child of about 9 and her mother. I could hear the girl saying, 'Why can't we do what I want. We ALWAYS do what you want. It's not fair.' The mother was clearly embarrassed seeing me nearby, so she dropped her voice as she said she was sorry her daughter felt that. This completely incensed the child who shouted, 'It's not what I FEEL! It's the TRUTH!'

What a wonderful moment! Here was a child completely at home with her anger, with an established sense of the truth of her feelings and an ability and confidence to call her mother out on any soft-soaping. As I walked away, I reflected on the number of ex-boarders I had seen who had lost the ability to do any of that at an early age. The trauma of being abandoned in the confusing environment of the school, with the overriding message that this is what is good for you, strips so many of their self-belief and the confidence to risk fully expressing their feelings and objections to anybody – even to themselves.

This is so much more pronounced when the trauma involves an abandonment in a country other than the one previously considered home and the ensuing sense of separation from family and everything familiar. The accompanying shock, the profound sense of isolation and the inability to grasp the immensity of the time involved in the separation leaves the child unable to hold on to so many of the certainties that had made up their experience of life so far. A woman who had been left behind when her parents moved abroad once said to me:

I think the moment they left me part of me froze, and I have never unfrozen.

It reminds me of another incident that happened in my early twenties when I was on a flight from the far east to the UK. Beside me sat two very small boys, clearly brothers, probably around 7 or 8, in their school uniforms. The flight was well over 12 hours long. The two were sitting at the back of the plane, in seats that would not recline. For the entire flight they sat almost entirely in silence, bolt upright in

DOI: 10.4324/9781003515517-3

their seats, with their hands folded in their laps. I don't think they moved once. Any attempts by the stewardesses or by myself to engage them were politely responded to, in the briefest terms, before they returned to their silent vigil. It is hard to describe in words the effect of sitting with these two traumatised and frozen children, with no apparent way to reach them in their grief, or to do anything to help mitigate the effect that this horrible journey was going to have on the rest of their lives.

'Shock'

The moment of separation and shock was vividly described to me by my client 'Miriam', left by her parents in a foreign country at the age of 5. Miriam had been brought up in Africa, the eldest child of devoted parents, and her memories of her very early years are extremely happy. The birth of her sisters preceded a brief period in the UK before the family moved to a new country, and Miriam was taken to a school in a third country nearby.

In her first session, Miriam described being on a climbing frame as her parents were leaving. She remembers the feel of the bars, the colour of the metal and the smell of it. But then all memory, all colour and texture stop. She lived the next few years in a kind of fog, retaining little memory of any of it, never showing anyone or acknowledging to herself the extent of the trauma she experienced. Her description of being on the climbing frame was so vivid that it stayed with me all the following week, as if I was holding that little 5-year-old in my heart during the time between the two sessions. Miriam struggled to attend her second session. She was taken over by doubt: thoughts that therapy was all nonsense and unnecessary. But she managed to make it back. I felt she had left that small child with me for the week.

Such a process of 'projective identification' may be used as a way of communicating, particularly with trauma that is unmanageable and beyond words.[1] Miriam had to disown her distress and confusion in order to survive. Of course, it was also important for me to be sure that it was a communication coming from her: having myself been an expatriate boarder from an early age, it was entirely possible that it could have been a triggering of my own trauma. But this seemed so specific in context – the look and feel of the climbing frame, the particular age of the child – that I was convinced this was a way for Miriam to safely deposit her small child for the week, and return to pick up the work again the following session.

Like so many ex-boarders, Miriam struggled to accept that what happened to her was traumatic. For years she had told stories of her school life as exotic and exciting. For her, as for others, the therapeutic journey is about taking in the profundity of what happened and the residues of the child's survival it leaves behind. Early in her therapeutic journey I told her about a talk I had been to by Lemn

Sissay, a man brought up in children's homes, who had commented how awful it was that boarding school children must live without hugs.[2] This had a profound effect on Miriam: she recognised that Lemn had experienced a traumatic childhood, and found his compassionate words about his boarding experience as a moving affirmation that what had happened to her was deeply wrong.

Accepting this as trauma was particularly difficult for Miriam as her parents were both missionaries, and the school she was sent to was a missionary school. The notion that God was somehow behind her abandonment, that it was being done for the greater good by an omnipotent force was deeply embedded in her understanding, even at the age of 5. The dissociation that she automatically engineered was the only way she was able to survive the apparently heartless and abrupt dislocation in her life. She accomplished this dissociation with such success that she convinced herself completely.

She remembers her father, on recently seeing a photo of Miriam with her sister, by then both at the school, saying how sad her sister looked, but how she, Miriam, was clearly fine. Miriam could see why he said that, and it helped her to recognise the depth of self-deception that she had employed. In adult life she has been constantly assailed with feelings that catastrophes are waiting around every corner and that bad events are her fault. She described never really feeling happiness, nor that her needs or wishes mattered, nor having any agency over decisions about her life.

The home country

While Miriam was taken to another, unknown, country to board, other children are 'sent back home' to the UK. However, this is not how it seems to a child whose life experience has often been in a completely different country and culture: that their parents call the UK 'home' can be deeply confusing. For those children, the sense of being alien, of the place they arrive in as being foreign, is denied by the language used and produces a profound disorientation. They conclude it must be *their* fault that it all feels so 'other' and that they cannot settle happily in the place their parents view as 'home'.

'Catherine', sent from her home in Malaysia to the UK at age 9, never shared her home life with her school friends as she knew they would have no understanding of it. Feeling alien at school did not make it easy for her back with her family either. As the eldest and the first to be sent, she returned to a functioning and happy family that had apparently got on fine without her. She felt an outsider there too and noticed that in later adult life she often retreated to the kitchen to cook or wash up, to 'justify her existence', as she put it. It took a while for Catherine to acknowledge in therapy that part of her loss was not just her parents but included the household members, the kitchen she knew so well and the cook with whom she had happily spent her childhood – all left behind. So, as an adult, being in the kitchen became a way of linking herself to that happier experience of belonging.

Catherine's way of coping with what happened to her was to retreat into a world of thinking where everything could be understood intellectually. So, her therapy tended to be about the recognition of ideas and thoughts rather than feelings and sensations. She rarely cried in a session, but she did take notes. She did a lot of reading, and the book When the Body Says No has been important to her.[3] She began to recognise that her retreat into her head had detached her not only from her feelings, but also from her body. Always having managed independently, she is sad that she has never had a relationship of any length.

Second mothers

Catherine's difficulty in recognising the importance of household staff, nannies or *ayahs* is not uncommon, as the loss of these significant people is rarely acknowledged by anyone around the child, yet it can have an extremely profound effect.[4]

'Robert', who was brought up in India, experienced his mother as cold and rejecting, but he had an *ayah* he barely talked about until well into his therapy. The extent of his attachment to her became clear when he became involved with two women: one English who loved him, and of whom he was very fond but unable to feel passionate about, and the other Sri Lankan with whom he had little in common but whom he found extremely sexually arousing. The link between these two women and his two childhood attachments, mother and *ayah*, helped him to make sense of his emotional confusion and to eventually get some resolution of his dilemma.

Another man, 'Peter', also had a 'second mother', his *amah*. At nine his parents left Malaysia, dropping Peter at boarding school in the UK, before the family travelled on to live in Kenya. His memories of his boarding school were sparse, but he vividly described the first night. He had the habit of rocking himself to sleep, but the reaction of the other boys in the dormitory made him realise, with despair, that even that had been taken away from him. Otherwise, he remembers being alone a lot, and wandering around the grounds. He had no memories of having friends.

During holidays, when he was able to join his family, Peter's experience was also deeply alienating. His siblings had a completely new life, with a household of people he did not know and with whom he felt he had no place. He remained as a boarder for three years. Perhaps it was his parents' recognition of the damage that it was doing him that led them to return to the UK. But he never settled comfortably in school after that, struggling with crippling social anxiety. Years later, when he was referred for therapy by his GP, an identity as an outcast seemed to mark his life, working in alienating menial work, living in a rented room and ringing the Samaritans almost every evening when he had drunk himself into a state of despair.

He took the opportunity of his referral very seriously and told me later that he was completely taken aback that someone would be prepared to spend their time helping him, and even more surprised when, as the work became more intense, I offered him twice weekly sessions at a reduced fee. Peter's gratitude for this remained long after the therapy was over, but the positive feelings were not the only ones he struggled with.

Peter recounted how he had had a brief sexual relationship early in his twenties; he felt very strongly for this woman, but he was deeply confused because he also had other much darker feelings. He described waking with her in the mornings and being preoccupied with murderous feelings, and shocked by how easy it would be to follow these through. The confusion this brought him led to an early end to their contact. Early on in his therapy I began to feel some discomfort as I walked in front of him up the stairs to the sessions. I mentioned this and he was able to confess to harbouring murderous fantasies towards me as he followed me.

The fact he had such suppressed rage was not surprising: opening himself up to the possibility of trusting someone was extremely scary for him, having felt so betrayed in his childhood. What was surprising was that he was able to tell me about these feelings; this meant we were able to look at them in the context of his distrust and fear. It became clear that it was the awareness of his confusing and often violent or sexual feelings that led to his acute social discomfort and his conviction that others would be repelled by him, were they to be revealed, which he felt sure that they would. This would lead to blushing and stammering in some social situations.

Much of the early work with Peter was to help him to understand the nature of these feelings in the context of the traumatic and alienating experience of his early abandonment and his sense of confusion and betrayal by those he had put his trust in. Gradual acceptance that feelings could be understood and that *feeling* things was different from *acting* on them led to a gradual ability to feel more comfortable with them and to recognise the origins of his inability to let people close or to trust. In one very memorable session he suddenly said:

> I have realised that the monster that I have lived with, caged up inside, is nothing more than a sad and lonely little boy.

My work with Peter began in the 1990s, and, although I had some substantial experience as a therapist before then, I had not done much work with ex-boarders. Nor had I done any specialist training in ex-boarder work, which was not available until much later. Today it would be a very important part of the work to introduce the concept of the 'inner child' and to encourage the gradual relationship between the adult in the room and the child inside, who has been repressed, but whose presence has dominated life since. However, Peter's statement arose from a profound insight out of his own experience, rather than any notion that had been put to him.

Peter left his soulless job with the encouragement of a friend. He had spent time helping her out with child-minding in the holidays and had found great satisfaction in working with children. With references from her, he was able to take a job as a SEN teaching assistant in a senior school. He proved to be an enabling and empathic support to many of the young people he worked with. Gradually he became more integrated into his life. He joined some local groups. A big step was when he started to take short holidays, travelling to foreign cities, that he greatly enjoyed. These were the first events that he initiated for himself and brought to fruition purely for his own enrichment. They gave him a tremendous sense of satisfaction.

Little soldiers

The difficulty in initiating events in adult life was a common theme for all three, Miriam, Catherine and Peter, and I have found this repeated in others sent to boarding schools in another country. There can be a sense that life has somehow happened to them, orchestrated by others, rather than a sense of having agency in important decisions and life choices along the way.

I have noticed that this is particularly so for those who are the eldest child in their family: it seems a special trauma for the first to be sent. Younger children at least have a sense that this is what can happen in life; seeing their elder siblings being sent away, they have some idea that this is what may happen to them. Of course, this has its own difficulties as the dreaded day comes nearer. But for the eldest, the experience comes out of the blue. Nothing can really prepare them for what will happen; the shock may leave an underlying sense that life is what is *done to* them, rather than something they can make happen.

The issues for younger children are as profound but often different. They can feel reassured that they are following in the footsteps of their sibling but may then be shocked to find that they never see them, even if they are at the same school. Some find that their sibling disowns or, in some cases, is actively unkind when they do see them, with family jealousies being played out at school. One woman described how she begged to be sent away to keep her brother company; once there she had no contact with him but was left feeling to blame for having asked to go.

A major factor for all these children is the absence of adults to comment on their lives and choices: the child is living, quite literally, in a different world. No one in my practice had any sense that their parents were interested in their school experiences. In fact, the best way of engaging with parents was to focus on their lives and disregard their own. Thus, the parents' lives become central, while the child's remains, at best, of secondary importance. Every child needs to learn about life through sharing experience, and it is the comments of a loving adult that help a child get a sense of themselves, their relationships and their capabilities. The child separated from their families by great distances is deprived of this.

'Sarah', sent at 7 from Japan, took a long time in her therapy to really be able to make contact with her own experience. Almost all her emotional life was centred on trying to give her two young children all the attention that she possibly could. This led to her having long periods of extreme anxiety about the issues they encountered, which were at times quite serious. During one session towards the end of therapy she came to a realisation of her own distress as a child and dissolved in deep crying. Through her tears, she said:

Now I know what a therapist is. You are a witness.

I understood that she meant: a witness of what was done back then, a presence that now confirmed the distress and the confusion the child had disowned.

I remembered hearing the talk of a group of mothers when my own child was at primary school. Their children were in Year Six and were going on a school trip for a week. The women were discussing the enormity of this coming separation, when most had only been apart from their children for a night at a time. They were not talking about how it would be for the children, but how *they* were going to survive it. If this was an example of mothers with healthily attached children, I wondered, how did some parents manage to send their children to another country for months – and sometimes even years – at a time? What profound breaking of bonds does this entail?

As a rule, reasons for the dislocation are attributed to the father's work. Perhaps this old-fashioned explanation is because most of the people I have worked with have been aged 40 or above. For some, like Miriam, religion is in play; for others, the children of the military or diplomats, the service of the country is a factor. Alternatively, they may be children of aid workers and have been given a strong sense of the privilege of their positions. These factors can make the concept of duty primary, and the child can imagine that their suffering is part of the sacrifice needed to serve the cause. It is as though the child becomes a little soldier, enduring what comes as a stalwart contributor to 'the greater good'. This belief can make it all the more difficult for them to access any sense that what is being required of them is unmanageable or beyond their maturational capacity.

For other children it is simpler, in that their father's work is temporarily overseas because they are part of a multinational corporation, or their work involves overseas contracts. Whatever the reasons for the separation, it is likely that the father's work is primary, and that he drives the educational choice, while the role of the mother can be more hazy. Some have had the boarding experience themselves and come from a background where it is not questioned; some are described as cold. Such coldness may be the mother's way of surviving the trauma of losing her child, particularly if she suffered a comparable separation from her own parents. Others are portrayed as unwilling collaborators. One man described how his mother never came to the airport to say goodbye because she was too grief stricken. But I have also noticed that some people find it very hard to describe their mothers at all.

Fractured families

'Matthew', who was initially sent away from Europe and later from Singapore, could only really tell me that his mother was a good cook. It sounded more like a child's view of their parent rather than the assessment of an adult. The use of child language can give strong hints about the degree to which part of the person has remained frozen in time. As a therapist, I have found it very important to look out for times when language changes. For example, one person I see will go from quite a sophisticated use of words to very simple overuse of one or two, in this case 'horrible' and 'stupid'. When she uses these, I am alerted to the possibility that what is being described links to much earlier experiences that were probably disorienting and disruptive. So, Matthew, who had a good facility with language, could only think of his mother as a cook, perhaps because thinking about her as a person brought up too many memories that had to be suppressed to survive all the years of separation.

Matthew came into therapy after he had had a panic attack while on holiday; it was triggered by the experience of someone lacing his coffee with some kind of alcoholic spirit. He deduced that the coffee reminded him of years in his public school when he had survived by being constantly inebriated, hiding alcohol in cups of coffee or tea. Christine Jack has written about trigger objects that can restimulate the trauma of separation in later years.[5] The panic attack scared Matthew and brought him into therapy.

In his first session, I told Matthew I could not work with him if he was drinking. He said that he would try to stop, and indeed for the remainder of the time we worked together he drank only occasionally. He had social contact with a therapist at some point, so he knew that therapy could take time, which, I think, gave him a sense of security. He said that he had no feelings and had never felt love in his life, despite having a wife and two children.

Matthew started boarding at 8 when his parents lived in Europe. Previous to that, he remembered happy times at home and said he had been close to his mother. His brother was three years older, and they did not get on. His father moved later to work in Singapore. There being no UK relatives, Matthew remembers being left at school for some exeat weekends, while others he spent with friends' families. A host family arrangement broke down when the father involved sexually abused Matthew during the course of the weekend. He chose the wrong boy: Matthew was a feisty child, who attacked anyone who bullied him, however big they were, and chose the dinner table to describe in graphic detail what the father had done to him. He was not invited back, and point blank refused to write a thank-you letter after the weekend, even though he got punished.

Subsequently, Matthew suffered sexual abuse by a teacher at school. In fact, sexual abuse by masters seems to have been rife at his prep school. In contrast Matthew remembers the boys taking great comfort in getting into bed together and experimenting sexually. Another refuge was in art. His work was so promising that the art master gave him the key to the art room. All that changed, however, when he went up to the senior school. There, violence and bullying were the norm, with a complete absence of any staff control; nights were disrupted by older boys having fun tipping the younger ones out of bed while they were sleeping. Not sleeping safely has a tendency to increase any underlying hyperanxiety. The comfort of other boys vanished too: any sign of intimacy between boys brought severe consequences from their peers. His art work diminished, his defences broke, and the drinking started.

All the ex-boarders I have worked with live with a degree of hyperalertness, a finely tuned awareness of what is going on around them, as a way of protecting themselves from the unexpected. With Matthew, it seemed that he had developed a coat of armour that kept him separate and safe from others. Patience seemed to be what he needed. The work was slow; but gradually he began to identify feelings, to experience moments when the child inside him surfaced, to begin to have flashes of happiness, an experience he said he had never had before. He was very close to his son and became a bit of a mentor to his son's friends and to other young men at work. As he was very open about being in therapy, he found friends opening up to him, which increased his self-worth. Being alongside him required taking things at his pace. In his final session, Matthew said:

Now I know there is at least one person in this world I trust.

It felt like his parting gift.

Although he was never really able to describe his mother, Matthew remained closely in touch with her. I have noticed that the ties of such children to their parents in adult life frequently remain central – even if the relationship can appear to lack depth and ease. One woman told me that her parents' neighbours remarked what a close family hers was. However, in reality many months of separation, due to being sent 'home' to board, had taken their toll. Although they all visited frequently, too much deep feeling remained repressed and denied; the number of visits, witnessed by the neighbour, in no way reflected real intimacy.

It has seemed to me that one way to understand such relationships is to recognise that the shock of separation may have left a part of the relationship stuck at the time of the trauma for both parties. Consequently, the abandoned child within the ex-boarder may still relate to their parent as they did in childhood, while the parent may struggle to allow the child they lost to fully grow up and individuate. Both sides seem to collude in trying to recreate the lost relationship. Sad as this is, I have not yet come across the example of a family who have managed to achieve it.

Epilogue

There are some moments in life when the privilege of being a psychotherapist can bring great gifts. I was walking into a café near my house when a man, sitting just by the entrance, said 'hello'. It took me a moment to recognise Peter: it was some years since I had last seen him. He was sitting in the sun with his friends. I knew that by this time he was married to a woman who loved him, and he looked entirely at ease and integrated into the life he was living – an outcast no more. We talked briefly, carefully, because his friends were there. As we came to the end of the brief catch-up, he deliberately caught my eye, looked at me deeply and directly, and said quietly 'Thank you', and then more emphatically, in case I hadn't heard, 'Thank you'. There was no mistaking the depth of that communication.

Notes

1 Schaverien, J. (2011) 'Lost for Words', *Therapy Today*, 22(3): 18–21.
2 Sissay, L. (2019) *My Name is Why*. Edinburgh: Canongate.
3 Maté, G. (2019) *When the Body Says No: The Cost of Hidden Strength*. London: Penguin.
4 Coles, P. (2015) *The Shadow of the Second Mother*. London: Routledge.
5 Jack, C.T. and Devreux, L. (2019) 'Memory Objects and Boarding School Trauma', *History of Education Review*, ahead-of-print DOI:10.1108/HER-01-2019-0001.

Chapter 4

Beyond the Glass

Making Visible the Boarding Experience for Women

Nicola Miller and Ruth Tudor

Introduction

For women, boarding trauma is particularly elusive. Ex-boarder women can find it hard to grasp the nature of the experience they had at boarding school when they were girls and emerging young women. Should they seek therapeutic help, they frequently see no reason to link their experience of boarding school with their current distress. The questions 'What happened to me there?' or 'What's so bad about what happened?' appear bewildering.

Drawing as our primary source on our experience of running therapeutic workshops for ex-boarder women[1] – including our specialised private practices as well as our personal experiences – this chapter attempts to make sense of some of the elusiveness of the boarding experience for women and examine how it comes about and may be addressed.

Throughout the chapter, we use the word 'sexuality' to refer to a sense of experiencing oneself as a sexual being with liveliness and energy, in addition to the conventional meaning of the potential for erotic intimacy. It does not reference current debates about gender.

As therapists working predominantly with female ex-boarders – in groups as well as one-to-one therapy – we are clear that we are working with the effects of delayed, and sometimes prohibited, adolescent growth in girls and young women who have been institutionalised. And we are working towards re-associating where dissociation has been necessary for survival. We understand the effects of the boarding culture on young women to be pernicious, regardless of their future adult sexual orientation or gender identity, and we maintain that women's issues have meaning and relevance for the whole of society.

While boys' boarding schools were consciously designed to raise men by encouraging 'masculinity' and associated qualities of resilience and adaptability, no such thought went into the design for women, who, in consequence, fail to be nurtured or seen *as women*. Our argument is that this is not simply a matter of neglect, but rather an active systemic process of *making invisible* the power and sexuality of

DOI: 10.4324/9781003515517-4

girls and young women, obfuscating their particular experiences. While this occurs throughout mainstream culture, the boarding school system further legitimates and intensifies it.

Traditional boarding school design and ethos tends to invalidate and deny women's embodied selves in a way that boys, with their contact sports, homoerotic traditions, communal bathing and so on, do not experience. The making invisible of girls' bodies occurs within a normalised context of abandonment and neglect. The silencing of the impulse to protest and the denial of the actual experience get rewarded and then used to exemplify acceptable or desirable characteristics of 'ideal' girls and young women. 'Ideal' girls do not make a fuss or take time and attention for their own needs, so shame is a key tool in controlling and shaping girls in boarding schools.

This elusive quality of girls' boarding is mirrored within the therapy literature, where published accounts of boys' experiences of boarding exceed those of girls, and the experience of women is assumed to replicate that of men. Hence it is important to tease out what is distinctive about what happens to girl boarders. While many accounts by male ex-boarders – for example, Renton's[2] and Spencer's[3] – tell of horrific incidents of bullying, physical violence and sexual abuse, girls are less likely to locate the precise nature of their trauma. When they do occur in girls' schools, acts of physical violence or sexual abuse are likely to be underreported. Research is urgently required in this area, and there is a plethora of reasons why it may be going unseen.

We are therefore up against two challenges: exposing the developmental trauma that engenders self-hatred and the mistrust of self and of other females and recognising that physical violence happens at girls boarding schools and is overlooked because of gender. We view this invisible trauma as an attack on the concept of femaleness itself, which we refer to as 'internalised misogyny'. Lacking explicit, obvious acts of horror, female ex-boarders and their therapists alike can underestimate or completely miss the aggressive and violent nature of this misogyny and the devastating trauma of the ordinary ongoing daily misery of navigating boarding life – lack of contact, lack of friendship, missing adults, managing their own bodies in space, being feminine and being seen and not being seen.

Inevitably, this phenomenon raises challenges in constructing narratives of experience. In our work, we are increasingly mindful of the need to develop and use a language that evokes, describes, and does justice to what is atmospheric, elusive, out of awareness, marginalised and not yet realised. The author Antonia White beautifully captures this elusiveness in the titles of her novels: *Frost in May*,[4] *The Sugar House*,[5] and *Beyond the Glass*.[6] In the women's workshops, as in our client work, we often hear expressions of self as being 'under water' or 'behind glass'. These descriptions evoke an experience of being removed from real life, of life happening *over there* or of never having been born as a woman.

In this chapter we attempt to get beyond the glass.

Visible yet invisible

Women leave their boarding school with not so much a skewed, partial, or narrow sense of inhabiting their sex identity – as men do regarding 'masculinity' – but with little sense of themselves at all; or perhaps with a multiple of internalised figures and structures that are hard to grasp.

Recalling her own experience, Ruth remembers everyday moving around as a painful and shame-inducing experience. For years, in therapy and in relationships, she searched for obvious, visible acts of cruelty to prove her trauma. She eventually realised that the quiet terror of corridor life – without the respite of home and mother – *was* the trauma.

> I feel my body most acutely when in motion, out in the open, making my way to maths or science or drama. Moving, but awkward; gawky, with my too big face and the too loud step of my stiff, ill-fitting, regulation shoes. I keep to the edge, eyes down, hyper-aware of every other body. I don't want to touch or be touched. Some girls jostle each other, move in groups, but I am aloof, careful. This is a dangerous balancing act. I'm treading fine lines between belonging and separateness, between seen and not seen, between cool and standoffish. I have just turned thirteen and my stupid body just got stupider.
>
> At night, curled into myself under my blankets, I smell different. I smell more. How much more worries me. I know I am not clean. I wash daily but I feel grubby. The peeling paint in the dormitory, the tiles in the toilet cubicles, with their edge of mould, the orange stains in the bath are inside me, dirtying me.

In this account, we see how the imperatives to be seen and to belong conflict with the shame of being visible – of being seen as unloved, unlovable, unsupported – and the consequent impulse to hide. We also see how the aggression and severe neglect in her environment, becomes internalised as 'bad' within the identity of the child.

When we speak of such experiences in therapeutic groups or one-to-one, there is often a powerful surge of recognition and relief at something essential being voiced. Our female ex-boarder clients begin to open up, to value their own hidden suffering and speak about it as trauma. One woman was astonished to see a photograph of herself on a Facebook thread from her school. In the picture she appears calm and competent – not something she ever felt:

> I felt virtually nothing all the time, but I was high achieving – becoming head-girl and winning prizes.

She said that the only clue in the photograph as to how 'bad' she felt was in the set of the jaw and the shoulders.

Another client described how she employed a designer to re-do her garden. This woman did not like the work but said nothing, paid the man, re-did the work herself and lived in fear of him visiting and finding out. She lacked a sense of a right to have her own home as she wanted it and felt shame that she might disappoint the designer, and that he would disapprove of her. Similarly, another woman recounted wetting herself at a dinner party, aged 18, because she could not navigate leaving the table and finding the toilet. Such hidden nightmares can be easily overlooked.

One participant in a workshop was aghast and awestruck when it dawned on her how much she had contained and suppressed. Her longing for home, her terror of being shamed or of getting something wrong, her feeling of inadequacy, her loneliness, her revulsion at the overwhelming physicality of growing up at school with hundreds of other girls – all were held quietly inside.

This capacity to contain intense feeling far away inside herself, beyond form and wordless, has developed within a situation where the child is unseen by parents who care for her and might respond to her relationally. Living within this absence, she hides her vulnerability. When she herself is unaware of her vulnerability she cannot feel fully alive, and this is often what leads women who have boarded to seek help.

The therapeutic groups provide an opportunity to witness and be moved by others: frequently someone else's material evokes another's own unease. Habitual and dissociated responses to discomfort include leaving the room, eating something, offering tissues and so on. Although these responses may seem unhelpful, at such moments we can recognise more explicitly how girls were taught to abandon and betray their impulse to self-expression.

Softness and sensuality

Typically, girl's school uniforms are made in block colours, not patterns, and of harsh materials such as tweed, lacking sensory pleasure or comfort as if designed to blot out feeling and sensitivity to their bodies. Girls often wear shirts, ties, tunics, jackets and hats in a style not dissimilar to boy's uniforms. In this way, girls' needs for tenderness and soft sensuality gets denied and obfuscated. In Ruth's account of corridor life, we saw how the physical environment – cold, harsh, sharp, ugly – actively impedes the development of girls into women. The architecture of the school gets internalised. Girls become tough when their relationship to sensuality and gentleness is uninvited and unattended.

A moving feature of the workshop for ex-boarder women is the change in clothing choices that we regularly see over the two weekends: more colours, more soft fabrics come in as they begin to reclaim their vulnerability, regaining their own agency and ability to relax into their female bodies. To be clear – we are not speaking here of the manicured femininity of celebrities or Royals as portrayed in the media, but rather an internalised capacity for softness that is often lacking in our ex-boarder clients. Nor are we advocating a particular way of being – we are keen to widen the repertoire of ways to be female – but we bear witnesses to such softening as recovery from boarding proceeds.

Girls' boarding schools lack a homoerotic tradition, and so female homosexuality is also denied. Without contact sports such as rugby or boxing, girl-on-girl touching is unusual and may only occur when a girl is sad. This sends its own message to the unconscious about when touch may be appropriate, becoming associated with sadness and need rather than with joy, pleasure or the gift of receiving.

Some women recount a secretive preoccupation with women's bodies that felt shameful. Having a 'pash' (a passion for another girl) was confusing. 'Was I gay?', many ex-boarders wonder. Part of our therapeutic work is hearing such stories, fantasies and fears and confirming the need for all girls to have support with this necessary developmental process. In the absence of parents who recognise and positively acknowledge her body, a girl at boarding school learns that her female body is a private matter that must be managed in secret. Knowing and understanding her body means struggling with something to be intuited alone with whatever resources are available. Puberty, therefore, raises very particular challenges in such a context.

At puberty children lose control of their bodies. Hair, blood, new body smells, skin eruptions, and mood swings occur: any attempt to control the body is doomed. Jane Dunn tells us how Antonia White thought she was turning into an animal when she began to grow hair.[7] In the absence of guidance from a grown woman, girls must depend on random information from other girls about puberty, sex, men and reproduction. This key stage of development is unlikely go well for girls at boarding school, who are neither supported nor seen. As therapists, we have found that we need to help our clients see that puberty in these circumstances has been compromised and encourage them to tell their unique stories.

Power, violence and vulnerability

The stereotype of the ideal feminine also affects the emerging adolescent boarder. A girl may have ideas about the ideal woman as maternal, warm, kind and caring. This can lead to the construction of a 'nice' 'false self'. Such a way of being lacks power and sexual aliveness. We have noticed that, for some women who attend the workshop, a rejection of the perceived feminine way of being occurs, in favour of a compensated and distorted experience of self as powerful only when in control or in authority. Often these compensations feel more manipulative than powerful. The key is how they are experienced in a relationship. For example, occasionally someone buys cakes for the other participants in a way that suggests an underlying need to demonstrate their kindness or to exert some power in the group. Some women may continue in this limiting way for the rest of their lives, unless it is compassionately exposed.

One workshop participant recounted how, at her school, new girls were allocated 'little mothers' – other girls aged between 12 and 16 years old whose job was to take care of them. She spoke about how she often felt cruel, even murderous, towards other girls – particularly younger girls – and worked hard to publicly 'nice' herself. It was confusing, and the shame of her *not so nice* impulses silenced her internally. 'I am quietly and politely evil', she had told her first therapist many years previously. This therapist had rushed to reassure her and validate her goodness, which only compounded her shame and heightened her confusion.

In the workshop, she began to understand that her difficult, hateful, and split-off feelings of rage and violence had validity. This allowed her to finally share her feelings and have her experience welcomed, not brushed aside; the relief was overwhelming. She could then accept that her conflicted feelings were the consequence of being a child required to mother other girls, while feeling abandoned by her own mother and in need of mothering herself.

One of the interventions at the workshop, which is hungrily received by many participants, is the validation of impulses towards cruelty towards self and others. Lies, gossip, being ignored, a harsh look in the corridor – these are all aggressive acts that a girl must endure alone. We need to include the possibility of violent fantasies and actual violence to the self and how these can be denied and dissociated. Being ignored, or having feelings reinterpreted in a way that denies their existence, can in themselves be thought of as acts of aggression. The malicious look in a cutting glance from one girl towards another expresses this. A common act of cruelty we hear about in the workshops is the treatment of teddies – hung out of windows, thrown at great heights, hidden from their child owner. Such behaviour is normalised at boarding school, and clients deserve to have such acts reframed as violent.

Power and aggression can get turned inwards, in many forms. One woman expressed outrage that females have to pay for sanitary products when males do not. In her adult life she was passionate about equality for women, while feeling herself to be intrinsically worthless. It emerged that, at age 13, her periods stopped soon after they started. Asked how she felt about this, she cautiously admitted to feeling superior to other girls, and therefore powerful. Cycles of physical pain, mess and self-consciousness could be forgotten. Furthermore, she drew satisfaction from knowing her parents would not need to be told she had insufficient money to buy both stamps for letters home and sanitary products.

Such covert independence concealed her immense suffering and illustrates the power of the psyche to survive by somatisation: her child's body took control, thereby validating her power to look after herself. It resumed menstruation on leaving school, but her adaptation was still active. As an adult, she continued to feel 'in control' and be little impacted by hormonal issues that she heard other women describe. In her therapy she realised how she continued to conceal her vulnerability through only engaging in adult relationships when she felt safe, or in a position of authority.

During the therapeutic groups with ex-boarder women there is often a moment when the rage being re-associated is a palpable presence in the room. We sometimes then fetch a sports punch-bag. While some of the women eye it with horror, others are excited and want to have a try. If they can connect their bodily anger to words and phrases that express why they are angry or at whom, the force of the punches grows. This is key: the feeling of rage had a cause – hurts, cruelties or betrayals – and can be re-associated with that cause. The more aggression expressed outwardly, the more genuinely powerful they may feel in the body.

With support, a woman can often stay aware of this power and allow it to move around the body, using sensation and breathing to regulate and prevent being overwhelmed or spinning out into renewed dissociation. Often, the rage then turns to tears and a longing for mother; the woman may then allow herself to be supported in her tears. In this way, she may experience her power and vulnerability together, embodied, and met in relationship with one of the facilitators.

The therapist's capacity to be present in their body, in particular standing in as a mature parent to a sexually developing child, is crucial for a healing relationship to be effective. This does not necessarily need naming for the participants, but it is a requirement for repair work with ex-boarder women at this level. A girl child needs a sexually alive, responsive and boundaried adult to help her body regulate feelings and receive mirroring that is grounding and affirmative.

Who shall parent the boarding girl?

In her seminal work, *Boarding School Syndrome*, Joy Schaverien shows how the attachment of a girl to her mother is central to the development of her identity through puberty, adolescence and to the brink of adulthood.[8] A Channel 4 documentary, *Leaving Home at Eight*, which followed 8-year-old girls and their mothers as they go through their first term at boarding school, sheds light on this issue.[9] In the film, we hear a great deal from the mothers about their suffering and conflicted emotions; however, we get little sense of their capacity to reflect on their daughters' emotional turmoil or empathise with their distress. The mothers seem comforted to remind themselves how their children are loving their new friends and all the exciting activities now available to them. We note too how little the fathers feature in relation to their daughters, and parenting seems to be stereotypically the responsibility of the mother. Sent away from mother, father and the family to live in an institution, who will now mother the little girl?

The documentary clearly shows how rapidly the girls come to rely on each other for solace, companionship and distraction. Other 8-year-old girls are internalised to function as mother, while 'Mummy' herself is idealised and protected. The activity-filled routines of institutional life are also internalised as ideal containers and protectors of the developing young psyche. As we watch, we see the pathology building up: the 'grown-up' children soon recognise there is no going back to being the little girls they were, when the only world they knew was Mummy's, where they belonged without question or awareness. Shock, fear, grief and denial follow and can be seen in their faces, while the rapidly developing self-sufficient child adapts to survive and belong as best she can.

Mummy isn't here. Get on without her!

Adapting and conforming offers relief, but truth gets sacrificed. Some of such hitherto unconscious compromises and hidden truths regularly surface at the workshops:

> Mummy is wonderful and I love her; I must be wonderful too if I'm to be loved. Mummy is powerless, poor mother needs my love and protection, if I disappoint her or make her sad, I must be a horrible person.

For the girl who decides mother is useless and despises this perceived weakness, problematic consequences also ensue. A 'useless mother' supports her venting of rage, disappointment, of distancing herself from the mother 'she-must-not-need'; but, ultimately, as she enters the adult world, such adaptations and beliefs no longer serve her. As a grown woman, any relationship is potentially vulnerable to receive these projections, which may play out, for example, with a boss, partner, daughter, friends or other workshop participants. They become the incompetent or 'useless' ones, not me – or, conversely, 'I am useless or powerless'. Either way, the vulnerable child's feelings are surfacing and need addressing before more autonomy can be accessed in the current situation. It will be hard for a girl to individuate and separate from her same-sex parent until she can let go of her idealisation-protection-aggression bond with her mother and grieve her own abandonment. Her therapist will be needed to provide – temporarily, at least – the reparative experience of a safe relationship with a significant adult.

Developing children need a parental presence: in a dominantly female environment, adaptations or compensations must suffice to mitigate the male absence – particularly of 'Daddy' – for the little girl. We observe how significant the environment became to many ex-boarder women: we often hear descriptions of powerful attachment to place, beautiful grounds, secluded space, such as a music room, or the view of a tree. These are present, consistent, non-judgemental and fulfil a significant role for her – a role filled not by a person but by a non-human being. We cannot say the environment is necessarily a substitute for fathering, but we are noting the absence of embodied 'Daddy' for the girl boarder.

This absence we believe impacts the girl who is schooled to be tough, like 'Daddy' – independent, conforming, achieving rather than sensual or soft. Women often carry the sense of 'male absence' as normal into their adult relationships; they are not always anticipating a benign male 'presence' – or able to relate to it should they encounter it. Without an internalised good mother or father, ex-boarder women can find adult relationships challenging.

'Celia'

The following clinical vignette illustrates the effect of the maternal wound, the ongoing attachment of the child to an idealised, weak or 'bad' mother, as it plays out in adult female relationships.

'Celia' spoke to her therapist Nicola about a current situation where a female colleague shut down conversation when any emotional charge arose. Celia had felt dismissed and found it infuriating and intensely painful. Her response was to withdraw and blame herself for what she believed must be her emotional oversensitivity or inadequacy.

Hearing her intense distress and anger, Nicola was reminded of the fragmented nature of friendships at school: part-time friends, part-time family. On hearing this, Celia recalled a particularly close friend at school who was unexpectedly removed because her parents could no longer afford the fees. She tells Nicola how, years later, they met up again and Celia had hopes of renewing the friendship. However, she quickly became frustrated by her friend's unwillingness to talk about their experience of school or discuss anything at all personal, or indeed to commit to arrangements to meet. As in the situation with her colleague, Celia felt dismissed, infuriated and hurt. There was evidently a pattern emerging: the 'other' was 'rejecting' and 'useless', while Celia felt pain and rage, then withdrew and felt 'bad'.

Nicola encouraged Celia, who was herself an experienced therapist, to look at this situation from another perspective, asking what Celia imagined her friend's capacity for intimacy might be in the light of her experience. Celia's body softened, she sighed and said 'She was a child; maybe she's scared ... I don't know'.

Then her eyes started to fill and she said, 'Maybe this isn't my fault at all?' A deep release of sadness followed about the very many losses she'd experienced, feeling her love rejected or denied and when no one had wanted to speak about feelings. One abandonment rolled into another, and her grief kept coming. This had been such a powerful theme throughout her life.

Over time, Celia began to see that not only did she have her heartbroken part, but also an angry frustrated part who lashed out to distance others and at the same time attacked and blamed herself. Repeatedly recognising, accepting and soothing or supporting these parts of herself, it became clear that Celia's angry part was not quite willing to let go yet. She wanted to fiercely punish someone – primarily herself. In this process she kept alive the memory of having been the victim of unbearable rejection while also still blaming herself for it.

Woman or child?

In the workshops, participants watch each other with curiosity and sometimes suspicion, which we welcome and contextualise:

Yes, you are women together. You may have strong feelings of resistance, dislike, trepidation, ambivalence. Which parts of others resonate with you?

When women become mirrors for one another in such a way, therapeutic groups can go deep very quickly, which can be alarming. Working slowly and sensitively, the level of trust begins to grow, it becomes 'safe to be unsafe' and participants open up about their vulnerability. This is inevitably linked to potentially dangerous feelings: sometimes violent, hateful, jealous, competitive or repulsive, even murderous. Whenever that which has been disowned becomes tangible, relief ensues; this allows a new narrative to arise, and acceptance follows. Therapists must pay minute attention to the body's activation cues – a still face, a rocking foot, a rush to pass the tissues.

While sitting with and paying close attention to our clients, we see how the survivor girl must hide. Janina Fisher's 'language of parts' is helpful when encountering the fragmented 'inner child' parts, who are often conflicted and contradictory.[10] Therapists must recognise that these are all 'child' parts, to use transactional analysis terminology, even though some are believed to be 'adult', or present as adult. This is painful and confusing and, in many cases, profoundly shameful to the client. To feel at all and to be seen to feel, can invoke the fear of judgement for a child without a safe or private space to go.

In the therapeutic relationship, we can expect such judgements to manifest in both therapist and client. Once accepted as part of the still-surviving 'little-adult' part, therapists can question their validity in current circumstances. For women who have created successful lives, dissociation – or the absence of feeling – can be what has made their survival, and even success at work, possible. The symptom that draws our attention to the trauma of having been culturally and institutionally invalidated, manifests precisely in the lack of emotional substance or affect, such as when an ex-boarder is able to tell a story without being emotionally present. This non-feeling *is* the feeling, and such a frozen emotional response is easily overlooked. As Patricia DeYoung explains:

> It's essential to remember that the return of dissociated memories of traumatic experience, including bodily and emotional feelings, is only part of the integration that needs to happen. They also need to make contact with the shame, past and present, that they can't bear to feel.[11]

'Rachael'

We end the chapter with a vignette from a woman's workshop, which illustrates much of what we have outlined above. 'Rachael' was a competent caretaker of others, a therapist who explained in the opening round that she was primarily 'there for her clients'. The facilitator was Ruth.

> Rachael is wearing dark trousers and big chunky shoes. One leg bounces out in a movement that seems involuntary. She's writing everything down and her upper body is alert, leaning into us, while her foot seems to be saying 'Keep away!'.
>
> I'm interested in the expression of this split and how incongruous her kicking out appears. Attentive to others, she has a competent kindly air: a safe pair of hands. At the breaks she's washing up, but she hasn't yet taken much time for

herself. I lean towards her and ask softly: 'So, Rachael I wonder what's happening for you. I see you're helping others, but what about you?'

She recoils. I've been too much. I breathe out, sit back in my chair; briefly I look away, then ask: 'I wonder if my concern is uncomfortable for you?' She looks interested. 'Probably it's too much, dangerous even?' I venture.

She nods: 'Yet I wanted your attention.'

'Maybe,' I say, opening my arms, letting the words be deliberately speculative, loose, airy. I need to let go of my own attachment to being right in this moment:

'Maybe my attention to you implies that you look like you're not coping. Implies you need something.' Rachael nods and tells us about her first term at school. She was 8. Someone hung her teddy out of the window. She got lost often, wandering the corridors, pretending to look like she knew where she was going.

The following day she asks for some time, then explains how much she's understood, using phrases like 'strategic survival personality', and so on.

But I can't take my eyes off her leg. 'Could we play?' I try. 'As if we're 8?' She nods and laughs nervously.

'Let's play with distance ... you let your leg bounce even more and I'll move away ...'

She looks alarmed.

'We're just playing,' I say. 'Try to be guided by the sensations. See if you can amplify your need for distance. We're playing. Just trying it out. Nobody will hold you to any of this.'

I'm far away now at the other end of the room. I tell her that although further away I feel more connected to her now. That taking space in this way might allow her to be more present. She's relaxing. Her breath is visible, and her energy seems less at the top end of her body.

'Come closer,' she says. I walk slowly. When I see her tense up, I move away again.

'Be curious – we're just playing,' I say, 'and you're in charge. You get to choose where you want me to be.'

When we're done, I say to the group: 'This is for all of you. You had no power to regulate distance, to protect your space, when you were at boarding school. You had to dissociate to manage it. Perhaps you felt ashamed that you wanted space and confused because maybe you wanted closeness.'

Afterwards, we reflected how children need to be received tenderly, with spaciousness and positive regard, as emerging beings, moving through transitions, as girls becoming women. Rachael's shyness had to be dissociated at school: the bold, more masculine part was more useful for surviving and stepped to the fore, became her frontline personality. She had needed this part; but these days, particularly in her personal relationships, it was no longer helpful to her. Her self-presentation had become intimidating, so she was even less likely to be welcomed in her shyness. She was betraying her shy part while unconsciously appearing to be competent. As facilitators, we needed not to be taken in or not to collude with this part of her.

Later in the day, Rachael linked both the dissociation of her shyness and our therapeutic play with boundaries to her difficulties in allowing others, including her partner, to see her and know her as a woman. She realised that she herself did not know what being a woman meant. Being able to express this in words felt hugely liberating to her, and she now felt the possibility to be curious about it. Listening to and valuing her own need for space or closeness gave her the possibility to be safer in relationship while exploring herself as a woman and as a shy being.

Notes

1 See https://www.boardingschoolsurvivors.co.uk/events-and-workshops/.
2 Renton, A. (2017) *Stiff Upper Lip: Secrets, Crimes and Schooling of a Ruling Class*. London: Weidenfeld & Nicolson.
3 Spencer, C. (2024) *A Very Private School*. London: HarperCollins.
4 White, A. (1933) *Frost in May*. London: Virago Press.
5 White, A. (1952) *The Sugar House*. London: Virago Press.
6 White, A. (1954) *Beyond the Glass*. London: Virago Press.
7 Dunn, J. (1998) *Antonia White: A Life*. London: Random House
8 Schaverien, J. (2015) *Boarding School Syndrome: The Psychological Trauma of the 'Privileged' Child*. London & New York: Routledge.
9 *Leaving Home at Eight* (2010) film, produced by All3media, UK: Channel 4.
10 Fisher, J. (2017) *Healing the Fragmented Selves of Trauma Survivors: Overcoming Internal Self-Alienation*. New York: Routledge.
11 DeYoung, P.A. (2015) *Understanding and Treating Chronic Shame*. New York: Routledge, p. 140.

Chapter 5

Good for Girls? Co-Educational Boarding Reviewed

Amelia White

A memoir

Aged 11, my brother, who was three years older than me, went off to boarding school. I stayed at home and went to a local school. Overnight I lost my sibling for him only to return in the holidays. Our father had died when we were very young, and my brother had always been on a pedestal for me, and I missed him.

When the school opened its doors for girls, I asked if I could go too. We went to work with extra maths tutoring, working at a scholarship, doing three-day entrance exams. Finally, I was awarded a place at this prestigious school. 'What fun', I thought, just as Darrell from Enid Blyton's *Mallory Towers* had felt when she was off to boarding school.[1]

Never was it made clear to me that, once I crossed that threshold of the boarding house, I would hardly see my brother and would feel like I would never come home again. My childhood was over.

I barely remember my first day, but I was immensely proud of the fact that I did not feel homesick or shed a tear when my mum left. Although in recent years, I have understood that the cough and projectile vomiting that occurred throughout my first term were probably somatic symptoms of suppressed grief.[2]

I do remember my 'nursemaid' at the time, a girl in the year above, leading me away from my mum; I turned my back quickly without even a hug and walked away. This is a tendency I have to this day when it comes to goodbyes. That was the moment I broke my attachment and dependence on my mum and became an independent resilient girl, with only myself to rely on. I was 11.

Letting the girls in

Wellington College and Marlborough began introducing girls in their sixth forms in the 1970s and 1980s, and over the past 20 years there has been a popular move away from traditional single-sex boarding schools towards co-educational schools. Soon there will only be four remaining boys-only boarding schools left in the UK: Radley, Eton, Harrow and Tonbridge.[3]

DOI: 10.4324/9781003515517-5

In recent years, many single-sex boarding schools have had to close, since fewer parents have been choosing such schools, placing them in financial difficulty. By opening their doors to girls, schools gain a financial advantage, while offering parents the convenience of sending their children to the same school; this is also more in line with a cultural change towards egalitarianism. Alex Peterken, the head teacher of Charterhouse, which started to take girls in 2021, believes that co-education helps militate against a 'macho, alpha-male culture, based on hierarchy and order'.[4]

Speaking to *The Educator*, Loren Bridge, Executive Officer of the Alliance of Girls' Schools Australasia, stated that:

> Many parents believe that co-education is better for boys because girls can have a positive influence on boys' behaviour.[5]

Despite research demonstrating that girls do better academically in single-sex schools and are less likely to feel a bias and be pushed into stereotypically girls' subjects,[6] advocates claim that co-ed boarding offers a better preparation for children as it is more representative of society and the workforce. The website for UK Boarding Schools claims that:

> Co-educational schooling demystifies the opposite sex and helps children to build relationships and confidence from an early age. Co-educational schools provide a mutually supportive environment for both boys and girls to live and work together and learn from each other.[7]

If these benefits are true, we must wonder how single-sex educational institutions that were originally designed to forge officers and gentlemen have evolved into ones that enable girls to thrive.[8]

This chapter asks why this transition to co-education in boarding schools occurred in recent decades and whether or not it is good for girls. My source material is informed by personal experience as well as my clinical practice, where I regularly see women who went to co-educational boarding schools; but my primary source comes from a specific questionnaire that I made public on three social media platforms, beginning March 2024, in order to better explore this topic. My questionnaire invited women to report on their experience as girls at co-educational boarding schools.

With a guarantee of anonymity, more than 40 respondents allowed me to use their words, which graphically illustrate this chapter. Most of those who responded to my questionnaire, as well as the women in my practice, were aged 30 upwards, having left co-educational boarding schools at least 10 years ago.

What emerges from their testimony forms the backbone of my argument and may shock some readers. It is to be hoped that the improvements in pastoral care over the last two decades have meant there have been some changes. However, it is unlikely that these unmothered girls, prematurely thrust into the charged erotic field of adolescent boys incarcerated in hyper-masculine institutions, will leave school without a significant impact on their emerging self-esteem and gender identity or their ability to develop healthy sexual relationships. At least, this is what these voices imply.

Living together away from home

In general, co-educational schools operate lessons and social activities in mixed groups, while the boarding houses, where the girls live, are single-sex until sixth form. Therefore, girls spend most of their time with their own gender. So, similar hierarchies and competitiveness, with older pupils increasing their power each year, apply within the boarding house, as they would within a single-sex boarding school.

With their attachment to their parents broken, it becomes essential for girls to form bonds and attach to one another. One ex-boarder told me how they used to practise 'honesty rings', which involved the girls in their year in their house sitting in a circle in the 'lav ends' (the bathroom area); they would take it in turns, one by one, to tell a girl what they liked about them, what they did not like about them and what that girl needed to change. This regular activity would be cruelly escalated whenever there was a vendetta against any one particular girl; then all the others would lay into her, destroying her character and shaming her. They were 12 years old.

The degree of envy, competitiveness and bullying experienced or witnessed within their boarding house frequently causes girls to grow up with a mistrust of each other. Many continue as adults to feel wary of other women. When asked what they learned about other women, some respondents to the questionnaire replied saying that they learnt that women were 'bitches'. One woman writes:

> My friends at school were more advanced than me in many ways and I always felt inferior to them. Living with this feeling 24/7 with no escape, for many weeks at a time, cemented it in me, and has been a present feeling all my adult life. It has had a major impact on many of my relationships with other women. I am constantly in alert mode and fearing being judged. I have one or two trusted friends but yearn to be confident enough in myself as a woman.

When asked who their female role models were, some women mentioned older girls, but most said they had none. Instead, they described stern, cold housemistresses and matrons to whom they would never turn for emotional support:

> There was a woman who ran the boarding house when I joined, and she was a cold-hearted authoritarian bitch at the end of a dark corridor. My chemistry teacher always had lipstick on her teeth. After that, I don't remember any other women.

Clearly, the principal female role model missing at any girls' boarding schools is their mother. To manage the repeated separation that occurs with every half-term and holiday, girls must repeatedly detach themselves from their mothers, both physically and emotionally. One woman described how she was desperately home-sick for months; and then she gave up. She never felt close to her mother again and never missed her. With no mother present for daily care, support and advice they must either turn to one another or develop an internal protector, *in loco parentis,* like the 'strategic survival personality' described by Nick Duffell.[9]

Maternal presence is especially important during developmental stages. Going through puberty only with other girls for support and to compare themselves to is a frequent generator of shame and humiliation for many. They are obliged to try to make sense of their changing body and menstruation in an environment without privacy or love. Here is an example:

> One time I couldn't figure out what to do with blood-stained pants and tried to get it out with soap and water, I must have made a bit of a mess as I got in trouble, but I still had no idea what I should do about it.

The developing female body is a particularly sensitive area when coupled with ethnicity differences. Reporting on the experiences of girls of colour at boarding schools, journalist Mollie Cohen noted how many felt 'othered'. The lack of black female role models led girls to feel shame about their hair or their body shape being different:

> She said she had no reference point to show her that her curves were normal. Her bigger thighs were just her body shape, but all she was able to compare her-self to were the 'perfect,' skinny bodies of her white peers.[10]

In co-educational boarding schools, values such as rationality, endurance and emo-tional repression, which could be described as hyper-masculine, are prioritised over more classically feminine values, such as nurture, care and empathy. Feeling shame about their changing bodies rather than celebrating them, girls often supress the feminine part of their identity and take on the more esteemed masculine traits. This impacts girls' gender identity formation at a crucial age and has problematic implications for when they are older and in intimate relationships.

Boys and exploitation

What gets even more confusing for girls at co-educational boarding schools is the added importance of being attractive to the boys – gaining their approval and val-idation. Many women have shared that they had little role modelling for healthy relationships, and with the absence of parental or pastoral care, they were left vul-nerable to sexual exploitation.

In puberty, girls receive an influx of sex hormones such as oestrogen and they have to make sense of new emotional responses and sexual feelings. The absence of parental love, physical touch, hugs and soothing can leave girls with a greater need for attention and physical contact. This leaves them more vulnerable to exploitation and pressure to engage in sexual relationships at a younger age than they might be emotionally ready for.

> At our school, the boys in the top year [18-year-olds] would choose a 'fruit bat' from the youngest year [11-year-olds]. One boy used to visit me in break-time. I do remember him bringing me chocolates and cards and asking me if he could give me a peck on the cheek, all of which made me feel uncomfortable. Mentally I felt pressure to be more sexual than I felt – attention from boys, but also pressure from peers to have boyfriends and be sexually active much younger than I was ready for.

One woman shared how she became obsessed with the idea of finding a boyfriend who would find her attractive, so she emitted some very desperate signals. She became absorbed with her looks, her weight and body image, trying to pursue perfection. She battled both anorexia and bulimia all throughout her boarding career.

Some women shared how, on arrival in the sixth form at boys' boarding schools, they were given scorecards, or marks out of ten, according to their looks. Isolated from girls in these institutions until now, many boys had already formulated ideas and fantasises about women, so, with the girls' arrival, they acted out their sexually objectifying mindsets.

Such girls then find themselves in a double bind: they must try to work out how to be like one of the boys and to become their friend, at the same time as being sexually desirable. Many women recalled this situation they found themselves in as 'Catch 22'. If they were not sexually active with the boys, they were called frigid, yet they risked being branded a 'slag' or a 'tart' if they were. If they were sexually active with a boy, it could be bragged about in the boys' dormitory and spread around the school as gossip.

One female ex-boarder recalled an incident in which she encouraged a male friend, whose plan was to go out onto the playing field one Saturday night with a girl who had a reputation for being 'loose' and to remove her clothes before running off with them. Such shaming behaviour illustrates the fine line that the girls were trying to negotiate. Going along with misogynistic views and behaviour might get you favour with the boys but to the detriment of your fellow female friendships. Another woman confirmed how girls climbed the social ladder by ganging up with boys against other girls.

> I learnt that we were weak and there for the boys' pleasure. Either a slut or frigid. Boys could touch me however they wanted and not much I could do about it. Boys were superior.

What has to always to be remembered, when considering boarding, is the absence of parents. One housemaster in charge of 50 girls in a boarding house is unable to keep an eye on them and know what they are up to in a way that parents of a child living at home can. They may have to sign in at night, but there is no parent to question them about where they have been or who they have been with. Importantly, there are no parents to counter the views of their peers or provide healthy role modelling of relationships.

Although children are confined within the school gates, many schools have extensive grounds where children may roam unseen and unaccounted for:

> There seemed to be a lot of drinking & sex around. I don't feel like we were particularly nurtured by our house mistresses, they felt more like there to check we came in on time in the evenings.

The breaking of attachments that occurs when girls board often means that they keep their school life separate and secret from their parents, perhaps only sharing superficial aspects of school life, like hockey matches or academic success, rather than sharing their internal feelings or turmoil. This accounts for how much abuse remains unknown by parents and the lack of monitoring over adolescent relationships. All of which leaves young girls vulnerable.

> There was no guidance, no one to talk to, no compassionate adult to help and guide you towards developing as a woman. The boys at school were seen as predatory. As a result of both home and school, sex has rarely been something I have enjoyed, and I have major issues with intimacy.

Sadly, many women also shared stories of being groomed and abused by male teachers, or knowing girls in the school who were. Young girls who miss love and nurture from their fathers are vulnerable to older men offering them kindness and care; girls frequently mistake grooming and abuse for being in a 'relationship' with a male teacher. One respondent shared how her drama teacher encouraged the pupils to act out rape scenes during class; another shared how she was shown porn during a science lesson. The lack of pastoral care and supervision shown for these girls leaves them vulnerable; it may also contribute to girls supressing their femininity to keep them safe from the male gaze.

Identity and internalised misogyny

In many co-educational boarding schools, there was, and still is, a gender imbalance, with a disproportionately higher number of male pupils. One example is how much emphasis is put on boys' sports, while provision for girls felt secondary and less important. This can leave girls feeling like they are in boys' schools, but inferior to the boys and second-rate, as one woman stated:

> Maleness is the default and femaleness is an afterthought.

Here are some relevant comments from the questionnaire:

Men at school were seen as superior to women. They were authoritative and I was fearful of them. This has stayed with me, in many respects, all my life and I am still watchful when in the company of men and I always feel inferior to them.

The boys were the leaders in the school too with girls very much treated as inferior/lesser beings. Girls were expected to be obedient and compliant and good. I had to fit into the patriarchal culture and learnt that the choice was either to be a 'good' girl or be punished and humiliated. I learnt to follow rather than lead, to accept the sexual advances of boys, and to tolerate and endure the sexualised behaviour of male teachers.

Girls were in the minority at school, and I suppose I got used to seeing myself in that way. I didn't trust women as much. I wasn't interested in women. Didn't feel much pride in being a woman. We were a curiosity group that had only recently been invited into the club of the school rather than an intrinsic part of the school community. We were also expendable. The boys boarding houses would have occasional discos and rather than inviting girls from the school to them, they would invite 'fuck trucks', – groups of girls from a nearby single sex school would literally be bused in for the evening. Looking back the teachers must have organised it, but it seems ridiculous and disturbing now. My relationship with women is complicated still.

Another way that some girls gain favour and a sense of being needed is to provide a mothering role for the boys:

> It was an old-fashioned upbringing where women had certain roles to carry out and there was a lot of 'looking after' men and trying to keep them happy. There was an air of being subservient to men and these were all lessons I learnt well.

In *Almost Boys*, a recent book about co-educational boarding in the 1960s, Isobel Ross suggests that girls assumed the tasks of giving boys the mothering, mentoring and friendship they needed as well as satisfying their sexual needs.[11]

Many of the women clients in my practice who went to co-educational boarding schools carry an inner misogyny that affects their self-esteem and self-worth as well as how they are in relationships. They may distance themselves from other women labelling them as feminine, frivolous, pathetic, wet, emotional or weak. One respondent noted that she felt prejudiced against women who use soft voices and demure demeanours, reading this as 'fake'. Another told me how she admired 'tomboy' types of women because they weren't 'pathetic'. She had internalised the view that stereotypical females were weak and frivolous.

It is not unusual to encounter such views across the wider society, for growing girls need the mirroring of positive, empowered female role models to learn to embrace and be proud of their own feminine characteristics. Mother is the obvious candidate for the job, but it is rare for me to meet a woman who went to boarding school who does not have a precarious relationship with their own mother. Such women often carry much grief and unexpressed anger towards their mothers for abandoning them, which may become internalised aggression. It can take much work from both sides to heal the rift caused by having attachments broken before the daughter is ready.

This precarious mother relationship can compound the negative experiences about womanhood that the girls take away from co-educational boarding schools, further impacting their feelings of worth and identity as women:

> It has taken many years to understand the language of women – and to not find all things traditionally female foolish – haircuts, make up, gossip, fashion. Being in a co-ed school with ratio of one girl to three boys made me feel more comfortable with men than women in adult life. I didn't feel any affinity with groups of women, and I would actively avoid them, finding the dynamic silly and embarrassing.
>
> Men were full of banter that I felt more familiar with, and it felt more down to earth. My inner misogynist was very strong and to some degree still is. I notice how critical I am of women sometimes and wonder why I hold them to different standards to men. I had a natural acceptance of men being the dominant presence and not to be challenged until my 40s.

Such internalised misogyny is dangerous while it remains unconscious. Female therapists who attended co-educational boarding schools, for example, may need to watch out for their blind spots when it comes to working with mixed-sex couples. There may be a part that gets pulled to align with the male in the couple against the female, repeating a pattern from schooldays.

Relationships with men

One argument used in favour of co-educational boarding schools is that they provide an environment that demystifies the opposite sex and mirrors the workplace. Evidently, in comparison to a single-sex boarding school, this is so, but school is not the workplace: girl boarders are children who need guidance, care and support when going through adolescence so they can learn develop emotional and sexual boundaries.

Girls who attend co-educational day schools are not in the same position. Such girls are able to mix with a different sex and then go home to be part of a family who may offer needed guidance. This could take the form of a conversation round the dinner table, or it may involve watching *Love Island* with their parents and debating whether particular relationships are healthy. Boys also need to be parented, see mutual respectful relationships modelled and misogynist views challenged.

In comparison to single-sex boarding schools, co-ed girls may grow up more at ease with boys and be more comfortable later having men as friends. Certainly, the testimony of those who completed the questionnaire attests to that. It is unclear, however, to what extent this is due to their unconscious misogyny towards women and feeling more at ease with dominant male characteristics and what the cost is to female friendships.

I was always drawn in the past to spending time with men rather than women. I always wanted to be one of the boys and never liked social events where the genders are split off into separate groups. I think I can be wary of men but also at the same time more at ease with them than women.

One of the largest consequences for all ex-boarders is a difficulty in forming healthy intimate relationships; this is prevalent for women who went to co-educational boarding schools:

I am good at forming male friendships because I see myself as 'one of them'. I've never learnt how to flirt and have no idea if a man finds me attractive.

On leaving school, many young women find themselves being promiscuous, believing this to be expected and a means of getting attention from men. Others attach very firmly 'like a limpet' to men who will have them, causing them to be in controlling, coercive relationships.

Another consequence of imbibing the hyper-masculine values of emotional repression, independence and self-reliance can leave women in relationships without love and nurture. Either because they are unable to offer it, or they are unable to receive it:

I had relationships with anyone who would have me, and my two marriages ended due to my inability to accept love or to have sex.

Another woman told me how she went through a very promiscuous phase at university and had a lot of one-night stands:

It was definitely about attention and affection even though I knew it wasn't good for me. My first serious relationship was with a man who was extremely violent and abusive. I had zero reference points for a loving healthy relationship and just went in headfirst with someone who showed me interest and affection.

The confusion between love and sex is apparent, and the lack of healthy role modelling and guidance offered to such girls can leave them stumbling in the dark when it comes to creating relationships in adulthood. The broken attachments and abandonment wound from being left at the school gates by their parents, deeply affects how women are in intimate relationships: either keeping one foot out of relationships to prevent being hurt or becoming anxiously attached and supressing their own needs and desires to prevent their partner from leaving.

The combination of having an abandonment wound and being raised in a hyper-masculine institution with a subtext that you are there for the pleasure of superior boys is a dangerous combination. It inevitable deeply affects girls' identity development, confidence and self-esteem.

Conclusion

Unfortunately, co-educational boarding schools do not provide the rosy outcome for girls that some advocate. I frequently hear tales of appalling conditions for girls at these schools and a lack of pastoral care; many leave school with low self-esteem and a confusing sexual identity that they carry throughout their lives.

Hopefully, pastoral care is becoming increasingly rigorous, and schoolchildren should be getting safer. For misogyny and sexist viewpoints and behaviour to change, however, conscious action to challenge and monitor adolescents is required, and yet the last 20 years' growth in mobile phones and the internet continues to make pornography freely available. It is unlikely that we are going to see a huge change in girls' perceptions of themselves. In fact, things seem to be getting worse for girls in all schools. Co-education may well continue mirroring the societal picture, where women feel inferior to men and that their voices are marginalised.

A survey, 'It's Just Everywhere', carried out by the watchdog organisation UK Feminista in 2017, found that over 37 per cent of female students questioned had been sexually harassed at school, compared to 6 per cent of boys.[12] The detrimental impact on girls' self-esteem suggests that girls learn to 'take up less space': to position themselves at the edges of corridors, playgrounds and classrooms. Girls continue to adopt strategies to avoid being noticed and singled out for unwanted attention, even if this means they miss out on more positive attention and recognition of their achievements.

Girls start to separate from their parents during their teenage years and often seek the wider approval of their peers and start exploring themselves sexually. This is a crucial development stage; but when a girl is away at co-educational boarding school, she is living and sleeping side by side with her peers, unable to go home for support, advice and reassurance from her family.

The attachment breakdown between mothers and daughters means that a girl at a co-educational boarding school may only seek advice from her peers, or not at all. She is without love and nurture, which leaves her vulnerable and she may seek attachment from an unsuitable male. Due to the misogynist values prevalent in schools in which men have more authority, she may be less likely to assert her own wants, needs and desires as a woman. The confusing messages about her own feminine identity and what is expected of her influences her friendships and trust of other women; it also impacts how she responds to men in both friendships and in intimate relationships.

Therapists working with women who went to co-ed boarding schools need to be alert to their clients' defensive rhetoric that it was 'fine' with boys there. Careful exploration is needed into their complex relationship with their mother, alongside their sexual and gender identity formation and how these things impact them today as a woman. The therapeutic repair work often calls for the re-parenting of a teenage girl going through puberty: this requires a safe adult who can give her the guidance and reassurance that she did not have at the time, with considerably more input than the client's façade may lead the therapist to suspect.

Notes

1 Blyton, E. (1980) *Mallory Towers*. Hampshire: Dragon.
2 Schaverien, J. (2015) *Boarding School Syndrome: The Psychological Trauma of the 'Privileged' Child*. London & New York: Routledge.
3 Young, F. (2023) 'Westminster School and the Sad Decline of Boys' Schools'. Retrieved from https://www.spectator.co.uk/article/westminster-school-is-wrong-to-go-co-ed/.
4 *The Economist* (2018) 'England's Single-Sex Schools Are Struggling to Recruit Pupils'. Retrieved from https://www.economist.com/britain/2018 /04/28/englands-single-sex-schools-are-struggling-to-recruit-pupils?, 29 May 2024.
5 Henebery, B. (2022) 'Single-Sex Schools vs. Co-Ed: Which Education is Better for Kids?' Retrieved from https://www.theeducatoronline.com/k12/news/singlesex-schools-vs-coed-which-education-is-better-for-kids/281599.
6 FFT Education Data Lab. (2023) 'How Does Performance in Single-Sex and Mixed Schools Compare Subject-by-Subject?'. Retrieved from https://www.ffteducationdatalab.org.uk/2023/10/how-does-performance-in-single-sex-and-mixed-schools-compare-subject-by-subject//, 10 May 2024.
7 UK Boarding Schools Guide (2022). Retrieved from https://www.ukboardingschools.com/co-ed-schools//, 25 May 2024.
8 Duffell, N. (2014) *Wounded Leaders: British Elitism and the Entitlement Illusion – A Psychohistory*. London: Lone Arrow Press.
9 Duffell, N. (2000) *The Making of Them: The British Attitude to Children and the Boarding School System*. London: Lone Arrow Press.
10 Cohen, M. (2020), *What it Means to be Black in a British Boarding School*. Flo London. Retrieved from https://www.flolondon.co.uk/all-posts/what-it-means-to-be-black-in-a-british-boarding-school-Bk0AX?rq=schools.
11 Ross, I. (2024) *Almost Boys: The Psychology of Co-ed Boarding in the 1960s*. Cheltenham, UK: Goldcrest Books.
12 National Education Union and UK Feminista (2017) 'It's Just Everywhere – A Study on Sexism in Schools and How We Tackle It'. Retrieved from https://ukfeminista.org.uk/wp-content/uploads/2017/12/Report-Its-just-everywhere.pdf, 10 May 2024.

Chapter 6

Boarding School Syndrome and Intimate Relationships

Elizabeth Carter

Introduction

> A man who during childhood was frequently threatened with abandonment can easily attribute such intentions to his wife.

This quotation comes from a lecture delivered before the Royal College of Psychiatrists by John Bowlby in 1976 as part of his series for *The Making and Breaking of Affectional Bonds*. Bowlby went on to explain:

> He will thus misinterpret things she says or does in terms of such intent, and then take whatever action he thinks would best meet the situation he believes to exist. Misunderstanding and conflict must follow. In all this he is unaware that he is being biased by his past experience as he is that his present beliefs and expectations are mistaken.[1]

I choose this extract because it encapsulates the issues that I will investigate through my clinical observations of boarding school syndrome and the impact it can have on adult intimate relationships.

When young children are sent away to boarding school, they experience repeated separation from their parents, which can lead to a rupture of emotional attachments. This rupture can ripple through their relational life as adults, wreaking havoc on their experience of and their capacity to love and be loved. The unconscious hypervigilance that ex-boarders frequently adopt can mean that they fail to recognise the difference between hostile situations and intimate opportunities.[2]

There is always a cost to enforced survival. Those in intimate relationships with ex-boarders may ultimately suffer the cost of their partner surviving boarding school. On entering therapy, ex-boarders' partners may present with marital or relationship problems or difficulties with intimacy or lack of affection; they frequently recount feelings of loneliness and despair, sometimes appearing in the

DOI: 10.4324/9781003515517-6

wake of other life events, but for which they do not know the cause. They may feel desperate for help without recognising the significance of boarding school syndrome,

> … they can sense the wounded ex-boarder but may not recognise the source.[3]

The childhood trauma experienced by the adult ex-boarder may often remain concealed by a socially confident and successful façade until difficulties begin to surface within their intimate relationships. The intimate relationship is therefore a key factor that can bring the boarding problem into awareness. Hence, in this chapter, I explore the wider impact of being sent away to boarding school at an early age and propose the causal effects that manifest through the relational lives of ex-boarders. I illustrate the issues associated with boarding school syndrome through experiences described by one female client, whose partner was a male ex-boarder, and I consider the implications for therapeutic support, using attachment theory as my primary model.

Wounds of love

It has been suggested by psychotherapists, including Nick Duffell and Joy Schaverien, that early boarding ruptures emotional attachments and subjects the child to living without love.[4,5] The young boarding child has to dissociate from emotions, vulnerability, sexuality and dependency and repress their true feelings in order to survive. Clearly, this may significantly impact intimate relationships in their adult lives. According to Simon Partridge, the boarding school system itself may also reinforce an insecure attachment style, particularly an 'avoidant attachment style',[6] normalising a distorted view of intimacy with often devastating consequences for the ex-boarders and their partners.

Emotional attachments formed between a child and their caregiver can provide a secure foundation from which further healthy relationships are able to be formed and maintained. Conversely, insecure attachment styles, such as avoidant, anxious or disorganised, arise from inconsistent, neglectful or traumatic caregiving experiences.[7] Young children depend on their primary caregivers to support them in their growth and development, and this includes the giving and receiving of love throughout their childhood. Research has shown that early patterns of attachment with caregivers can be repeated in adult intimate relationships and shape the ability to form healthy, secure attachments in later life.[8] Thus, the unique upbringing of children in boarding schools can cast a long shadow over their romantic and intimate relationships.

Children sent to boarding school at a young age, traditionally at 7 or 8 years old and sometimes as young as 4 years old, experience a sudden and significant disruption in their attachment relationships. The early years of boarding school, marked by homesickness, emotional isolation and strict institutional norms, can rupture attachments and severely impact the formation of emotionally secure bonds No wonder the trauma of boarding is sometimes referred to as a wound of love.

The institutional environment often leads to the development of coping mechanisms, predominantly the psychological defences of dissociation, repression, denial, omnipotence and mania, that are maladaptive in the context of intimate adult relationships.[9] The child may dissociate in order to survive and begin to function from what Duffell calls the 'strategic survival personality', which, as a façade of resilience and of a skilful self, can protect the vulnerable and prematurely independent child, but in adulthood this self-protection can become self-punishment.[10] Additionally, boarders find themselves caught in a double-bind, where, internally, they are aware of the privilege of boarding school and parental sacrifices made to enable such an expensive education. This engenders fear of communicating their unhappiness – or even unhappiness generally – and results in self-negating behaviour.[11]

As adults, ex-boarders may continue to function from their strategic survival personalities, appearing confident and successful, while sacrificing loving attachments and good relationships. Hypervigilance and self-reliance replace dependency and vulnerability, resulting in a survival state of hypervigilant anxiety. A pattern of learned behaviours that revolve around problems with intimacy, are evoked by the psychological and emotional challenges faced by individuals who attended boarding school at a young age, now known as boarding school syndrome.[12]

The traumatic experience of early boarding can disrupt the child's relationship with themselves and, as a result, impair their ability to articulate feelings and understand emotions, which is a cornerstone of partnership skill. Instead of developing a secure representational model, where self-reliance is balanced by an openness to be helped, fear of abandonment and pain of rejection can prevent the ex-boarder from allowing themselves to rely or depend on others.[13] A person who struggles with intimacy and trust in relationships, often idealises the other while avoiding closeness. Sometimes, such avoidance can be observed through a series of idealised and intense erotic encounters, which may persist even within marriage, reflecting deep-seated fears and grievances against tender expressions of love.[14]

Adults who boarded as children may feel threatened by intimate connection and abruptly cut themselves off from feelings of dependency. They may abandon their partner through an act of compulsive self-reliance, which can be experienced as 'a violent attack or abrupt rejection'.[15] Or they may abandon the other so that they are not the one who gets abandoned.

Dissociation and repression encourage defensive psychological reactions, such as 'projective identification', through which partners may feel the disowned feelings of despair or loneliness as if they were their own. It is as if the lonely and sad young boarder's disowned feelings finally get felt; the problem is, however, that the partner experiences these emotions inside of them and believes them to be theirs, because they feel so real, while the ex-boarder carries on.

Furthermore, masochistic and sadistic tendencies, where self-defeat preserves pride, can be utilised to deny the vulnerability and to preserve and protect the pride of the ex-boarder. This will leave the partner feeling hurt, abandoned and unloved.

The ripple effect of boarding

Boarding school is often a family tradition, so it is possible that these dynamics are inherited at the same time as being conditionally developed, as Philip Larkin poignantly suggests:

Man hands on misery to man, it deepens like a coastal shelf.[16]

Furthermore, writing in the journal *Attachment*, Simon Partridge suggests that there are consistent avoidant attachment patterns in the British upper-class culture which feed into and are fed by boarding school syndrome. He proposes a first stage of boarding school syndrome as:

usually (be*ing*) a member of a family *where an avoidant/dismissing attachment pattern predominates*: where physical contact is sparse or non-existent, in which emotions are discouraged or inexpressible, where intra-familial relationships are already 'detached' or 'professionalised' through nannies or au pairs.[17]

Through the lens of attachment theory, the transgenerational impact of early boarding on intimate relationships seems inextricably linked. The well-known metaphorical 'stiff upper lip' in British culture represents the repression of emotion and of traumatic experience, which traditionally – and particularly in military contexts – was viewed as an expression of fortitude, courage and resilience. In the past, say Capstick and Clegg:

maintaining a stiff upper lip involved the ability to exert high levels of cognitive control over the subjective, visceral, and emotional domains of experience.[18]

These values were often reflected in boarding schools, as well as traditional boarding school families, and are perhaps illustrative of an avoidant attachment style, where inhibition of attachment feelings, compulsive self-reliance and avoidance of close relationships persist in place of seeking love and care from others.[19] Early boarders who originated from a family entrenched in this culture may experience the trauma of the extensive and repeated separation from the parents as a reinforcement of their past.[20] This is perhaps reflected in the formation and function of the strategic survival personality, particularly what Duffell calls the compliant survival strategy.[21] Therefore, this transgenerational aspect may not only reinforce boarding school syndrome, but perhaps even idealise it from a cultural perspective, 'this is how we have always conducted our relationships'. There are persistent consequences for intimate relationships if these patterns do not get addressed and understood.

Ex-boarders who develop strategies to survive, notably the compliant survival strategy, and continue to function from a detached 'false' self, are unlikely to seek psychotherapy, as their past has taught them that the only care they receive is the care that they give themselves.[22] However, partners who experience the disowned feelings of the ex-boarder through projective identification, difficulties with intimacy or inexplicable problems in their relationship often seek out psychotherapy. Working through separating their own feelings from those of their partner, within a strong therapeutic alliance, while gaining an understanding of the impact of boarding school, may support their relationship towards greater empathy and healthier communication.

Clinical example

I would like to illustrate my thesis through an example of a female client who presented for therapy with acute feelings of anxiety, confusion and despair after a sudden and unexpected breakdown in her relationship. Although the client was aware of her partner's boarding school background, it was not an issue that she had initially thought of as relevant or significant when entering therapy.

The client, who I call 'Olivia', had experienced an abrupt detachment from her partner with whom she had been in relationship for over a year. Both were divorced, and Olivia described feeling settled and ready for the next chapter in her life when she first met her partner, who I call 'Richard'. The couple had known each other for many years previously, and the relationship started with an intensity of emotion and excitement that Olivia described as equally reciprocated.

Richard had vocalised his sexual desires towards Olivia from the outset, but he had explained that he was still in the course of processing past emotional complications, so it would take some time for him to be able to express them. Olivia also experienced sexual desire towards Richard and felt that she could understand his predicament, yet she sensed an underlying emotional conflict. Although this triggered some apprehension, Olivia was comforted by his apparent honesty. They had both experienced the breakdown of their own marriages but continued to prioritise their parental responsibilities. She described how they felt deeply committed to their own children, while also making time for each other, which seemed to Olivia to be balanced and an indication of mutual values.

Reflecting on the initial stages of the relationship, Olivia acknowledged their sexual attraction towards one another and, although there may have been a misconceived reliance on sex as intimacy, she felt that they were developing a close emotional connection through thoughtful dialogue. However, Richard had expressively denied this, perhaps as a defence against fear of dependency, which in boarding school may have been repressed in order to survive the broken attachment of being sent away at such a young age. Olivia found this confusing and vacillated between feelings of connection and intimacy to an inexplicable sense of abandonment or loneliness.

After a few months, Richard broke off the relationship for the first time. Olivia experienced this as an abrupt and forceful rejection, particularly following his previous compelling expressions of love and closeness. This can be framed as an example of boarding school syndrome, as Schaverien says:

> It is not uncommon for boys who are sent to boarding school at an early age to yearn for an idealised mother. The separation is a rupture that came too early. Later, in adolescence, separation from the internalised mother ... is not possible because there has been too little actual closeness. From then on, all women seem tantalising; offering the hope of the idealised love object but also the constant threat of abandonment. This contributes to a pattern of women being idealised and then denigrated – loved and hated.[23]

During the following weeks, Olivia reflected on her difficult feelings, which felt somewhat unrecognisable in realistic response to the situation. She described it as a deep longing and heavy loss; but this seemed incongruous with her rational experience.

After some time apart, Richard recontacted Olivia, and although she sensed an avoidance of their past, she cautiously reconnected with him. Each time Olivia felt that there was a development in their relationship or that there was a deepening of feelings, Richard seemed to withdraw from her, sometimes disclaiming any desire for a close relationship. This is perhaps indicative of an insecure avoidant attachment style. Olivia was often left with an overwhelming sense of sadness and rejection, with intermittent, but intense anxious feelings. While Olivia was in therapy, Richard reconnected with her and withdrew on a number of occasions. She felt that she was tied to him and often found it difficult to focus on her own needs.

Richard was not Olivia's only contact with the world of boarding schools. Both she and her younger brother attended private schools but were not sent away to board; they have a good relationship and have always remained close. Olivia had friends who were sent off to boarding school and she remembers thinking how fun and exciting it must have been and how 'lucky' they were. Such fantasies illustrate the cultural perspective of the privilege of boarding school and what young boarders were sent away believing in.

Olivia described her mother as warm and caring, but she could also be passive aggressive and 'often got upset and angry with her'. Her father was 'traditionally strict but fair'. Both had been sent to boarding school. During Olivia's early childhood, her mother provided stability and consistency, staying at home to care for the family while her father frequently travelled for work. Olivia recalled some parental conflict, and her parents divorced when she was 9 years old. She remembered developing night terrors, and she missed her father at this time, often fearful that she may never see him again. She felt loved by both her parents even though there was very little physical contact from her father.

Initially, her father remarried and Olivia felt a sense of responsibility in caring for her mother, which subsided with conflicting feelings when her mother met a new partner. Although there were periods of emotional turmoil for her, while she adapted to her changing family dynamics, Olivia felt that there always remained a sense of safety and security, particularly with the consistency provided by her mother. She and her brother predominantly lived with their mother and stepfather but regularly spent time with their father and stepmother. Both new partners had children from their previous relationships and Olivia felt that overall, their relationships had developed to be positive and amicable.

Olivia's ex-husband had not attended boarding school; they separated after 15 years of marriage. A breakdown of trust and feelings of loneliness in her marriage had triggered anxious feelings, resentment and relentless conflict leading to the eventual separation. Olivia acknowledged that her relationship with Richard provoked unresolved attachment issues linked to her childhood and her past relational experiences. She explored the roots of her anxiety as a response to misplaced fears of abandonment and a need for love and security. This was perhaps most acutely experienced in the periods of absence when her father would leave for work trips, followed by the divorce of her parents.

Olivia was self-reflective and she recognised that unmet childhood needs in her relationship with her emotionally unavailable father might be linked to her relationship with Richard. In particular, how she might have become more vulnerable to her anxious responses in relationship with him. She expressed how her fears of loss and abandonment might have been behind her avoiding conflict and not expressing her needs within the relationship. This, she wondered, may have contributed to 'waiting' for Richard, as she 'waited' for her father to return home. In doing so, perhaps this amplified Richard's boarding school syndrome patterns and his defensive sense of control in the relationship. At the same time, it disempowered Olivia who disowned her own power to say what she wanted, leaving Richard to choose whether to return or not.

During one important therapy session, Olivia reflected on her increasing self-awareness, yet she felt perplexed as to why she still felt that she was the failure in the relationship with Richard. She described him as being contagious in his charm, charisma and enthusiasm; despite his socially confident and articulate exterior she found him also to be warm, kind, sensitive and loving. However, she was at a loss with how to communicate with him because he seemed to retreat at any sign of vulnerability, and she feared such communication with him would lead to his departure.

Richard had been sent to boarding school when he was 8 years old, following in his father's footsteps, and had told Olivia how much he had enjoyed it; it had been a positive experience for him and made him who he was today (perhaps demonstrating the compliant survival strategy). His family promoted traditional British values, but, behind a façade of strength and solidarity, Olivia sensed an array of unspoken vulnerabilities, reflective of the boarding school experience. She indicated to me that he did not seem open to talking about it in therapy.

Breaking through

Eventually, I was able to discuss with Olivia the potential trauma associated with being sent away to boarding school and the significance of boarding school syndrome. I also recommended she watch the documentary film *The Making of Them*.[24] Inspired by these ideas, in a later session Olivia expressed how she had once felt inexplicably tied to Richard's feelings and consequently found it difficult to focus on and understand her own experience, instead always turning her thoughts to him.

Over time, Olivia seemed to appreciate the insights that emerged in our conversations, noting the change of perspective within her. She expressed that she felt a greater empathy and compassion towards Richard, as well as a greater capacity to discern what feelings might belong to her and what belonged to him. In doing so, she was better able take ownership of her own feelings of fear of abandonment in a way that allowed her to express more directly how she felt and what she thought about the confusing dynamics within their relationship.

Our work together seemed to help Olivia distinguish between her and Richard's feelings, and consequently to set boundaries within the relationship by challenging Richard about his defensive behaviours, despite it sometimes being scary for her. This allowed her to challenge her own defensive approach to the relationship, without identifying with Richard's projections, which before she had felt no choice but to embody.

Even though the practitioner may recognise this as projective identification, it takes time for a client to disentangle themself from this web of unclarity. When a partner begins to extricate themself from this pernicious sticky mess, the therapeutic advantage for the ex-boarder is that they now have the chance to confront their own childhood trauma rather than projecting it onto the one who is trying to love him. So such a breakthrough can be important to both partners.

Consequently, Olivia felt empowered to make choices of her own making, rather than through the fear of abandonment that had once dominated the defensive behaviours in the relationship. With increasing self-awareness through therapy, she felt more confident in herself and in her capacity to address conflict early on, without being governed by the fear of abandonment. Despite remaining somewhat disorientated about Richard early on, she felt her capacity to distinguish feelings of her own from the projections in the relationship was empowering. This allowed her to feel confident in addressing conflict and setting boundaries – a platform from which she felt the relationship could move forward in a healthier way.

Afterword

I will leave the final word to journalist David Thomas who, in a 1994 newspaper review of the same film I recommended that Olivia watch (*The Making of Them*), remembered his own schooldays and wrote:

You can't love your parents because it hurts too much. And you most certainly can't love your fellow-pupils because there is an overriding taboo against any hint of homosexuality. So, after a while, you just get out of the habit of loving. As I dare say many of those Boarding School Survivors – not to mention their wives – will testify, getting back into the habit can be a very difficult task.[25]

Notes

1 Bowlby, J. (2005) *The Making and Breaking of Affectional Bonds*. Oxford & New York: Routledge.
2 Duffell, N. and Basset, T. (2016) *Trauma, Abandonment and Privilege: A Guide to Therapeutic Work with Boarding School Survivors*. Abingdon & New York: Routledge.
3 Duffell, N. and Basset, T. (2016) *Trauma, Abandonment and Privilege: A Guide to Therapeutic Work with Boarding School Survivors*. Abingdon & New York: Routledge
4 Duffell, N. (2000) *The Making of Them: The British Attitude to Children and the Boarding School System*. London: Lone Arrow Press.
5 Schaverien, J. (2015) *Boarding School Syndrome: The Psychological Trauma of the 'Privileged' Child*. London & New York: Routledge.
6 Partridge, S. (2021) 'Boarding School Syndrome: Reconsidered in Social Context and Through the Lens of Attachment Theory', *Attachment*, 15, 269–278. Retrieved from doi:10.33212/att.v15n2.2021.269.
7 Bowlby, J. (1973) *Attachment and Loss: Vol 2, Separation*. Harmondsworth: Penguin.
8 Firestone, R.W. and Firestone, L. (2004) *Handbook of Closeness and Intimacy*. London: Psychology Press.
9 McGinley, E. and Varchevker, A. (2013) *Enduring Trauma Through the Life Cycle*. London & New York: Routledge.
10 Duffell, N. (2000) *The Making of Them: The British Attitude to Children and the Boarding School System*. London: Lone Arrow Press.
11 Duffell, N. and Basset, T. (2016) *Trauma, Abandonment and Privilege: A Guide to Therapeutic Work with Boarding School Survivors*. Abingdon & New York: Routledge.
12 Schaverien, J. (2015) *Boarding School Syndrome: The Psychological Trauma of the 'Privileged' Child*. London & New York: Routledge.
13 Bowlby, J. (2005) *The Making and Breaking of Affectional Bonds*. Oxford & New York: Routledge.
14 McGinley, E. and Varchevker, A. (2013) *Enduring Trauma Through the Life Cycle*. London & New York: Routledge.
15 Duffell, N. and Basset, T. (2016) *Trauma, Abandonment and Privilege: A Guide to Therapeutic Work with Boarding School Survivors*. Abingdon & New York: Routledge.
16 Larkin, P. (2003) *Collected Poems*, London: Faber & Faber.
17 Partridge, S. (2021) 'Boarding School Syndrome: Reconsidered in Social Context and Through the Lens of Attachment Theory', *Attachment*, 15, 269–278. Retrieved from doi:10.33212/att.v15n2.2021.269.
18 Capstick, A., and Clegg, D. (2013) 'Behind the Stiff Upper Lip: War Narratives of Older Men with Dementia', *Journal of War & Culture Studies*, 6(3), 239–254. Retrieved from doi.org/10.1179/1752627213Z.00000000021.
19 Bowlby, J. (2005) *The Making and Breaking of Affectional Bonds*. Oxford & New York: Routledge.
20 Partridge, S. (2021) 'Boarding School Syndrome: Reconsidered in Social Context and Through the Lens of Attachment Theory', *Attachment*, 15, 269–278. Retrieved from doi:10.33212/att.v15n2.2021.269.

21 Duffell, N. and Basset, T. (2016) *Trauma, Abandonment and Privilege: A Guide to Therapeutic Work with Boarding School Survivors.* Abingdon & New York: Routledge.
22 Bowlby, J. (2005) *The Making and Breaking of Affectional Bonds.* Oxford & New York: Routledge.
23 Schaverien, J. (2015) *Boarding School Syndrome: The Psychological Trauma of the 'Privileged' Child.* London & New York: Routledge.
24 *The Making of Them* (1994) film directed by Colin Luke for Mosaic Pictures, first broadcast BBC *40 Minutes*, 9 January 1994. Available on YouTube http://youtu.be/2uRr 77vju8U.
25 Quoted in Duffell, N. (2000) *The Making of Them: The British Attitude to Children and the Boarding School System.* London: Lone Arrow Press.

Chapter 7

How Do Counsellors in UK Independent Schools Experience the Effects of Working with Boarders?

Virginia Sherborne

Introduction

The impetus for the research study presented in this chapter came from two sources: my own experience teaching in an elite girls' boarding school in the UK during the late 1990s and my professional interest in trauma when I later became a counsellor. By the time I took up the boarding post, I had spent seven years teaching classics in both boys' and girls' independent day schools.

Several aspects of life at the boarding school struck me as odd, even disturbing. For example, the boarding houses were arranged for age-cohorts. This meant the 11-year-old new girls had no older girls around to comfort and encourage them. The 13–14-year-olds were forced together round-the-clock in what I considered 'a toxic hormonal soup'. Siblings were separated. It seemed as if the system had been designed by someone with no knowledge of normal human children. I was also struck by the flattened energy level of the boarders as they went about their activities, so different from the peaks of energy familiar to me from day schools.

By 2016, I was an experienced counsellor. When choosing my research topic for an MA in trauma studies, I considered if I could find a way to explore the boarding experience from the inside. I knew there was a dearth of peer-reviewed studies on the effects of boarding in UK independent schools, though there were accounts from therapists working with adult ex-boarders. Whilst I didn't think school leaders would give permission to interview their pupils, I realised I could ethically interview counsellors working with those children and young people (CYP).

The question I chose to address was: *How do counsellors in UK independent schools experience the effects on themselves of working with boarders?* I hoped my study would inform good practice for counsellors and shine a light into the realities of boarding in the twenty-first century.[1]

Study design

I chose interpretative phenomenological analysis (IPA) methodology for my study because this qualitative approach tries to engage with the reflections of

DOI: 10.4324/9781003515517-7

people who have had a major experience in their life as they try to make sense of it. My study aimed to explore how counsellors made sense of their experience of helping CYP who were themselves trying to make sense of being at boarding school. I followed Smith et al.'s six steps to analysis.[2] Ethical approval was obtained from the University of Nottingham. I followed their ethics guidelines and the BACP's (British Association for Counselling and Psychotherapy) Ethical Guidelines for Researching, to honour five key principles throughout: integrity, rigour, respect, trustworthiness and responsibility. I aimed to interview counsellors with current UK independent school boarders among their clients. To recruit participants, I asked professional contacts to publicise the study. I emailed any counsellors named on boarding school websites, plus contributors to the BACP's journal, *Children, Young People and Families*, who mentioned they worked with boarders.

Paying attention to reflexivity was crucial so that I could note how my assumptions, background and behaviour affected the study's conduct. I explored in personal therapy my choice of topic in the light of my life experiences. These included attending Nick Duffell's diploma course on working therapeutically with ex-boarders during the study's interview stage. I was provided with a complex set of perspectives simultaneously: from the interviewees, the therapists on the course and the tutors. Individual face-to-face semi-structured interviews were planned, starting with an open-ended question: 'Please tell me what it's been like for you working with boarders.' Further prompts enabled me to collect relevant data. The interviews, lasting around an hour, were audio-recorded and transcribed verbatim. Seven counsellors came forward, one of whom was excluded as they had only recently started. The six participants formed a fairly uniform group: all female and in mid-life; no ex-boarders; three in the south of England, three in the Midlands/ north of England. They chose pseudonyms.

Results

During data analysis, I developed three overarching themes, with sub-themes for each:

1 Outside/inside
   a) The professional
   b) Outside/inside.

2 Culture and expectations
   a) The foreign students
   b) Money and expectations
   c) What really matters.

3 Parent+child[3]
   a) The parent substitute
   b) The distressed child.

Theme 1: Outside/inside

a) The professional

All the participants came to the school as well-qualified professionals, describing their interactions with senior management teams (SMTs), staff, parents and pupils. All reported a sense of achievement in developing the counselling service, feeling appreciated by the SMT to different degrees:

> 'I am assured by my line-manager ... the impact has been profound.' (Jane)

> 'I feel frustrated sometimes, or almost deskilled in a way, that what I'm saying is not important enough.' (Lucy)

Rebecca felt fulfilled when a pupil who had been detained on a mental health section recovered. However, she also felt isolated, 'on a desert island', experiencing the SMT as fearful of counselling, 'until you've got a child who *has* tried to commit suicide. Then they love you!'. Lucy expressed shock at the lack of emotional awareness in school staff, also feeling rather isolated in her role:

> 'They look at more the educational side. "Let's get on with things." And I'm there for the emotional side. But I feel like I'm the only one that is, sometimes!'

Holly and Anne encountered SMT resistance to pupils arranging support groups. There was mistrust of young people organising together and tension around the limits of the counsellor's influence.

The counsellors brought in specialist knowledge about child development and mental health, seeing their psycho-educative role as important. Anne described holding parental information sessions about stress: 'It was kind of interesting ... because they hadn't thought about their own role.' Four participants were anxious about their clients' future mental health; for example, 'I do worry that some of these young people are going out there into responsible roles, when they'll be making big changes to the world' (Lucy). Oatcake, Anne and Lucy described what they noticed about boarders compared to day students regarding attachment:

> 'A wariness of being dependent on other people. And so, they kind of shut themselves out, off, in a way, so they become more insular.' (Oatcake)

> 'They're quite happy being distant sometimes. It's almost like they just get on with it.' (Lucy)

Another aspect to this theme is the counsellors' sense of themselves as ethical practitioners. All mentioned issues around boundaries and confidentiality/trust. Tension and misunderstanding could be heightened because of the school's position *in loco parentis.* There could be 'a lot of bad feeling ... so I do feel a bit protective [of pupils]' (Holly).

b) Outside/inside

The counsellor is essentially an outsider crossing the boundary into a closed world, bringing their own professional and cultural perspective. Five counsellors provided data relating to this theme. Two used a 'little bubble' metaphor: Holly valued her freedom to come and go, bringing healing in, while Lucy, self-employed, tried to 'keep on the outside', so she could independently represent the children's interests. She seemed to value and feel comfortable in her role of witnessing, advocating and empowering and felt 'glad I've had the privilege to work in a different setting'. Anne, whose father is an immigrant from an ethnic minority, experienced enhanced self-esteem as an outsider in the boarding school:

'I thought I wasn't good enough, which was a part of my cultural history. That's been really good, to change my own *beliefs* about myself. My expertise, my knowledge, my experience, that actually is very respected.'

The counsellors talked about the impact of the children being '*inside*'. For Rebecca, the overtones of this word were a reality: 'It's prison, for a lot of them.' Lucy said: 'Counselling for these students is the only way they can let things out. There's no freedom.' The counselling room itself became an 'inside' place, with safety and freedom from the 'outside' world of the school. Anne described a room where children found 'your own space and your own time and nobody's going to tell you what to do'. However, she wondered whether what the clients received was counselling or actually special one-to-one time, which they craved.

Finding a safe space was mentioned often. The boarding school presents itself as a safe place for children to grow up, and four interviewees mentioned some children valued this safe haven. Anne said 'some of them are positively better off as boarders' due to the consistent support provided. Holly called it 'posh fostering', where children could 'find peace', and Lucy used the term 'sanctuary'. For other boarders, the lack of freedom to leave meant they could not get that 'distinction' (Oatcake) and feel safe at home when there were difficulties with staff. Despite idyllic school grounds, some boarders felt 'claustrophobic' (Lucy).

The 'Outside/inside' theme also relates to the idea of surface-versus-underlying reality. The counsellors were uniquely positioned to access the child's internal world. Anne and Jane mentioned the boarders presenting a false façade:

'"My heart inside is breaking. I am so unhappy." I hear that in this room quite regularly. And yet they daren't tell their parents, and most of the teaching staff are unaware of it.' (Jane)

Theme 2: Culture and expectations

a) The foreign students

The foreign students constituted another set of outsiders. Five participants' data related to this theme. Interacting with foreign students and their cultures proved fertile ground for the counsellors to undergo personal change.

Holly experienced a beneficial personal process of accepting difference, but felt concerned about the language/cultural barrier hindering pastoral care: 'There can be a lot of stuff going on that is not noticed and that could be traumatic.' After initially finding the language barrier difficult, Oatcake mastered new skills. Rebecca found it 'enriching' when foreign children brought gifts from home, making an ethical choice to accept, to meet the child's need for deeper understanding. She also explained, 'walking in their shoes ... has benefited me tremendously in how I communicate with my own children'. Jane expressed admiration for how the foreign boarders coped in a new culture and language. Contact with them changed her: 'I do feel more open-minded, more interested, more educated and ... I'm very aware of how much there is I don't know.' At Anne's school, in contrast, there was a sense that different cultures could not understand each other. Asian boarders were put in segregated accommodation, with some telling Anne they 'always feel different, feel isolated'. This made Anne 'uncomfortable'.

b) Money and expectations

This theme applied to Anne, Rebecca and Holly. Many of Anne's expressions of 'surprise' were linked to her encounter with the culture of the rich and their entitlement. Huge fees meant huge expectations of the boarders to succeed – as well as on the school to make this happen. She explained: 'There's no language around failure.' Rebecca had strongly negative reactions to this privileged outlook. She experienced intense frustration: 'Sometimes you wanna shake them and bring them back to life. You know, this is not the way the world is.' Rebecca also felt frustrated, with compromises being made around staffing because: 'It's all about money. It's a business.'

c) What really matters

Holly experienced the boarders as deprived, despite their huge wealth:

> 'They might have lots and lots of money, but ... a lack of love. So, I will come home and sort of ... hug my children a bit more. I don't view people with a lot of money as having it all.'

She also attributed a change in her values due to working with boarders: 'My belief system is stronger: love and listening to people and not controlling them.' She really valued good relationships and letting people be themselves.

Oatcake found herself 'becoming more responsive generally'. She experienced an atmosphere in her religious boarding school of 'genuine love and care' that impacted her personally.

Theme 3: Parent+child

We now move into the more intimate space concerning the parent and child relationship.

a) The parent substitute

All participants talked about the confusing reality of an institution trying to be a substitute for parents. Exactly how close and how warm was this relationship supposed to be? Which staff were supposed to be the substitutes? What did '*in loco parentis*' actually mean?

Oatcake tried to tease out the nuances:

> 'I suppose they, to some extent, are treating me a little bit like say a houseparent or something like that. And I have to be careful to make sure there is that distinction between the caring and the help even in the therapy that I do with them. It has to have that slight professional detachment, and yet I still have to be able to show them that I do care. Whereas the pastoral staff in school I think are more like relatives and friends.'

Jane said she felt troubled:

> 'I think to myself we're expecting school staff to somehow or other parent a child and I don't think we're supposed to be doing that, and we're not the parent, you know.'

Lucy described herself as 'a significant other', explaining:

> 'If your parents are not there, young people are resilient and they look for other people to take that role. That motherly figure or that fatherly figure. And that can be educational staff as well. And I think boarding school staff probably need a bit more teaching in that area! They are like another parent to those young people, sometimes, and they don't realise that.'

Holly described the close relationship with clients as a 'privilege', saying: 'They get very attached to you, almost like you are a substitute parent. So, there's quite a depth of feeling, quite a bond sometimes, which is rather lovely.'

Both she and Lucy joked they sometimes felt a maternal impulse to take a child home with them to look after, but of course that would be unprofessional. Rebecca too found the parental element of her job tricky: 'You become part of their lives, which can be, yeah, incredibly difficult. You become almost like a foster-parent. You become that secure attachment.'

Another parental aspect for the counsellors was the idea of being attuned to individual children's needs. A parent living with their child can witness their child's developmental stages and needs thanks to the close contact, but when the child is boarding, that proximity vanishes. The school cannot replicate this level of intimate knowledge, whereas counsellors are trained to tune in to individual clients. Anne felt 'discomfort' when children's needs were overlooked. She mentioned the quality of houseparents, how some were 'more caring and attuned, more vigilant to notice things than others'.

Five participants mentioned the importance of close contact between parent and child, particularly close physical contact. Oatcake's awareness of how its lack impacted clients also affected her own relationships:

'The importance of having family close by, to lean on and support you, when things are going wrong. And perhaps make a bit of an effort to let my family know that I'm there if there's something going wrong and keep in touch more, maybe. Understanding how the boarders … can't just go for a cuddle with mum, if something's wrong, has probably just been a reminder.'

Jane felt 'uneasy' as it was clear what distressed children needed: 'Seeing … housemasters and matrons trying to help, actually all it needs is a parent coming and giving them a hug and saying "Let's go through this together".' She found herself affected:

'I realise how important that physical proximity and touch is. Some of these young people are not getting that, even at times of crisis and need. So I've been very conscious that the people in our lives are very precious. And that we do need to be connected to them *physically*.'

b) The distressed child

As school counsellors, my participants naturally dealt with upset pupils. They used evocative phrasing to describe the ruptured attachments some experienced:

Oatcake: 'suddenly they've been turfed out of the family.'
Jane: 'very lost and alone.'
Holly: 'ripped away from your family, ripped away from a loving environment.'

Jane gave vignettes of 11 distressed children, far more than anyone else. She sensed ongoing personal impact from this work – she'd been 'left with quite a profound sense of unease'. Among the matrons, she witnessed deep distress 'when they're *desperately* trying to fill a hole left by parents'. For some students she felt the decision to board was 'abusive' and at times she felt 'very conflicted'. She was not the only participant to feel conflicted. Anne stated: 'I don't judge parents, but I do sometimes feel really cross with them.' Rebecca struggled with frustration each year when the international boarders arrived, 'because you always know there's one or two in the group who will be suicidal'. She needed a strategy to cope: 'I've almost learned to detach myself, because you have to.' Oatcake acknowledged her own response to the distressed child: 'There's a sadness there ... I get a sense of ... well ... poor child.' The last two words were almost inaudible, as if unbearable to say out loud.

Another aspect of this theme was 'overwhelming demand'. The way the school has to take over the parental round-the-clock on-call role could cause confusion and difficult boundaries. Anne described the school nurse as 'firefighting a lot'. Lucy worried about 'those I *don't* see' and that she might miss someone's call, yet handing over the task of emergency responder was important as 'this job ... can take over if you're not careful'. Jane described the overwhelming demand: 'I'm having to keep an eye on how draining it is, because it's a bottomless pit.'

For Holly's clients, the school's relentless work ethic exacerbated some clients' distress: 'It's workaholism. There's ... no space to breathe or to *be*.' She saw it as part of her role to challenge this, empowering the children. However, she also at times felt pressure: 'It can leak in, and you think: "Oh my gosh! Oh, I'd better start doing *this*."' Her language showed her sense of contamination. She saw having a work-life balance as very important, becoming more aware of this over time. Oatcake experienced the demand differently. She noticed herself becoming more 'responsive', which she linked to working with boarders: '*Having* to say, initially: "Yes, OK, I'll come." Because that was my job, and there was no one else there to do that.' For her, being ready to respond unhesitatingly was meaningful.

Discussion

Personal change through exposure to trauma

The data from this study reveal how the counsellors experienced personal change, both negative and positive. Research shows how professionals, including therapists, can be affected by working with traumatised people.[4,5] Negative changes identified include *secondary traumatic stress* (STS), *vicarious traumatisation* (VT) and *moral injury* (MI). Positive change has been theorised as *vicarious posttraumatic growth* (VPTG). Symptoms of STS include intrusive imagery; avoidance; physiological arousal; distressing emotions; and functional impairment.[6] Vicarious traumatisation encompasses the painful psychological shattering of assumptions about oneself, other people and the world that happens from ongoing exposure to traumatic material.[7] Assumptions can become negative in five key areas: trust, safety, control, esteem and intimacy.[8] Moral injury involves negative self-judgement after transgressing core moral beliefs or feeling betrayed by authorities.[9]

It has been understood since ancient times that humans can experience psychological growth from struggling with life trauma, the phenomenon termed *posttraumatic growth* (PTG). Five domains for PTG have been suggested: personal
strength, new possibilities, relating to others, appreciation of life and spiritual
change.[10] Trauma professionals experience vicarious PTG through being affected
by and coping with their clients' emotional distress.[11] Aspects of this VPTG cover
changes in values and priorities; spiritual growth; personal strength; and personal
relationships.[12] Other specific aspects include becoming a better professional and
developing greater awareness of social injustice and human resiliency.[13,14]

Participants' experiences of negative effects on themselves

In the participants' accounts we can see examples of secondary traumatic stress. All
the participants showed emotional distress, such as discomfort, unease, anger, sadness
and anxiety. Two stood out as experiencing more distress than the others: Jane and
Rebecca. Rebecca spoke of needing to detach herself, a form of avoidance. Neither
of these two mentioned seeing clients outside the boarding school. Both expressed
anxiety about the overwhelming demand. This chimes with Hensel et al.'s finding
that the strongest indicator for predicting STS is the *proportion of time* spent working
with trauma survivors rather than the actual number of clients.[15] The unease, discomfort and conflict participants reported may be examples of moral injury, where a
caregiver has not intervened despite ongoing trauma affecting a child.[16] The discomfort of collusion may be amplified if a school is the sole employer. We can compare
the situation of Lucy who felt free to speak out, having various sources of income.

The counsellors' use of an attachment model to conceptualise boarders' issues
points towards trauma occurring through shattered assumptions around secure
attachment.[17] Researchers recognise that a hallmark of adolescence is 'striving for
emotional self-sufficiency and autonomy' but that 'adolescents at times rely on
their parents for help in regulating emotion'.[18] Just as toddlers need a secure base to
explore from, so adolescents need an available parent to move out from and back to
in their own individual rhythm, based on their own developmental needs. Boarders
cannot follow this rhythm and so may not manage the transition to healthy adulthood. In the boarding world, there does not seem to be enough awareness that
healthy attachment develops not only in early childhood, but throughout adolescence and into adulthood.

Participants' experiences of positive personal change

My study participants ascribed positive changes in themselves to working with
boarders. We can map these changes against those aspects of VPTG experienced
by professionals working with trauma survivors. Holly was clear she had *changed
her values and priorities* due to exposure to the relentless work/achievement ethic
and its effects on her clients. She prioritised authentic living, feeling less controlling and more accepting.

Jane, Holly, Oatcake and Rebecca mentioned positive effects *on their personal relationships* with their own children. Holly hugged her children more; Oatcake made more effort to be there for family; Jane really valued physical proximity, explicitly linking this growth with witnessing the distress of children deprived of physical closeness at times of need. Rebecca communicated better with her children. Of the five participants who mentioned having children, four experienced positive effects on the relationship, plus Lucy said she 'appreciated' her children had not been in boarding. Holly and Lucy's fantasy of taking children home with them could be viewed as a rescuer/healer countertransference from doing trauma work.[19] A higher level of identification in professionals may enable them to metaphorically apply the traumatic event to their own lives, thereby increasing their levels of STS and VPTG.[20] Empathetic work with boarders may particularly affect the counsellor's personal parent-child schema.

Regarding *enhanced professional identity*, Holly and Rebecca described fulfilment in enabling young clients' trauma recovery, giving examples of apparent PTG in them. This would fit with Cohen and Collens' suggested link between witnessing a client's recovery/growth and the professionals' VPTG.[21] The positive effect of exposure to cultural differences was reported by three participants. Oatcake felt initially scared sometimes but used the term 'growth' to describe her increased confidence in working with foreign boarders. Rebecca's communication with her own children was enhanced, and Jane felt more open-minded. Lucy also expressed her sense of achievement, feeling appreciated by students and SMT. She valued her role in witnessing, advocating and empowering. She felt privileged to work in a different setting, hinting that being accepted in a different class environment mattered. The transformational effect of the encounter with wealth and privilege was striking in Anne's interview. Being respected as a professional by the elite transformed her internalised oppression and the effects of transgenerational racism. It even seems to have had a wider positive effect on her self-esteem, beyond her professional identity, to how she saw herself as a person. Her experience shows the power that resides inside 'the bubble', the power to influence and mould the individual's sense of self, the same power that passes on entitlement and has, in other boarding contexts, been used to change people's cultural identities. Anne's experience may correspond with the VPTG aspect *developing greater awareness of social injustice.*

In summary, participants showed the following aspects of VPTG: changes to values and priorities, enhanced relationships, awareness of human resiliency and growth relating to professional identity. They also experienced effects typical of STS and moral injury. They were experiencing personal changes typical of professionals working with traumatised clients.

Recommendations for practice

At least 80 per cent of school counsellors identify with a person-centred/humanistic or integrative orientation.[22] This was true of all my participants. They used an attachment model to conceptualise their clients' issues. However, 'trauma-focused cognitive behavioural therapy (TF-CBT) [is] a well-established treatment for trauma ... potentially salient for clinicians interested in supporting PTG in their work with youth posttrauma'.[23] I suggest a more explicit use of a trauma model could be helpful, leading the way to actively talking about PTG as a possible outcome for children.

Productive rumination has a key role in developing this. It is a constructive processing of trauma, facilitated, according to Hensel et al., by 'continuing distress and efforts to reconcile one's post-trauma reality'.[24] This process, via the recognition and expression of emotions, enables the generation of good solutions to problems. Currently boarding schools do not facilitate productive rumination nor the expression of negative emotions about boarding. Instead, they distract children with relentless activities and discourage group sharing of distress. Counsellors can support the process of PTG by changing this culture and enabling CYP to talk about traumatic experiences with each other and with skilled, well-supported adults they trust.

Boarding schools must begin to take responsibility for trauma they cause. Trauma screening from pre-admission and continuing throughout the school career would allow traumatised children to be identified and helped. Testing would help schools meet their duty of care to safeguard and promote the safety of children, including 'preventing the impairment of children's mental and physical health or development'.[25] Resulting data would potentially settle the question of whether the boarding experience 'in and of itself represents a primary trauma'.[26]

Boarding schools also have a duty of care to staff. My participants described the distress of matrons and other support staff. Recognising that staff are having to deal with trauma would allow for better support and training in self-care. Counsellors working with current boarders need support to manage the effects of trauma on themselves. Their supervisors therefore need to be trauma informed. My participants also highlighted isolation as a difficult issue. This can affect any school counsellor but may be more likely for boarding school counsellors. Forming peer interest groups would provide regular support and a forum for discussion.

Limitations

The sample size of six is small but appropriate for IPA methodology, as it allows similarities and differences to be recognised in a homogenous group.[27] The participants were not solely working with current boarders, so any VPTG and STS they experienced could relate to other client types. This study was limited to boarders at fee-paying schools in the UK. Therefore, it does not address issues relating to state schools, special schools or schools abroad.

Conclusion

By interviewing counsellors who work with current boarders about their personal experiences of change, this study shines a light into the heart of the twenty-first-century boarding experience. Participants benefited from a sense of enhanced professional worth, thanks to their engagement with these high-status institutions. However, they also described negative effects matching those experienced by professionals working with traumatised individuals. It is time for boarding schools to acknowledge the risk of trauma to children in their care. They must take steps to mitigate negative effects both on their pupils and on those striving to support them.

Notes

1 I received invaluable supervision from Professor Stephen Joseph.
2 Smith, J.A., Flower, P. and Larkin, M. (2009) *Interpretative Phenomenological Analysis: Theory, Method and Research*. London: Sage.
3 This theme is written as a single word to convey the potential closeness of this bond.
4 McNeillie, N. and Rose, J. (2021) 'Vicarious Trauma in Therapists: A Meta-Ethnographic Review', *Behavioural and Cognitive Psychotherapy*, 49(4): 426–440.
5 Weiss-Dagan, S., Ben-Porat, A. and Itzhaky, H. (2022) 'Secondary Traumatic Stress and Vicarious Post-Traumatic Growth Among Social Workers who have Worked with Abused Children', *Journal of Social Work*, 22(1): 170–187.
6 Hensel, J.M., Ruiz, C., Finney, C. and Dewa, C.S. (2015) 'Meta-Analysis of Risk Factors for Secondary Traumatic Stress in Therapeutic Work with Trauma Victims', *Journal of Traumatic Stress*, 28(2): 83–91.
7 McCann, I.L. and Pearlman, L.A. (1990) 'Vicarious Traumatization: A Framework for Understanding the Psychological Effects of Working with Victims', *Journal of Traumatic Stress*, 3: 131–149.
8 McNeillie, N. and Rose, J. (2021) 'Vicarious Trauma in Therapists: A Meta-Ethnographic Review', *Behavioural and Cognitive Psychotherapy*, 49(4): 426–440.
9 Brock R. (2011) 'How Do We Repair the Souls of Those Returning from Iraq?'. Retrieved 1 November 2021 from Huffpost Communities.
10 Cohen, K. and Collens, P. (2013) 'The Impact of Trauma Work on Trauma Workers: A Metasynthesis on Vicarious Trauma and Vicarious Posttraumatic Growth', *Psychological Trauma: Theory, Research, Practice, and Policy*, 5(6): 570–580.
11 Cohen, K. and Collens, P. (2013) 'The Impact of Trauma Work on Trauma Workers: A Metasynthesis on Vicarious Trauma and Vicarious Posttraumatic Growth', *Psychological Trauma: Theory, Research, Practice, and Policy*, 5(6): 570–580.
12 Manning, S.F., de Terte, I. and Stephens, C. (2015) 'Vicarious Posttraumatic Growth: A Systematic Literature Review', *International Journal of Wellbeing*, 5(2): 125–139.
13 Cohen, K. and Collens, P. (2013) 'The Impact of Trauma Work on Trauma Workers: A Metasynthesis on Vicarious Trauma and Vicarious Posttraumatic Growth', *Psychological Trauma: Theory, Research, Practice, and Policy*, 5(6): 570–580.
14 Manning, S.F., de Terte, I. and Stephens, C. (2015) 'Vicarious Posttraumatic Growth: A Systematic Literature Review', *International Journal of Wellbeing*, 5(2): 125–139.
15 Hensel, J.M., Ruiz, C., Finney, C. and Dewa, C.S. (2015) 'Meta-Analysis of Risk Factors for Secondary Traumatic Stress in Therapeutic Work with Trauma Victims', *Journal of Traumatic Stress*, 28(2): 83–91.
16 Kilmer, R.P., Gil-Rivas, V., Griese, B., Hardy, S.J., Hafstad, G.S. and Alisic, E. (2014) 'Posttraumatic Growth in Children and Youth: Clinical Implications of an Emerging Research Literature', *American Journal of Orthopsychiatry*, 84(5): 506–518.
17 Janoff-Bulman, R. (2002) *Shattered Assumptions*. New York: Free Press.
18 Allen, J.P. and Miga, E.M. (2010) 'Attachment in Adolescence: A Move to the Level of Emotion Regulation', *Journal of Social and Personal Relationships*, 27(2): 181–190.

19 Cash, A. and Weiner, I.B. (2006) *Wiley Concise Guides to Mental Health: Posttraumatic Stress Disorder*. Newark: Wiley.

20 Manning-Jones, S., de Terte, I. and Stephens, C. (2016) 'Secondary Traumatic Stress, Vicarious Posttraumatic Growth, and Coping Among Health Professionals: A Comparison Study', *New Zealand Journal of Psychology*, 45(1): 20–29.

21 Cohen, K. and Collens, P. (2013) 'The Impact of Trauma Work on Trauma Workers: A Metasynthesis on Vicarious Trauma and Vicarious Posttraumatic Growth', *Psychological Trauma: Theory, Research, Practice, and Policy*, 5(6): 570–580.

22 Cooper, M. (2013) *School-Based Counselling in UK Secondary Schools: A Review and Critical Evaluation*. Glasgow: University of Strathclyde.

23 McNeillie, N. and Rose, J. (2021) 'Vicarious Trauma in Therapists: A Meta-Ethnographic Review', *Behavioural and Cognitive Psychotherapy*, 49(4): 426–440.

24 Hensel, J.M., Ruiz, C., Finney, C. and Dewa, C.S. (2015) 'Meta-Analysis of Risk Factors for Secondary Traumatic Stress in Therapeutic Work with Trauma Victims', *Journal of Traumatic Stress*, 28(2): 83–91.

25 Department for Education (2023) *Keeping Children Safe in Education: Statutory Guidance for Schools and Colleges*. London: Dandy Booksellers.

26 Lee, J., Wardman-Browne, J., Hopkins, E., McPherson, S. and Cavenagh, P. (2024) 'It's Not All Down to Boarding' in P. Cavenagh, S. McPherson and J. Ogden (eds), *The Psychological Impact of Boarding School: The Trunk in the Hall*. London & New York: Routledge, pp. 53–68.

27 Smith, J.A., Flower, P. and Larkin, M. (2009) *Interpretative Phenomenological Analysis: Theory, Method and Research*. London: Sage.

Chapter 8

The Use of EMDR for Boarding School Trauma

Susannah Cornish

Introduction

In this chapter I hope to explain how eye movement desensitisation and reprocessing therapy (EMDR) can be an effective treatment method for adults who have experienced various types of trauma at boarding school. EMDR is a treatment method that 'rewires' parts of the brain where implicit memories are stored, by using bilateral stimulation, which activates both hemispheres of the brain. This can be done with sounds, touch or eye movements.

I will focus on two clients who have been kind enough to let me use their stories (which have been highly anonymised). I am indebted to them. These vignettes describe single-incident major trauma, but I have also used EMDR for complex trauma.

There are many types of trauma experienced by children at boarding school. I have used EMDR with both male and female ex-boarder clients who:

- were mercilessly bullied by teachers or other pupils;
- felt intense abandonment at a young age when their parents left them at school, often without even saying goodbye;
- cried themselves to sleep during the first weeks and months of school;
- had to deal with the shame of dyslexia at boarding school;
- were outed for being gay in the years when being gay was risky in an all-boys school;
- suffered from the trauma of anorexia;
- seen and/or heard fellow pupils be abused;
- were physically and sexually abused themselves.

I also used EMDR with one female client in her mid-40s who was traumatised after being left at boarding school at the age of 6 years old.

All of these clients had one thing in common, they had to deal with their trauma without the presence of a caring adult, only of other children, also trying to survive.

DOI: 10.4324/9781003515517-8

Children have to survive at boarding school, and adult clients often arrive in the therapy room in survival mode. The aim is for them to leave therapy in a thriving mode. Is this ever possible?

Duffell and Basset's Recognition–Acceptance–Change (RAC) model[1] is a useful treatment concept. It offers a framework for ex-boarder clients to recognise and accept the impact of boarding and then hopefully go on to change and start living as mature, loving and functioning adults outside the therapy room, instead of being driven by their needy inner child.

However, ex-boarder clients have developed strong defences, which, when developed in childhood, were absolutely necessary for survival, but in adulthood they often serve to keep other people out of their lives, especially therapists. The 'boarding school survivor' can often disown their own vulnerability by projecting it into others, either by bullying other children at boarding school, or, in their adult life, onto their partners and their own children as well as onto their therapist.

Partridge talks of 'a terrible violence, disguised by privilege', being done to children and parents when children are left at boarding school for the first time.[2] This is the start of what can become a traumatic journey for some children, a journey that can lead to post-traumatic stress disorder (PTSD) or complex PTSD. The experience of this terrible 'violence' makes boarding school clients feel that the world is a dangerous place. Children are very adaptive and use dissociation from their emotions to survive, employing a 'strategic survival personality', which has three main types: 'complier', 'rebel' and 'crushed'.[3] John Bowlby's attachment theory is a useful model for understanding boarding school clients and their broken attachments,[4] and this has been eloquently discussed by Anne Power.[5]

EMDR

In *A Very Private School* (published while I was writing this chapter), Charles Spencer describes the abuse that went on in boarding schools in the 1970s.[6] Although now historic, it appears that abuse of one sort or another in boarding schools has continued long since. In an interview with Julia Samuel,[7] Spencer describes how EMDR helped him deal with the trauma of violence and sexual abuse he experienced at boarding school, turning technicolour memories into dull grey memories. Similarly, I have noticed how ex-boarder clients have very definite memories they wish to target from boarding school. When small children are abused and mistreated, they live with the trauma for years afterwards in a deep cesspit of shame, reliving the trauma on a daily basis, which grinds down their self-worth.

There are numerous ways to treat trauma. I find my training as an EMDR therapist to be very effective with ex-boarder clients, who often intellectualise, talk too much or find it hard to connect with their emotions.[8] I use EMDR as a standalone treatment method, or part of talking therapy. I believe that polyvagal-informed EMDR[9] to be particularly important for this client group. Polyvagal theory (PVT)[10] describes the processes of the autonomic nervous system (ANS) and how the vagus nerve mediates between the mind and the body with 'afferent' and 'efferent' nerve networks. This way of working keeps me alive to the boarding school client's tendency to dissociate.

The nature-nurture make-up of the client determines how damaging the particular trauma is and how long the impact will be felt in later life. We are all unique individuals, so EMDR processes are equally unique. EMDR helps clients deal with single-incident major traumatic and disturbing life events, which may not in themselves appear to be major traumas but are registered in the client's nervous system.

I am perpetually surprised at how effective EMDR can be with early childhood traumatic memories, particularly with ex-boarder clients. This client group often struggle to access their emotions as they have been conditioned to have a 'stiff upper lip'. After all, men who originally went to boarding school were being groomed to be stationed overseas for the sake of the Empire, and the women who originally went to boarding school were taught all the skills to be the wives of such men. Emotions were meant to be swallowed right down or, better still, cut off completely. However, EMDR seems to tap into these emotions very quickly and effectively. The client is in control of the process, and I merely facilitate their journey. This client group often arrive for therapy with a high level of disturbance, sometimes following a breakdown or relationship breakup, and leave therapy in a much calmer state.

EMDR treatment methods

Ex-boarder clients often struggle with affect regulation. When processing, it is best for clients to stay in their 'window of tolerance'. This means that the client is fully present with me in the therapy room and not completely cut off or overstimulated. The sympathetic and parasympathetic systems – the twin branches of the ANS – can work together and the client is able to experience 'dual awareness'.

In terms of PVT, this is when the client is operating in the ventral vagal circuit, which is one gear of the system that slows things down: the parasympathetic. In this mode, a client is fully regulated, coping well and able to manage stress.[11] If a client is outside their window of tolerance and becomes *hyper*aroused, they activate their sympathetic circuit and can experience such things as panic, anxiety or anger. If they become *hypo*aroused, they enter the dorsal circuit, which is another gear of the parasympathetic system and which can shut things right down: the client becomes numb and dissociates, which complicates EMDR processing.

I can assess whether there is a likelihood to dissociate by administering the dissociative experiences scale, which is a self-report questionnaire that measures dissociative experiences, such as de-realisation, de-personalisation, absorption and amnesia. If clients score highly, I do more preparation work with them and I am more attuned to their tendency to dissociate. I can then employ different techniques to bring them back into the therapy room.

The key with these clients is their need to feel safe: they need to be secure enough to feel their emotions with me in the room. Therefore, there needs to be co-regulation in the consulting room. This is because whenever a young child has been traumatised, for example while at boarding school, their 'neuroception' – a subconscious process that helps us evaluate risk in the environment[12] – can become biased towards detecting danger.

Before we start to process their memories, I teach clients coping mechanisms – affect-regulation skills. A safe or calm place is created.[13] For this, I ask clients to visualise an entirely imaginary place where they would feel calm, on their own, where there is no risk of making any connections with negative events or people. This place is 'tapped in' using some form of bilateral stimulation, usually a 'butterfly hug'. This literally involves the client giving themselves a hug with their arms wrapped around themselves and performing alternate taps with their hands on their arms.

There are different forms of bilateral stimulation: tapping, auditory, via headphones, sensory stimulation (with hand-held pulses) or eye movements (clients watch a light bar, wand or my fingers moving from side to side). I ask clients to use this calm place each day until the following session. This helps them build up resilience of their autonomic nervous system. Then when we actually start processing the trauma, the client can return to their safe place at the end of the session, thereby returning to their emotional and physiological equilibrium.

Next, I install a 'team of allies'. Laurel Parnell recommends three figures for each category: a nurturing figure, a protector figure and a wise figure.[14] These allies are used if the processing gets stuck. I ask clients to use people or animals from books or films or from public life, but not people they actually know. Installing a team of allies can often be hard; in particular, ex-boarder clients struggle to find a nurturing figure, since their main caregivers sent them away from home. These clients often choose animals rather than humans, as they seem to find it hard to trust other humans and let them close. I often use the metaphor of a fortress being built around themselves to keep them safe, which frequently resonates deeply.

EMDR rewires old traumatic memories by using 'adaptive information processing'.[15] The client is asked to share an image of the traumatic event and to identify the connected emotions, where they feel it in their body and any negative belief about themselves that activates the same neural network as when the trauma first occurred.[16] The client is then asked to name what they would prefer to believe about themselves now – a positive cognition. The neural networks become maladaptive over time and the process of EMDR re-activates the trauma by lighting up the particular neural network to treat it. The client is next asked to think about the worst part of the target memory, which activates the maladaptive neural network. In this way, the prefrontal cortex, the limbic system and the brainstem are all activated and then bilateral stimulation is used.

The client maintains dual awareness by keeping one foot in the present and one foot in the memory. The result is adaptive resolution of the traumatic memory.[17] This is measured by using subjective units of disturbance, on a scale of disturbance from 10, which is highly disturbing, to 0, which is no disturbance at all.

The 'magic bullet' client

'James' came to see me for EMDR having read an article about this treatment method. He wanted to stop reliving his old traumas. A senior manager in his early 60s, from the outside he seemed a happy and successful man, the father of three children and settled with his wife. However, he told me that he was not enjoying his life: he felt anxious a lot of the time and was unable to let go of the past. He suffered from panic attacks and could feel his heart turning over and feared a heart attack at any minute, even though a heart monitor confirmed he had a healthy heart. James described his life as anaemic. He did not want his past to be so present in his life. The aim for EMDR therapy was for his memories to be *part of his history* rather than to *govern* him.

James was sent to boarding school at the age of 11, as he had been taken into care because his father could not cope after James's mother had died. James recalls visiting the boarding school and having a meeting with the headmaster. The next minute he recalls seeing his social worker driving away down the long driveway, without a second look. He remembers the day as if it were only yesterday, even though it was over 50 years ago. James tells me he hated his life at the school. There was a member of staff, Mr Wormwood, who was a paedophile and who raped boys and hit them with a slipper. The other boys joked about it, but James was terrified.

James was in a hurry to start EMDR, so we met twice weekly and soon developed a safe therapeutic relationship. We installed a safe place for James. Not surprisingly, he chose a place outside, overlooking a river, sitting under a tree. James chose Julie Andrews in *The Sound of Music* and *Mary Poppins*, two wonderfully caring mother figures, as his nurturing figures. He clearly had a good bond with his mother until she passed away, which also helped our therapeutic relationship. The protector figure was Mr Dawson in the film *Dunkirk*, the captain of one of the little ships, played by Mark Rylance. His wise figure was Atticus Finch from *To Kill a Mockingbird*.

James knew exactly which memory he wanted to target. One evening at boarding school he had been called to visit Mr Wormwood. The other boys teased him that he was about to get the 'bum treatment'. At the time, James was a young, attractive, blonde boy. James walked into the room clothed in his pyjamas and dressing gown, but somehow ended up over his abuser's knee with his pyjamas round his ankles. Initially, he was uncertain about what happened next and whether it happened more than once. James recalls that Mr Wormwood fondled his bottom and joked about how hard he would slap him. For the next 40 years he questioned himself about his sexuality and punished himself with the question whether he had enjoyed the experience.

The negative belief about himself at that traumatic moment was that he was unsafe. The overwhelming emotion was one of shame, but also revulsion and vulnerability. There was a sense of real terror. The level of disturbance was nine.

We started to process the memory using bilateral eye movements. James immediately experienced heat on the back of his neck and his legs became restless. James felt the emotions in his body very quickly. His face turned red and he explained that he felt shame. I believe his restless legs were a trauma response, as he was in flight mode. This happened just after one set of eye movements: the speed of EMDR, on reflection, is remarkable.

I gently suggested, being aware of my tone of voice, that it was not *his* shame, but that it belonged to someone else. I stayed attuned to his process to keep a sense of safety. We continued, and James felt something in his thighs and explained that Mr Wormwood was very good at teaching and James wanted to try hard for him, but he came to the realisation that Mr Wormwood was a paedophile. We continued to process, and James had a sense of being unsafe and had a realisation that other adults must have known what was going on in the school. These adults could have taken action to stop the abuse, but nobody did anything. I reassured him that he was doing really well to keep him regulated and to keep him within his ventral circuit.

We continued with the bilateral eye movements, and James recalled he was almost able to separate himself from the situation now that his head was out of the way. He started to feel sick, and the feeling was one of humiliation. I suspect that James dissociated in that moment of torment as a young boy. He started to stare off into the distance. I did not want James to drop into his dorsal circuit and reassured him that he was doing really well. I needed him to maintain his dual awareness, otherwise the processing would become stuck.

I quietly asked what he wanted to happen in that moment. He wanted an adult to walk in, and I asked if he wanted to imagine that happening as if for real. The power of imagination in EMDR is exceptionally powerful. We processed this interweave. In his imagination a female teacher walks in on the scene and he is naked and Mr Wormwood is trying to regain his composure. James reports, with a smile, that it is almost farcical as the female teacher questions why there is a naked boy in Mr Wormwood's study. I smile with James, co-regulating.

Next, James relives the memory as his adult self and chooses to not even walk into the study, taking back control. After the next set of eye movements, James takes his adult self into the study and puts his arm around his younger self and confronts Mr Wormwood, calling him a paedophile; James tells and his teacher has no come-back, as it is now known. James takes control of the situation and states that he will not do what Mr Wormwood wants him to do. Further processing brings James to the realisation that Mr Wormwood was mentally very unwell and in need of professional help.

At the end of the session, we return to the original memory and James reported no sense of terror. The level of disturbance was zero. The years of nagging doubt and shame were over. There was a realisation that he was not raped, unlike some other boys.

James returned the following week, and I was keen to check the level of disturbance. However, James was beaming and reported that EMDR was a magic bullet, which he could not quite believe. He was free of the constant torment of that memory and he could live his life in peace. James was able to process the trauma in one session of EMDR.

The client who could fix himself

'Ollie' presented as a very polite, engaging client in his 40s, working in the technology sector. He was seeking talking therapy, and we started working online during lockdown. Ollie was in a long-term relationship with a very controlling, fiery and passionate woman from New York, who sought to control every aspect of his life and bullied him. Ollie felt stuck. He loved the sex, but he was beginning to feel pulled in different directions. He was very distressed, and this took the form of skin complaints.

Ollie comes from a family of ex-boarders, but he found boarding school hard and he felt very angry a lot of the time. He sometimes expressed his anger by slapping his own head; he reported self-hatred and very low self-worth. He was offered therapy at school but refused it, telling me he thought he could sort out his own issues. He also refused the medical route of antidepressants, since he believed he could fix himself.

We started to talk about how he survived at boarding school, and there was recognition that he was angry, which was, perhaps, his disowned vulnerability. He realised he was a late bloomer. He was bullied and felt very lonely. He shared with me that he had been sexually abused by a much older and bigger boy at boarding school. He did report it to a teacher at the time, but he was ignored.

Ollie had a tendency to talk a lot and intellectualise, perhaps in an effort to remain hidden: I imagined that in order to keep on surviving he felt he needed to keep me out. After 18 months of talking therapy, we agreed to process some traumatic events from Ollie's childhood using EMDR. The talking therapy had already enabled us to develop a safe therapeutic relationship, which is essential for successful EMDR.

We did some resourcing work. Ollie's safe place was lying down on a grassy riverbank next to a tree, remarkably similar to James'. Ollie's safe place was meant to be a sunny, warm day, but when he was installing it, it suddenly became cold and there was a wave in the sky. He found it hard to maintain a safe place. I suggested he had a superpower that enabled him to zap anything in his safe place that was not meant to be there and he calmed down again. His nurturing figure was a mother hen, interestingly not a human figure. His protector figure was the character from out of town in a Western film, and his wise figure was Yoda from *Star Wars*.

Ollie wanted to come to terms with his response to the sexual abuse he experienced at the age of 13, something that he had carried around with him for far too long. Ollie found friendships at school a challenge. However, an older boy, Charles, had befriended him. Charles took advantage of the situation and one night, after everyone in the dormitory had fallen asleep, he grabbed hold of Ollie and kissed him and lay on top of him. Charles was six foot tall and 20 kilos heavier than Ollie. Ollie is not a big man. Unsurprisingly, Ollie froze and admitted that he felt isolated and frightened, which was his trauma response. He did not shout out and wake up the other boys in the dorm, which is often the case in such circumstances, since the brain quickly tries to work out the best way to survive the situation. Ollie felt completely powerless and unable to resist as Charles kept pushing. Eventually, Charles gave up and left, but Ollie recalls waking up the next day and feeling sick. The worst part of the experience for Ollie was the utter confusion and disbelief that it was happening and his own passive reaction. Ollie likes to think of himself as someone who speaks his mind.

The negative thought about himself was that by accepting the abuse he was 'weak'. He preferred to view himself as assertive and able to stand up for himself. We quickly reached Ollie's emotions of frustration and sorrow at his perceived weakness in accepting the abuse. He was able to locate this emotion in his stomach and down his spine. The level of disturbance was high at 8 out of 10.

While processing, Ollie started to sweat profusely, as his emotions were pushed into his body. He has a tendency to somatise. I noticed Ollie was not breathing normally and I gently invited him to breath. He did not understand why he froze. I introduced an educational interweave, explaining that the body has to decide how to survive a trauma and one trauma response is to freeze. Ollie would have had no control over his response, which can be very alarming.

Ollie wanted to understand why Charles behaved in the way he did. He felt frustration that he could not have the final word. I invited Ollie to think about what he would like to say to his abuser. In a very adolescent tone, he asked, 'What is your problem, Charles?' But then he switched to his adult self, explaining that it must have been lonely for Charles with his urges and he hoped that he got the help he needed. I was moved to hear Ollie express compassion for his abuser.

We continued to process, and Ollie reached acceptance of the fact that he was just a frightened 13-year-old boy and, no matter how old you may be or however strong-minded, the unexpected can always catch you out. He was quick to process that he needed to forgive himself, accept it happened and embrace the fact there was nothing he could do. He accepted that he did the best he could do at the time in those circumstances. He realised that having friends could have helped him.

Ollie returned for his next session and the level of disturbance had gone down to 4 out of 10. The memory felt different, more in its place in Ollie's childhood history. We processed the sadness, and Ollie felt much calmer; the level of disturbance had come down to zero. We installed a positive cognition of being assertive.

EMDR helped Ollie to realise that he did the very best he could to protect himself at a time when he was unprotected by any caring adults. We finished our work together shortly after processing some other memories. Ollie reflected that EMDR calmed everything down in his system. When he thought of the abuse, he realised he no longer had an emotional attachment to the memory. He realised that you cannot change the past but you can move on, and EMDR had helped Ollie to stop living in the past. By the time we concluded our work Ollie had left his American girlfriend and met someone new who was far better suited to him. He felt optimistic about the future.

Conclusion

With the help of EMDR both James and Ollie were able to think about themselves in a more adaptive way. They both achieved adaptive resolution from their negative thoughts about themselves to a more positive outlook on their lives. Alan Schore writes:

> The intuitive clinician is implicitly learning the rhythmic structure of the patient's internal states, and modifying her behaviour to synchronise and couple with that structure, right brain-to-right brain. This interpersonal synchrony, expressed in a coupling of the therapist's and patient's right brains, also enables the patient's embodied subjective self to implicitly experience 'feeling felt' by the empathic therapist.[18]

I like the above reference to the right brain hemisphere, since EMDR is a right brain to right brain process. My task as a therapist is to be highly attuned to the emotion in the room and not to collude with the client's dissociative process, which is common with ex-boarder clients. Philip Bromberg explains:

> If the therapist is too long listening to the 'material' without being alive to his own internal experience of the relationship itself, a dissociative process often begins to develop in the therapist that may have started in the patient, but quickly becomes a cocoon that envelops both patient and therapist.[19]

The beauty of EMDR is that clients can be safely brought back to the here and now when they start to dissociate, as was seen with James. Some critics accuse EMDR of not being very relational and being too formulaic. However, when I process with clients, I 'feel'. I sit very close to them and I often experience the shame, the sorrow, the tears, the need for a hug and the need to laugh. I am emotionally synchronised with the client's process. There is nothing formulaic about the actual processing of the memory or feeling, as each client processes in a different way, which is personal to them.

EMDR has been very effective with boarding school clients, as it quickly gets to the emotions that have been shut down for so long. Both these clients were able to process their traumas in one or two sessions. In my experience, other client groups may take longer. This may partly be due to the 'doing mentality' of boarding school clients. As soon as the parents, social worker or nanny drive away on that first day at boarding school, these children are taught how to keep busy. Those in charge do not want a dormitory full of openly homesick children. There will be a meal to attend or an activity within the first hour of being a boarder. Then lessons start the next day and your life is dominated by bells and keeping busy. Some boarding school clients sometimes find talking therapy difficult as they do not feel they are 'doing' anything. But, EMDR can feel like a magic bullet.

Notes

1 Duffell, N. and Basset, T. (2016) *Trauma, Abandonment and Privilege: A Guide to Therapeutic Work with Boarding School Survivors*. Abingdon & New York: Routledge.
2 Partridge, S. (2007) 'Trauma at the Threshold: An Eight-Year-Old Goes to Boarding School', *Attachment: New Directions in Psychotherapy and Relational Psychoanalysis*, 1(3): 310–312.
3 Duffell, N. and Basset, T. (2016) *Trauma, Abandonment and Privilege: A Guide to Therapeutic Work with Boarding School Survivors*. Abingdon & New York: Routledge.
4 Bowlby, J. (1965) *Childcare and the Growth of Love*. London: Pelican.
5 Power, A. (2013) 'Early Boarding: Rich Children in Care, Their Adaptation to Loss of Attachment', *Attachment: New Directions in Psychotherapy and Relational Psychoanalysis*, 7: 186–201.
6 Spencer, C. (2024) *A Very Private School: A Memoir*. Glasgow: William Collins.
7 Samuel, J. (2024) 'A Talk with Charles Spencer About Childhood Sexual Abuse', YouTube. Retrieved from https://www.youtube.com/watch?v=R7YZHcLhrF8, 22 April 2024.
8 Shapiro, F. (1989) 'Efficacy of the Eye Movement Desensitization Procedure in the Treatment of Traumatic Memories', *Journal of Traumatic Stress Studies*, 2: 199–223.
9 Kase, R. (2023) *Polyvagal-informed EMDR: A Neuro-Informed Approach to Healing*. New York: W.W. Norton.
10 Porges, S. (2011) *The Polyvagal Theory: Neurophysiological Foundation of Emotion, Attachment, Communication, and Self-Regulation*, New York: W.W. Norton.
11 Childre, D. and Rozman, D. (2005) *Transforming Stress: The HeartMath Solution for Relieving Worry, Fatigue, and Tension*. Oakland, CA: New Harbinger.
12 Porges, S. (2011) *The Polyvagal Theory: Neurophysiological Foundation of Emotion, Attachment, Communication, and Self-Regulation*. New York: W.W. Norton.
13 Shapiro, F. (2001) *Eye Movement Desensitization and Reprocessing: Basic Principles, Protocols and Procedures*. New York: Guilford Press.
14 Parnell, L. (2013) *Attachment-Focused EMDR: Healing Relational Trauma*. New York: W.W. Norton.
15 Shapiro, F. (1989) 'Efficacy of the Eye Movement Desensitization Procedure in the Treatment of Traumatic Memories', *Journal of Traumatic Stress Studies*, 2: 199–223.
16 Bayer, R. (2023) *The Art and Science of EMDR: Helping Clinicians Bridge the Path from Protocol to Practice*. Eau Claire, WI: PESI Publishing.
17 Shapiro, F. (2001) *Eye Movement Desensitization and Reprocessing: Basic Principles, Protocols and Procedures*. New York: Guilford Press.
18 Schore, A. (2022) 'Right Brain-to-Right Brain Psychotherapy: Recent Scientific and Clinical Advances', *Annals of General Psychiatry*, 21(46).
19 Bromberg, P. (2011) *The Shadow of the Tsunami and the Growth of the Relational Mind*. New York: Routledge.

Chapter 9

English Landscape

An Archetypal Perspective on the Ex-Boarder

Sally McLaren

Introduction

The image in Figure 9.1 provides a focus for my paper. It is a picture of a fox roaming the English countryside and it hangs on the wall in my kitchen. It is part of the background of my life. Andrew Waddington's paintings express finite moments in a changing world, often symbolised by a bird or animal known to mankind for millennia.

This image has an archetypal or numinous quality, characteristic of images emerging from what Carl Jung would call the 'collective unconscious'.

Although Jung fully recognised the individual or personal unconscious, one of his greatest discoveries he called the 'collective unconscious' – deeper levels of the psyche that are common to all mankind. The content of the collective unconscious is made up essentially of archetypes that bring possibility and potential; for Jung, archetypes are spiritual.[1]

The issue I am addressing is one that has a long history in our society and is deeply embedded in the class system and the English landscape. It is therefore both an individual and a collective issue, but one that has largely been hidden behind a veil of silence, denial and collusion. I am referring of course to the public school system and in particular the practice of sending children away to boarding school at an early age and placing them in the care of an institution.

Primarily through my work with one particular patient, I will show how the archetype of the fox has emerged out of the shadows and into my consciousness as a symbol of work with 'boarding school survivors'.[2]

I will reflect on my approach to my clinical work and my analytic attitude, with reference to the ideas of Carl Jung[3] and those of contemporary Jungian analysts, August Cwik[4] and Donald Kalsched[5].

Throughout, I will draw attention both to the depth of the wound that results from this practice and to its hidden nature.

DOI: 10.4324/9781003515517-9

Figure 9.1 English Landscape by Andrew Waddington.

Source: Reproduced with permission from the artist, Andrew Waddington.

Guiding lights

As I introduce my patient, I notice an echo of the feelings that were a feature of the early years of our work: there is so much material. I do not know quite where to start, what to include or what to leave out. I feel overwhelmed and inadequate for the task.

I understand my feelings as countertransference, an unconscious communication between my patient and me, relating primarily to his own unwanted feelings of inadequacy.

My interest in the subject of boarding school began some years ago when a man walked into my consulting room with a photo of himself aged 7, in school uniform, on his way to his first day at boarding school: a small child in tie and blazer, smiling, full of expectation and hope.

My countertransference resonates with the overwhelming nature of the experience of the young child abandoned at boarding school by his parents, long before he has developed the capacity necessary to manage such a situation – a brutal severing of his most fundamental attachments, leading to a lifelong denial of any dependency needs.

The man standing before me, now in mid-life, appears confident, mature, articulate and charming. He has a loving family, good social status and ample financial resources. However, he tells me that in recent years he has realised that there is a hidden part of himself – a part that he does not know and now this makes him feel like there is a 'schizophrenic split' in his personality. It is a very sensitive, young and undeveloped part. He says he wants to 'get to know' this part of himself in analysis.

He remembered a repetitive dream as a child of a penis broken off – the feelings are of powerlessness and having no control. I get a sense of potential rage and violent emotions. Every time I feel threatened by my sense of inadequacy, I remind myself of his initial dream and this helps me to orientate myself and reminds me of the framework within which we are working.

> He is driving an articulated lorry into a large, dark warehouse. He is trying to park it amongst other lorries ... very carefully, inch by inch. He thinks he knows what to do, but he has not had the experience of other drivers who have been doing it since they were 17. He is anxious about what will happen if his foot slips on the clutch. The other drivers are Glaswegian, which he associates with dockworkers he has seen in Glasgow ... the banter, the carelessness, saying what they mean even if it is rude to others. He wishes he could be like that in relationships. We talk about him getting into position for analysis ... inch by inch ...

This dream has been a light that has helped me navigate my way through his analysis, bit by bit and inch by inch. It has contributed to my appreciation of this huge articulated lorry he brought with him into analysis and my awareness of the importance of slowly and carefully getting into position before unloading the lorry.

Duffell[6] describes the kind of trauma experienced by boarding school survivors as the trauma of persistent neglect over a long period, leading to dissociation, and the construction of a 'strategic survival personality'.

This resonates for me with Kalsched's work on the 'self-care system'. I suspected the presence of a harsh inner figure with archetypal roots, akin to Kalsched's 'Dis', which functioned initially as a survival technique in order to protect the innocent core self, leading to dissociation of all feelings.[7]

Duffell describes the developmental trauma of the child who has nowhere to take and process his feelings about normal developmental processes. And he describes the boarder's double bind:

> I know Mummy and Daddy love me. They have told me so. I know it's important to them to send me away to school and that it costs a lot of money and that I should be grateful.
> But I hate it. If they love me, why did they send me away?
> Either they don't love me or there's something very wrong with me for feeling like this. If they don't really love me, it must be because I am bad. If they do, and I feel like this, it must be because I am bad.[8]

The child is caught in a trap and the only way to escape is by shutting down on all feelings and thereby betraying himself. This is a wound to the soul. It is a wound from which many do not recover, and the shock waves continue to be felt in subsequent generations.

Kalsched describes patients who were 'robbed of their childhood by trauma and forced to grow up too fast, becoming self-sufficient too early'. He approaches 'the image of Rapunzel in her tower as an image of the inner condition of these patients – a condition that is both split and walled off'.[9]

The analytic third

Another light that has accompanied me is the writing of Jungian analyst August Cwik, and in particular his work on reverie, 'associative dreaming' and 'thirdness'. He writes,

> Listening analytically is not listening just to what is said but listening to what is just below the surface waiting to be said – or, as the alchemists so aptly phrased it, 'the search for what not yet is' (Petrus Bonus 1330). The royal road to apprehending this mercurial element is through the use of the imagination to inform one about the nature of the 'third thing' that is being co-created in the analytic situation. Ghent (1989) of the relational school, suggested that all analysts need to find their own 'credo' – an expression of his or her own beliefs about how therapy works. This is my 'credo' and orienting compass that guides me through the analytic day.[10]

Cwik's credo about how therapy works gives central place to the capacity of the analyst to listen and to listen in a very particular way 'not listening just to what is said but listening to what is just below the surface waiting to be said'. Arguably, never is this more critical and more challenging than in working with a 'boarding school survivor', whose very survival depends on keeping his wound hidden, not only from others, including his analyst, but also and more disastrously from himself.

I reiterate my intention of drawing attention not only to the *depth* of the wound that results from the practice of early boarding, but also to its *hidden* nature.

Cwik also highlights Jung's insight into a 'third thing' being created intrapsychically and within the analytic encounter. He explores how the state of thirdness is created and accessed through use of reverie and associative dreaming. He equates the analytic third to the unconscious-to-unconscious connection between the individuals, the relational unconscious. Jung argued that the unconscious itself could best be understood and related to as if it were another person, and we can apply this idea of personification to the notion of thirdness.

Cwik equates the notion of thirdness to the unconscious-to-unconscious connection between analyst and patient. This operates not only at the individual or personal level, but also at the shared, collective and archetypal level. It is deeply hidden. It is unconscious and therefore unknown and, indeed, at the deepest level it is *unknowable*. It is also the place of transformation – transformation for both parties.

In 'The Psychology of the Transference' Jung describes this third element thus:

The elusive, deceptive, everchanging content that possesses the patient like a demon flits about from patient to doctor and, as *the third party* [italics mine] in the alliance, continues its game ... alchemists aptly personified it as the wily god of revelation, Hermes or Mercurius.[11]

He also said,

Psychological induction inevitably causes the two parties to get involved *in the transformation of the third* [italics mine] and to be themselves transformed in the process, and all the time the doctor's knowledge, like a flickering lamp, is the one dim light in the darkness.[12]

The fox has come to represent this 'elusive, deceptive everchanging content' for me in my work with boarding school survivors.

The Book of Symbols, a product of the extensive research of Archive for Research in Archetypal Symbolism, drawing on Jung's work on archetypes and the collective unconscious, has been a rich resource for my reflective process. In it, the archetypal fox is described thus:

In Medieval legend, the labyrinthine passages of the wily Reynard's underground 'castle' allowed him to be everywhere at once and nowhere at all, while the shimmering fluidity of his vulpine intelligence anticipating and deluding all opponents, subverted the proper order of things ...Thus if we approach the ubiquitous, mercurial fox – like the unconscious – on its own terms, it may guide us through the transformational spaces between oppositional states of being – between wild forest and cultivated farmland, between unconventional, intuitive intelligence and collective social norms, and between animal, human and spirit worlds, both beneficent and demonic – in the service of wholeness ...[13]

Cwik describes the attitude of mind required to address the imaginal material arising from the analytic third as 'associative dreaming' and it is this that provides the 'compass' for analytic work. A vignette from early on in my work with this patient will illustrate this concept.

A closer look

One day, my supervisor suggests to me that it might be useful sometimes to write more detailed notes, that this might give her a better understanding of what is going on between my patient and me.

From the beginning of the next session, I concentrate hard, determined to retain every word. He lies on the couch and is silent. He says he does not know what to talk about. In the silence I find myself remembering a difficult time with a previous supervisor. As the relationship deteriorated, he asked me to produce ever more detailed notes. He was in the habit of writing notes himself in the session, but I began to wonder if he was not fully present in the room with me and whether this was contributing to the difficulties with him and limiting the effectiveness of our work together.

So, as I sit there in the silence with my patient, I resolve to forget about notes and focus on being fully present with this man bringing me his difficulties, placing himself in a vulnerable position on my couch.

Cwik suggests that, although Jung offers a deep theoretical understanding of 'reverie' and the 'analytic third', he fails to demonstrate how this is experienced and utilised in analysis. So, Cwik enlarges on the process, and I illustrate it in my vignette.

Jung had a sharp, intuitive understanding of the conscious and unconscious effects two people have on one another. He wrote, 'Emotions are contagious, because they are deeply rooted in the sympathetic system'.[14] Jung envisioned a diagram[15] that conveys all the possible conscious and unconscious connections both between and within the analyst and the patient. Cwik reproduces a version of this diagram to include the analytic third (see Figure 9.2). The focus in associative dreaming is on what is taking place in the mind of the therapist (on the left-hand side of diagram). This is the area of countertransference through which contents of the therapist's unconscious come into consciousness. Cwik writes,

> Many of the contents ... may not be accessible to the therapist without creating a particular state of consciousness that can allow them into awareness, observe and note them, and engage them in a kind of dialogue that yields some sort of understanding.[16]

It is a kind of analytic mindfulness or 'active imagination' with countertransference experiences. Furthermore, because of the hidden nature of the condition of the boarding school survivor, the capacity to be fully present and to be open to the unconscious-to-unconscious communication taking place under the surface is particularly important.

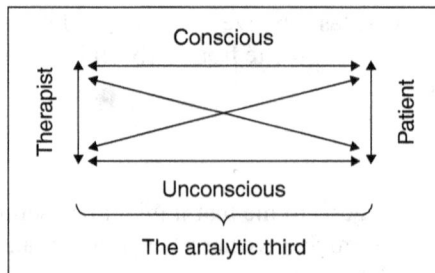

Figure 9.2 Variation of Jung's transference diagram to include the analytic third.

Source: Cwik A. (2011) 'Associative Dreaming: Reverie and Active Imagination', *Journal of Analytical Psychology*, 56(1): 16. Diagram reproduced with kind permission of the author, August Cwik.

I have described in this session the kind of dialogue going on in my mind, and now, returning to that session, I describe the fruits arising from the analytic third.

We are sitting together in the silence; then my patient tells me how after the last session he left feeling good and full of hope. He then had an appointment with the dentist. He has been troubled with a split tooth that has been causing him soreness for a long time. He went from feeling good to feeling bad. It is always one or the other – like at school – the freedom and hope in the holidays and then returning to and being abandoned in a place of no hope with no end in sight. The only way to survive was to shut down on his feelings. I suggest we stay with this story of the dentist and the split tooth. He had a filling done on this tooth when he was a teenager. This filling did the job at the time but over the years it has ceased to function. He does not know the dentist well. His first words to the dentist as he lay back in the dentist's chair, were 'I do not want to lose this tooth'. The dentist says he is not able to fix it straight away and he is not able to give him any guarantees. He will try to re-join the split parts and see if that works. But the split has gone right down to the roots and this has happened over a very long time. We explore some parallels: my couch and the dentist's chair, the dentist and me, the split tooth and the split in his personality.

As we near the end of the session he says he normally goes away with something he is able to put together in his mind – 'a model' – what to do to get fixed. But today he has not. Then as he sits up to leave, he says he does not know what to write in his notes today. I feel a sudden jolt. He told me a while ago that he has a coffee after seeing me and writes notes on every session. How could I have forgotten?

Afterwards, I write a page of notes, but then I give up and reach for my sketch pad and pens instead. I draw the split tooth, the dentist, the clock, the notes. I write 'time ticking by', 'no hope'. The split tooth, a shadowy black mass at its roots, looms large on the page and looks more like a penis.

The boarding school survivor often has a desperate need to feel that he knows what is going on, that he is in control, that there is a plan, a quick fix, a tidy solution. The alternative is to be overwhelmed with a sense of inadequacy, hopelessness and terror.

My patient tells me a few weeks later that he spent an extra hour writing his notes after the previous session, but it is 'becoming more like an art class'. He is developing the thoughts and ideas in his head as he writes, rather than just writing down what he remembers.

I think this was the first tentative sign of him moving from predominantly logical, rational, scientific thinking towards the opposite, a more fluid, non-directed and imaginative attitude.

We move on now to some months later.

Myth and synchronicity

The story of the ancient Greek state of Sparta had been in my mind from the beginning of my patient's analysis.

The Spartan family was quite different from those of other ancient Greek city states. In Sparta children were children of the state more than of their parents. They were raised to be soldiers, removed from the 'softening' influence of their mothers at age 7, like my patient, and housed in a dormitory with other boys.

Spartan children were taught stories of courage and fortitude. A favourite story was about a boy and a fox:

> The little fellow on his way to school saw some fox cubs playing together. They belonged to a man who was fond of pets. The boy picked one up and hiding it under his coat went on to school. The fox, restless and angry, began to gnaw the boy's flesh just above the heart. The child studied his lessons without a word or cry, though he grew pale and weak. Suddenly he sank down upon the ground, and when the teacher went to him and opened his coat, the fox jumped out and ran away. But the boy was dead. He would steal and suffer and die rather than be found out. That was the Spartan idea of manliness.[17]

This story resonated strongly with my experience of my patient.

When I tell my colleagues this story in a supervision group, the fox leads to associations with rats and then to the Pied Piper and then to Jimmy Savile. And I think of the headmaster of my patient's prep school. Boys were taken to his study for frequent beatings, trousers down, bent over the man's bed and thrashed brutally. Regular harsh beatings for minor offences are a common story from many ex-boarders.

This headmaster, *in loco parentis*, is a feared yet idealised figure in my patient's story. We might think of the headmaster as the harsh inner figure in Kalsched's self-care system, who must be defended at all costs. He is a Pied Piper figure who lures the children into following him without questioning, as they dance to his tune.

Both the abandoned child, frozen and undeveloped, and the authoritarian, persecutory headmaster have been internalised as dominating figures in my patient's inner landscape and can appear in his outer world through projection. They have an archetypal, larger than life quality and need to be brought down to size, as it were, and integrated as parts of himself.

As we walk down the street after the meeting, my supervision colleague suddenly exclaims, 'Look! A fox!'. And there it is, disappearing into the shadows between two houses where the rubbish bins are placed.

Returning to the transference diagram, Cwik draws our attention to one particular pole that was previously left out of the familiar transference diagram – the one descending from above depicting the influence of archetypal and/or synchronistic energies. (See Figure 9.3.)

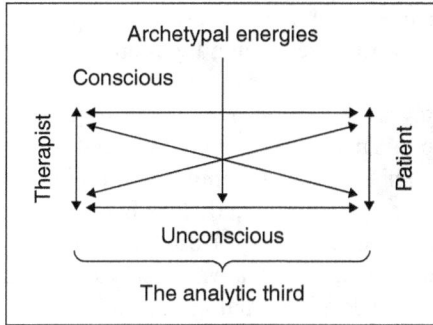

Figure 9.3 Revised transference diagram demonstrating presence of archetypal energies.

Source: Cwik A, (2017). 'What is a Jungian analyst dreaming when myth comes to mind? Thirdness as an aspect of the anima media natura', *Journal of Analytical Psychology*, 62(1): 114. Diagram reproduced with kind permission of the author, August Cwik.

This extract from my work would suggest the presence of both: a myth, containing archetypal themes, has come to mind and a synchronicity has occurred. Cambray suggests that it is in moments of synchronicity (or meaningful coincidences), when an archetypal field is constellated, that there is the potential for new patterns to emerge and transformation to take place.[18]

Survival

Everything is about survival, and this is central to an understanding of the inner world and behaviour of the ex-boarder.

The Book of Symbols tells us,

The nimble fox's notorious ability to transgress boundaries has made it one of the most successful survivors on the planet ...[19]

It is remarkable to me how often duplicity appears in the stories of all my ex-boarding school patients, particularly in the form of stealing and lying, and this can reappear in the transference. Stealing from the headmaster, stealing from peers, stealing from father. Duffell points out that, in a boy's development, it can be important not only to defy the authorities, beginning with one's own domineering father, but also to get away with it. Duffell writes too about a boy's compensation for lack of love in a world where the thing seen to be done is much more important than the thing actually done.[20]

My patient had a leading role in the leadership team of a charitable organisation. He and the chairman had been meeting for mutual personal support, sharing openly and making themselves vulnerable. However, he told me there had been increasing discontent with this man: several people were not happy with his leadership style. This was early on in our work together and I was unfamiliar with the history of this relationship.

I became increasingly uneasy about the persecutory and omnipotent nature of my patient's attitude to this man. He would tell me that the problems in the charity had been going on for far too long: it should be brought out in the open and the chairman should accept responsibility and 'face his own issues'. He saw it as his duty and responsibility to lead the way. I tried various ways over the months to challenge him about his role in this, in a way that would not simply ignite his sensitivity to criticism or close down the dialogue between us.

I wondered if his rage about this situation really belonged to the injustices he experienced in the boarding school system? He was trying to put right now what he could not as a child, when he was powerless and had no voice. However, I was to realise that the incident may have held far more significance than was apparent to me at the time. The chairman left the organisation eventually, probably finding himself in an intolerable situation and after some years of loyal service.

As my patient's analysis continued, it became increasingly clear to us both that, hidden behind my patient's charming and articulate persona, there existed a brutality and ruthlessness, born of his terror and his need to survive as a child, that might be triggered whenever he felt vulnerable or under the least apparent threat. This was so deeply hidden from himself and others that he was capable of betraying and destroying anyone who got in his way, with the support and collusion of those around him.

He realised that he lives much of his life constantly in survival mode, as many ex-boarders do: the stakes are always high and out of proportion. Guilt and shame began to emerge, holding their own terror.

Symbol and soul

One Easter break, I decided to spend some time reflecting on the progress of the work. I reproduce here my thoughts based on notes made at the time in order to illustrate the concept of associative dreaming in my reflective process.

> There is little that can be concluded at this stage of my work. I am reorientating myself. Perhaps the compass needs resetting. As a result of a recent dream my patient is questioning the goals he has set.
>
> And I am 'niggled' by the fox. My son and his pregnant wife are troubled by a fox who disturbs their dog at night. My analyst sees a fox through the window while I am on the couch one day. What have I missed? What is eluding me?
>
> One night, I take a break to watch some TV, a drama series called *The Split*. It focuses on the lucrative world of divorce law, four women from the family who represent clients going through often high-profile splits, while they themselves navigate their own complicated relationships. Children get caught in the 'fall

out'. In this episode a fox keeps appearing ... in the background ... in the shadows. I hear, 'The fox keeps me up', and 'Mum, the fox has "pooed" on the car again'. In one scene I see a fox being chased out of the posh kitchen where it has got right inside the fridge. And in another, a fox is being chased away from the rabbit's cage.

Is this the latest manifestation of the 'elusive, deceptive, ever-changing content that possesses the patient like a demon' and 'flits about from patient to doctor'? I read again the story of the fox and the boy.

If you met my patient, you would see a man who is confident, articulate and self-assured, like many ex-boarders. He has all the trappings of privilege and success. You might be intimidated by him or envious of him. You might think he is being self-indulgent coming several times a week for analysis. After all he was not actually abused – was he?

But you cannot see the fox gnawing into the flesh just above his heart, the fox who persecutes him daily, giving him no rest. You cannot see the fox and his gnawing, leaving him with a profound sense of inadequacy and despair. He has kept that fox hidden all his life under his coat and his suffering is not seen or acknowledged by anyone, including himself.

John Lennon famously proposed that the one thing a person could not hide is when they were crippled inside. But the boarding school survivor becomes an expert at doing just that.

And then, unexpectedly, Kalsched's latest paper on working with survivors of early relational trauma arrives in the post. He concludes:

In some cases of early traumatic injury there is relational work to be done with embodied emotion, connecting psyche and soma, and opening the imagination, before conventional analytic work can be initiated.

In these cases, to carry something consciously is not just a matter of adjusting our mental attitudes or of insight alone. We need what Bruno Bettleheim called 'an informed heart'. The great *coniunctio* that we're after with these patients – and that Jung discussed in reference to the dis-embodied 'opposites' – cannot happen without the body and its unredeemed, unknown, unremembered and frozen affects. In trying to heal our capacity to feel we're pursuing a consciousness of the heart. That for me is the numinous *mysterium* in what Jung called the 'Mysterium Coniunctionis'. The heart is the hidden third. And recovering a heart that can break is how we help ourselves and our patients recover the capacity to feel.[21]

Cwik concludes his paper:

Jung says, 'In the deepest sense we all dream *not out of ourselves* but out of what lies *between us and the other* ...' Then our analytic mindfulness begins to be a natural way of being in the world that engages all experience both inner and outer – truly to live and embrace the symbolic life through thirdness.[22]

Kalsched writes:

> In trauma work … we must learn to speak a soulful language, because it is uniquely the human soul that is threatened with annihilation by early trauma in a child's life.[23]

This requires 'binocular vision', one eye looking in and one eye looking out, on the part of the analyst; it is this that unites the two worlds of inner and outer reality in a living third thing.[24]

A few months later my patient brings me a dream.

> He is trying to bring to life a newborn baby in a polythene bag who is struggling to breathe. He feels panic-stricken, inadequate and ill-equipped for the job and that too much is being expected of him, but in desperation he starts to massage the baby's heart … And the baby begins to breathe.

And, also a few months later, my daughter-in-law gives birth at home to a little boy whom they name Kit. This is the couple who had been disturbed at night by a fox during her pregnancy. They did not realise – and neither did I until later – that 'kit' is another name for a baby fox.

The fox has emerged again in the analytic field in different ways over the years as my patient slowly recovers the capacity to feel, and begins to live life fully. It has also been instrumental in keeping me alert with other ex-boarder patients to the devious way certain aspects of their behaviour and the depth of their wounds may be kept hidden. The fox has helped me to keep in mind the duplicitous nature of their personalities, and helped to guide me through the transformational spaces between oppositional states of being – in the service of wholeness.

Notes

1 International Association for Analytical Psychology (IAAP), 'Contemporary Understandings of Analytical Psychology'. Short articles on key Jungian concepts, such as 'collective unconscious', 'archetypes' and 'synchronicity'. Available at https://iaap.org/jung-analytical-psychology/short-articles-on-analytical-psychology/. Accessed 26 February 2024.
2 I am grateful to my patient for his permission to use material from our work together.
3 Jung, C.G. (1935) 'The Tavistock Lectures', *Collected Works 18*. Hove: Routledge. Jung, C.G. (1946) 'The Psychology of the Transference', *Collected Works 16*. Hove: Routledge. Jung, C.G. (1963) 'Mysterium Coniunctionis', *Collected Works 14*. Princeton, NJ: Bollingen Foundation.

4   Cwik A. (2011) 'Associative Dreaming: Reverie and Active Imagination', *Journal of Analytical Psychology*, 56(1): 14–36. Cwik, A. (2017) 'What Is a Jungian Analyst Dreaming when Myth Comes to Mind? Thirdness as an Aspect of the Anima Media Natura', *Journal of Analytical Psychology*, 62(1): 107–129.

5   Kalsched, D. (1996) *The Inner World of Trauma: Archetypal Defences of the Personal Spirit*. London: Routledge. Kalsched, D. (2013) *Trauma and the Soul: A Psycho-Spiritual Approach to Human Development and its Interruption*. Hove: Routledge. Kalsched, D. (2020) 'Opening the Closed Heart: Affect-Focused Clinical Work with Victims of Early Trauma', *Journal of Analytical Psychology*, 65(1): 136–152.

6   Duffell, N. and Basset, T. (2016) *Trauma, Abandonment and Privilege: A Guide to Therapeutic Work with Boarding School Survivors*. Abingdon & New York: Routledge.

7   Kalsched, D. (2013) *Trauma and the Soul: A Psycho-Spiritual Approach to Human Development and its Interruption*. Hove: Routledge, pp. 86–126.

8   Duffell, N. and Basset, T. (2016) *Trauma, Abandonment and Privilege: A Guide to Therapeutic Work with Boarding School Survivors*. Abingdon & New York: Routledge. p. 35.

9   Kalsched, D. (1996) *The Inner World of Trauma: Archetypal Defences of the Personal Spirit*. London: Routledge, p. 148.

10 Cwik, A. (2017) 'What Is a Jungian Analyst Dreaming when Myth Comes to Mind? Thirdness as an Aspect of the Anima Media Natura', *Journal of Analytical Psychology*, 62(1): 107.

11 Jung, C.G. (1946) 'The Psychology of the Transference', *Collected Works 16*. Hove: Routledge, para. 384.

12 Jung, C.G. (1946) 'The Psychology of the Transference', *Collected Works 16*. Hove: Routledge, para. 399.

13 Ronnberg, A. and Martin, K. (eds) (2010) *The Book of Symbols: Reflections on Archetypal Images*. Cologne, Germany: Taschen, pp. 278–281.

14 Jung, C.G. (1935) 'The Tavistock Lectures', *Collected Works 18*. Hove: Routledge, para. 318.

15 Jung, C.G. (1946) 'The Psychology of the Transference', *Collected Works 16*. Hove: Routledge, para. 422.

16 Cwik A. (2011) 'Associative Dreaming: Reverie and Active Imagination', *Journal of Analytical Psychology*, 56(1): 19.

17 Shaw, C.D. (2008) *Stories of the Ancient Greeks*, Chapel Hill, NC: Yesterday's Classics, p. 153.

18 Cambray, J. (2002) 'Synchronicity and Emergence', *American Imago*, 59(4): 409–434, at 417.

19 Ronnberg, A. & Martin, K. (eds) (2010) *The Book of Symbols: Reflections on Archetypal Images*. Cologne: Taschen, p. 278.

20 Duffell, N. (2014) *Wounded Leaders: British Elitism and the Entitlement Illusion*. London: Lone Arrow Press.

21 Kalsched, D. (2020) 'Opening the Closed Heart: Affect-Focused Clinical Work with Victims of Early Trauma', *Journal of Analytical Psychology*, 65(1): 149.

22 Cwik, A. (2017) 'What Is a Jungian Analyst Dreaming when Myth Comes to Mind? Thirdness as an Aspect of the Anima Media Natura', *Journal of Analytical Psychology*, 62(1): 125.

23 Kalsched, D. (2013) *Trauma and the Soul: A Psycho-Spiritual Approach to Human Development and its Interruption*. Hove: Routledge, p. 117.

24 Kalsched, D. (2013) *Trauma and the Soul: A Psycho-Spiritual Approach to Human Development and its Interruption*. Hove: Routledge, pp. 6, 9, 31.

Chapter 10

The Effect of Boarding School on Sibling Relationships

Dawn Grundy

Introduction

When a child begins their boarding school life everything changes. The sudden loss of parental guidance, attention and support can break a child's attachment, compelling him or her to make personal adaptations to manage this change. Over the last 25 years, this has been well documented.[1,2] The loss of daily contact with family has an undeniable impact on the boarding child, but it can also be a mutual loss for other family members, friends and community left behind.

In this chapter, I explore a lesser-known effect – the potential impact of broken relationships on ex-boarders and their siblings. The existing boarding school literature only makes a fleeting reference to this, and yet research into the relationship between siblings shows it to be of significant relevance to children's regulation and security.[3] The problems arising for siblings through boarding is only now becoming fully apparent. In a recent article, Joy Schaverien, who coined the expression 'boarding school syndrome', recognised the 'impact on sibling attachments and … the suffering of those left at home'.[4] And, within my clinical practice, I have repeatedly heard about the deep importance of sibling relationships, and this is reinforced by anecdotal evidence from ex-boarders and their families.

The sibling experience is not a unitary one: differing scenarios include when one or more children are at the same or different boarding schools, where they might be separated in different establishments, or by difference in age or gender as well as the effect of separation on those siblings who remain at home.

To illustrate this little-known problem, we will hear the words of siblings who boarded in a variety of situations, as well as those who stayed at home. The examples of sibling relationships within this chapter have been anonymised for the privacy of those who were kind enough to describe their experiences and gave permission for them to be shared. This study will hopefully go some way to extending our clinical understanding of the varying and wide-ranging effects of boarding education.

DOI: 10.4324/9781003515517-10

The sibling experience

John Bowlby's attachment theory suggests that a child's attachment to their primary caregivers is the foundation for their emotional security and that this extends onwards into their relationships throughout life.[5] It has been recognised that this attachment does not need to be a singular bond with just a parent or main caregiver – it can be with several people.[6]

At a young age, when the brain is rapidly developing, the sibling relationship and the shared activities of siblings can have a profound bearing on developing self-worth. Play between siblings allows different experiences, behaviours and reactions to be tested out, so that children learn where boundaries lie and receive attentive feedback such as reaction, response, criticism and encouragement.[7]

Within a family, sibling relationships provide a practice ground for individual roles within a hierarchy; these include the exercise of competition, self-worth development, boundary setting and conflict regulation. Siblings inadvertently teach each other how to manage relationships and give plenty of experience of conflict and its resolution. Such lessons are the basis for understanding the social world and future intimate relationships. In the case of single-child families, some children may have developed close relationships with cousins or friends that mirror the sibling relationship.

Even though the traditional nuclear family is no longer the typical expectation, as family life is increasingly complicated by trauma, divorce, stepfamilies and so forth, a family is still a potential matrix for support, shared experiences, connection and history. In my practice I hear when these family experiences have not been realised, there are inevitably broken attachments, resulting in loss and hurt.

Boarding and attachment

The moment a child is left in a new unfamiliar school environment by their parents has been termed 'trauma at the threshold'.[8] The new boarder realises life has radically changed: they are now living alone but among many others. They have much to learn about their new boarding school life – the unwritten rules and regulations, the new environment and buildings to navigate, new peers and adults to get to know. There is little time to process what they have lost, and yet when they do, the feeling of loneliness can bring a yearning for home, for family – for familiarity and safety.

These feelings are often not expressed because the new boarder does not want to bring attention to themselves, so they are often repressed or disowned. 'Homesickness' is a form of disenfranchised grief, often unrecognised by others, possibly not even by the person themselves, and so not attended to.[9] Bowlby, however, believed that when a young child was dealing with the loss of their main caregiver it was comparable to an adult's experience of grief.[10]

This withholding of emotions can have a long-term effect. In 2015, Schaverien suggested that the loss of home and subsequent incarceration in boarding school had effects that she called boarding school syndrome.[11] The effects were identifiable as a variety of behaviours apparent in many adult ex-boarders and are now increasingly recognised.

To stay safe and manage their situation, boarding children have to shut down their emotions and develop a hypervigilance to keep them one step ahead of trouble, becoming pseudo-adults. In 2000, Nick Duffell proposed that boarding children, in order to manage the loss and broken attachments of leaving their home and family at an early age, regularly constructed a 'strategic survival personality'.[12] The strategies exhibit themself in a raft of insecure attachment behaviours, e.g. masking and defences from childhood that can last through to adult life. This is the response that Duffell calls strategic survival and he argues that boarders make a compensatory attachment to their own survival personality.[13]

For most children, the normal transition into adulthood involves the gradual detachment from family and home. However, for boarders, this transition happens *suddenly* and much earlier. Bowlby argued that successful separation from family and the ability to cope with the change is determined by the child's attachment security. Secure attachment comes from earlier experiences of being part of a family in which each member can navigate loss by regulating and supporting each other so that they feel safe. In families where support and regulation were compromised due to trauma, abuse or emotional detachment, children can become insecurely attached. This can result in children not feeling safe within themselves and struggling to build relationships with others.[14]

Arrival at boarding school means that their physical and emotional safety depends on their school and peer group. In a boarding school environment, where the one-to-one ratio of parent to child can never be achieved, a child is unlikely to receive the time from an adult to help them understand and regulate their feelings. With so many children living from their strategic survival personalities, the developmental process of puberty and adolescence that would normally happen within a family is compromised. After many repetitions of leaving home and family, children become accustomed to the loss and adapt by fully identifying with their survival personalities.

Schaverien discusses how boarding children can form a 'sibling matrix', a way to feel safe at school and form new bonds with their peer group, some leading to lifelong friendships.[15] In adulthood, the unspoken understanding of their childhood experience found in other ex-boarders brings a familiarity and allegiance. This 'old boys network' can prove invaluable in building business and social connections. It is one that both the parents may hope for and the schools promote. However, Schaverien notes that the sibling matrix support can also be elitist, separating ex-boarders from others in society. The camaraderie learnt at school can extend to the ex-boarder's long-term intimate relationships, causing an unconscious 'incest taboo' and so preventing sexual intimacy.

The 'special one'?

Every child has a right to feel special to their parents. As they compete for their parents' love and affection, a need to be special and to be seen as important often brings rivalry between siblings.[16] Siblings can hold very different perspectives of their experiences in childhood and their position within the family. Children are hard-wired to find favour with parents, family or peers in order to receive love and feel secure. Alfred Adler suggested that sibling conflicts are fuelled by a natural need for parental favour within the family and a desire to be recognised by their siblings as more important.[17]

Boarding school is not a place where it is easy to feel special and it can considerably amplify the competitive effects that siblings are subject to. Whether they are younger siblings who are left behind or the sibling not chosen to go to boarding school, such an alteration to their living experience can mean that their family ranking is changed forever. The older sibling is no longer available as playmate or substitute parent for additional guidance, support and solidarity. Whether they were sent away or left at home, siblings struggle to understand the other's experience.

The sibling relationship is universally marked by disagreements and is distinct to other relationships that children form.[18] Yet, when children are separated from family, their familiarity of daily family dynamics is much reduced; a loss occurs, and a compensatory narrative often fills the gap.

Children who are only children may struggle at boarding school having had no experience of living with or feeling part of a larger group.[19] In contrast, some single-child ex-boarders, have reported positive experiences connecting with same-age peers as their home experience was socially isolating. In difficult home situations, the boarding child may feel both relief of responsibility as well as an inability to support siblings at home.

Parents of boarders, ex-boarders or their siblings sometimes insist that there was rarely a cross word between brothers and sisters during holiday times. Some of these accounts of conflict-free home lives may be questionable: arguably, the return to the sibling relationship meant it was too precious to risk conflict and possible rejection, or that alternatively their boarding school personality was now too strategic to risk authentic emotional outbursts. Here again, boarding has the power to influence the narrative of home life.

For some parents, the struggle with the loss of a child to boarding school can result in their distancing from those children remaining at home. As a result, according to Ricky Emanuel writing in *Sibling Matters*, the remaining children can feel a loss of attachment with their parent, compounding their own form of grief at losing their sibling to boarding school.[20]

Clinical examples

Many ex-boarders in my practice frequently speak of having two different identities in each place – home and school. From the perspective of the boarder who returns home, life has changed: the family have had new experiences without them, their siblings and friends have grown and made new social connections.

'David' told me about how he felt he was no longer 'one of the team', unlike his younger siblings who had a connection with each other and parents. He described how he felt his role and sense of place within the family had gone. Already feeling separate, he never shared this with his family. In his late 50s now, he speaks of still feeling 'disenfranchised' from siblings.

'Peter' spoke of how he separated home from school; home was with family, but for him, as an only child and as for those with a large age difference between siblings, the return home might mean many hours alone. Such children can be lonely, missing the local friendship groups that had developed without them. In consequence, school could feel like 'home', since this is where they find social connection within their peer group.

'Charlotte', whose brother had been sent to boarding school, described how the loss of him at home radically altered the existing relationships within the family. She felt he would be welcomed home in the holidays as the 'special' child whose needs were always prioritised. She explained that financial constraints on the family from having to pay school fees meant she and her parents needed to budget and often did without; yet, when her brother returned, his every whim was seemingly attended to. School trips and extracurricular activities were paid for to help him fit in at school; and his favourite meals prepared on his return home.

Not only was Charlotte's sibling relationship broken, but also the close relationship that had existed between mother and daughter was lost when her brother started at school. In later life, her mother spoke of her inability to love her son while he was away. As a result, she felt unable to love her daughter as she could not balance her love while he was not there. As an adult, Charlotte reflected on her brother's resentment of her being the child at home with parents; this dynamic continued into their adult lives. Although he had gone away to school, she felt *she* was the abandoned one.

Many ex-boarders report a complex relationship to the meaning of 'home'. 'James', who boarded due to his father's nomadic work life, described returning to another new home and excitedly looking for his childhood games, only to discover that they had been discarded during his family's move. He felt his history had been wiped out; he reported that it was only recently, in his 50s, he had begun to feel at home in the place where he lived.

I recently heard from a middle child of three siblings – the only child in the family to attend boarding school – who found that on her return home her place at the table had been taken by her sibling. Of course, family life continues without the missing child and day-to-day memories are created, relationships grow between remaining siblings and parents.

Siblings boarding together

The loss of parental figures at boarding school means that sibling support and connection become more important to the siblings in maintaining family identity and loyalty. However, when siblings are educated at the same boarding school, factors such as their ages, or whether they are at co-educational or single-sex schools, will influence the connection and support that they retain: the situation can become extremely complicated.

In clinical work, younger siblings have reported being prematurely sent to board in order to support their older sibling. In such cases, the imagined contact and support were often not realised due to the customs and hierarchy of the boarding school institution. In the hope of supporting the boarding child, and seemingly unaware of the importance of parental attachment, parents may receive dispensation from the school to enrol a younger same-sex sibling before the normal intake age.

For example, a colleague told me what had happened to his mother. Her parents sent her away when she was just a little girl of 5 years, in the hope that her presence would stabilise her sister, three years older, who kept running away. But the elder girl seemed to think that associating with her young sister would make her a less popular figure in the peer group, so she avoided her at school.

A younger child may appear keen to join their older brother or sister because they are familiar with the school from visiting and perhaps want to emulate their grown-up ways. When the younger child arrives, the promised connection is rarely realised. The difference in ages means that the children are in different academic year groups, or they can be split between seniors and juniors in accommodation; even if housed together, the expectation will be to socialise within their own peer groups.

Bowlby advised that if children were housed in institutions, it should be within small family groups with varying ages and that siblings should be kept together to provide 'comfort and support'. He adds:

Nothing is more tragic and destructive of mental health than a system that divides children by age and sex and thus splits up families of brothers and sisters.[21]

The natural hierarchy between siblings still applies in the school situation and is important for advice, support and protection; yet the school structure means that the relationship is difficult to foster. Older siblings at school cannot protect their younger family members from the abuse of adult staff or older children. Their own survival needs must be met: fear for their own well-being and a need to obey the rules means there is often no way to actively protect the younger ones.

The sense of responsibility that the older child holds can be felt by both children. Elizabeth Routledge recounts her first experience of joining the boarding school that her older sister attended. A poem about the first train journey there with her sister describes this excruciating problem.

My sister is afraid,
It makes her hate me,
My blonde-child neediness,

Her freckled plumpness,
She resents being responsible for me
She has only just learnt how to be,
In this world away from family.[22]

'Hope', in her late 60s, four years older than her younger sister, spoke with emotion of how vulnerable her sister looked when she began boarding: she was small and wore an eye patch after recent surgery. Hope felt the irresistible need to protect her and find her a friendship group; yet she knew that she had to stay with her own peer group to protect herself. Until recently, she carried the guilt of feeling that she could have done more to keep her sister safe.

In a news report about Canadian residential schools for First Nations children, Debra Coucherne, who attended from the age of 6, echoes this need to protect her younger sister when she was punished for a misdemeanour with a whipping from a nun. She recalled:

I couldn't do anything to help her and that was one of my responsibilities, because it was just her and I all the time.[23]

In a further interview from the same report, Karen, one of 16 siblings, related how at the age of 6 she was split by gender and age from her two brothers and her older sister. Contact with siblings was not allowed and this even extended to breaking up new peer friendships that may have provided support. She explained how in adulthood she has struggled with both emotional intimacy and developing a sense of her own identity.[24]

'Howard', in his late 50s, described explaining to his younger brother that he would only be there to protect and support him in times of dire need. He feared if the other boys believed his brother was protected, he would then be targeted once Howard had left the school. He related this in a very matter-of-fact style: it was just the way it was, and his manner suggests this behaviour was normalised.

Siblings at different schools

Siblings who attend different schools experience a separation that is beyond their control.

'Ruth', in her late 60s, spoke about having a close relationship with her brother while living abroad with her family. Due to her father's work, both were sent to single-sex boarding schools. She spoke of them each being very unhappy in their respective schools: her brother began the lifelong habit of using alcohol and drugs as a coping mechanism. When they got back together in the holidays, their relationship displayed a disconnection that has never been recovered. Ruth recounted this story with heartfelt sadness.

Earl Spencer, younger brother to the late Princess Diana, described how he followed in his three older sisters' footsteps and started at a boarding school for boys at age 8. Due to his parents' separation, his childhood was split between households. He remembers that, at age 7, he found it 'shattering' to also lose his closest sister Diana to boarding school:

The one constant was the sister who was sent away to boarding school.[25]

Two children at different boarding schools with differing holiday dates meant that sometimes he did not see his closest sister for 13 weeks at a time. Spencer concludes that sending a child to boarding school 'shatters families'.[26]

In later life

Can adult sibling relationships be rebuilt after the breaking of attachments and a childhood where the boarder no longer experiences a sense of home? Home is a place that provides roots, so when there has been a strong disconnection, a sense of belonging is very difficult to rebuild. My clinical experience has taught me that the rebuilding of sibling relationships in adulthood cannot be taken for granted; however, they can be worked for and redeveloped over time.

One ex-boarder with such a background explained that her siblings now live in different countries and, although there is communication within the family, spending time together occurs very infrequently. Furthermore, those children who had to adopt a supporting role – for themselves, parents or family – may struggle when reuniting with siblings who have become 'parentified' or overly independent. For those who were separated at a young age, the experience of being a sibling is something they may never have had chance to develop. One ex-boarder woman told me:

I don't know what being a sister means.

Due to their family home being a long flight away, the only significant time she and her older brother had the opportunity to spend time together was for a month in the summer school holidays. Different school systems between England and Scotland meant staying separately with a local family or even the school matron during short holidays. Due to a four-year age difference, when they reunited the older brother often socialised with friends his own age rather than with her. In adulthood, sibling connection was only through their parents and, on their death, she effectively lost her entire family structure, including the access to shared memories and timeline.

In later life when parents become old or sick, the hierarchy between siblings may become re-energised, or conflict may occur. Who will now take ownership of the parental relationship and provide the care? Should it be the child who was sent away, who desires reconnection or feels resentment? Or should it be the child who stayed at home, who may feel they have served their time or have earned their parental care status? Such scenarios can prove difficult to negotiate, and yet therein lies a potential to reunite the siblings. As Chris Beckett and Hilary Taylor say, when parents die:

> The bond between brothers and sisters is all that holds the family together.[27]

Clinical example

'Alice' is the youngest of four siblings. Her eldest brother began boarding when she was quite young; the middle two siblings were educated locally, and, after failing the entrance exam for the local grammar school, Alice was sent to boarding school from the age of 11 to 18. She talked about her anger at being sent away from a home and community that she loved. At boarding school, she felt disconnected from the family and frustration with parents who seemed to not understand her needs. In her mid-20s, she developed a strong yearning to get to know her parents and family again. Reconnection with her parents proved possible, as they were still living together in the family home, and as the years passed their support needs increased, so Alice became more involved.

The siblings, however, remained disconnected. The eldest, who had boarded first, had lived abroad for many years, and the middle two siblings had moved forward with their own lives and relationships. Alice recognised that the disconnection between the four had started when the eldest brother had left for boarding school. He would return for exeat weekends and holidays in his uniform as someone who was 'exotic'. She remembers seeing him very distressed in the garden on a Sunday evening before returning to school, and she subsequently worried about him until his next visit. She was already at boarding school herself when he returned home for a couple of years; and when Alice left school, he had already left to work abroad. Her way of not losing her brother was to adopt the same interests as he had.

Later in life, when her parents needed more support, she managed to achieve some reconnection with her ex-boarder brother. Their shared boarding experience enabled them to collaborate together in their project of supporting their elderly parents. They found a mutual way of being and a connection that was different to that of their other two siblings.

Alice's desire to reconnect with her middle two siblings was less successful. Their lives and relationships had developed and, without having had the experience of boarding, they seemingly could not understand the importance of rediscovering what Alice felt she had lost. Her yearning for connection was shown in a need to understand whether they had missed her when she went to school, yet this experience seemed irrelevant to them, since it had all been normalised in their childhood.

In later life, when they came together as a four with ill parents, they found the time to sit together and talk through many family stories. These stories demonstrated the family fragmentation: most narratives featured three or less siblings;

very few included all four. Yet this time together brought a reconnection and a recognition of once again being family.

In conclusion

The sibling relationship appears to be secondary to the parental relationship, yet, when ex-boarders begin to recover and open up about their experiences, they consistently recognise strong feelings of loss about their siblings. For when siblings are separated, each has to meet their own needs in their different situations, and their lives and experiences are no longer shared. Siblings who stayed at home also had to manage a new situation without brothers or sisters and then find that, when they are reunited, their relationship has profoundly altered. The durability of the sibling relationship is therefore severely tested by boarding, and the long-term effects for the family from one or more of its members attending boarding school are complex.

For the boarding child, the transition from communal family life to living as a separate individual among many within an institution is crucial. To manage this change without family support, boarding children have to concentrate on their own strategic survival. Masking vulnerability works at the time, but this mask can stay in place and become the new normal. The loss of the sibling relationship then either becomes normalised or does not get experienced until the ex-boarder adult feels safe enough to start thawing out their frozen emotional self.

For many adults in recovery from boarding trauma, there may be a recognition of what has been lost. Next comes a desire to reconnect with and get to know their early childhood, to rediscover the roots of their family and home. As they age, siblings are the only witnesses to their timeline, and this often holds great meaning. Sometimes, where there has not been an opportunity to be brothers and sisters in childhood, a new reconnection is, unfortunately, unlikely.

The sibling relationship, with its irreplaceable value, can be one of the unexpected costs of boarding.

Notes

1 Schaverien, J. (2015) *Boarding School Syndrome: The Psychological Trauma of the 'Privileged' Child.* London & New York: Routledge, p. 2.
2 Duffell, N. and Basset, T. (2016) *Trauma, Abandonment and Privilege. A Guide to Therapeutic Work with Boarding School Survivors.* Abingdon & New York: Routledge.
3 Coldwell, J., Pike, A. and Dunn, J. (2006) *Family Relationships In Middle Childhood.* London: National Children's Bureau for the Joseph Rowntree Foundation.
4 Schaverien, J. (2024) 'Boarding School Syndrome and Sibling Relationships', *Attachment*, 18: 76–90. doi: 10.33212/att.v18n1.2024.76.
5 Bowlby, J. (2006) *The Making and Breaking of Affectional Bonds*, second edition. London & New York: Routledge Classics.
6 Rutter, M. (1981) *Maternal Deprivation Reassessed*, second edition. Harmondsworth: Penguin.

7   Gorell Barnes, G. (2019) *Sibling Matters. A Psychoanalytic, Developmental, and Systemic Approach.* London & New York: Routledge.

8   Partridge, S. (2007) 'Trauma at the Threshold: An Eight-Year-Old Goes to Boarding School', *Attachment: New Directions in Psychotherapy and Relational Psychanalysis,* 1(3): 310–312.

9   Doka, K.J. (1989) 'Disenfranchised Grief', in K.J. Doka (ed.), *Disenfranchised Grief: Recognizing Hidden Sorrow.* Lanham, MD: Lexington Books, pp. 3–11.

10   Wilson, J. (2014) *Supporting People Through Loss and Grief. An Introduction to Counsellors and Other Caring Practitioners.* London: Jessica Kingsley Publishers, p. 62.

11   Schaverien, J. (2015) *Boarding School Syndrome: The Psychological Trauma of the 'Privileged' Child.* London & New York: Routledge.

12   Duffell, N. and Basset, T. (2016) *Trauma, Abandonment and Privilege. A Guide to Therapeutic Work with Boarding School Survivors.* Abingdon & New York: Routledge.

13   Duffell, N. and Basset, T. (2016) *Trauma, Abandonment and Privilege. A Guide to Therapeutic Work with Boarding School Survivors.* Abingdon & New York: Routledge.

14   Bowlby, J. (2006) *The Making and Breaking of Affectional Bonds,* second edition. London & New York: Routledge Classics.

15   Schaverien, J. (2024) 'Boarding School Syndrome and Sibling Relationships', *Attachment,* 18: 76–90. doi: 10.33212/att.v18n1.2024.76.

16   Adler, A. (1924) *The Practice and Theory of Individual Psychology.* New York: Harcourt Brace.

17   Adler, A. (1924) *The Practice and Theory of Individual Psychology.* New York: Harcourt Brace.

18   DeHart, G.B. (1999) 'Conflict and Averted Conflict in Pre-Schoolers' Interactions with Siblings and Friends' in W.A. Collins and B. Laursen (eds), *Relationships as Developmental Contexts.* Hillsdale, NJ: Lawrence Erlbaum. Raffaelli, M. (1997) 'Young Adolescents' Conflicts with Siblings and Friends', *Journal of Youth & Adolescence,* 26: 539–558.

19   Parker, V. (2020) *A Group-Analytic Exploration of the Sibling Matrix: How Siblings Shape our Lives.* London & New York: Routledge, p. 69.

20   Emauel, R. (2019) 'The Impact of Sibling Loss and Illness', in D. Hinde and S. Sherwin-White (eds), *Sibling Matters: A Psychoanalytic, Developmental and Systemic Approach.* London & New York: Routledge.

21   Bowlby, J. (1990) *Child Care and the Growth of Love,* second edition. London: Penguin, p. 156.

22   Routledge, E. (2019) 'Whispering Walls', in N. Simpson (ed,), *Finding Our Way Home.* London & New York: Routledge, p. 117.

23   CBC News (2018) 'Residential School Survivor Says She Felt Helpless'. Retrieved from https://youtu.be/9GChd5_RT6A?si=l0-9dPLO9x769n46, 19 March 2018.

24   CBC News (2018) 'Residential School Survivor Separated from Siblings'. Retrieved from https://www.youtube.com/watch?v=jFDln2CykXY, 22 April 2018.

25   Samuel, J. (2024) *A Talk with Charles Spencer About Childhood Sexual Abuse.* Retrieved from https://youtu.be/R7YZHcLhrF8?si=-hcRLovNuJFd-8IE, 13 March 2024.

26   Samuel, J. (2024) *A Talk with Charles Spencer About Childhood Sexual Abuse.* Retrieved from https://youtu.be/R7YZHcLhrF8?si=-hcRLovNuJFd-8IE, 13 March 2024.

27   Beckett, C. and Taylor, H. (2010). *Human Growth and Development,* second edition. Los Angeles, CA: Sage, p. 19.

Chapter 11

Boarders from Military Families

Do They Ever Come Home Again?

Eric Blencowe and Rosemary Lodge

Introduction

The commonly held view that a boarding school education is a privilege is unsurprising: its privilege derives from the fact that independent, fee-paying schools, in which category most boarding schools fall, charge sums that preclude access from any but the most affluent in society.[1] Therefore, the majority of children attending such schools come from wealthier backgrounds and have higher social status.

However, there are some pupils who come from families without access to such resources, such as children from military backgrounds. Such families send their children to boarding school through funding sources such as the Continuity of Education Allowance from their institutions, principally the army, air force or navy. Boarding school can be an attractive option for these families because the families are subject to frequent relocation, both domestically and internationally, to serve on successive postings throughout the parents' careers. It is this frequency of change that may foster the belief in parents that their children would receive better continuity of education, and even care, if they were placed in a boarding school.

However, we now know from the existing literature[2] that sending a child to boarding school may have unforeseen and unintended consequences on the development of the child.[3] We also know, from recent research, that children from forces families have their own struggles to contend with, such as the frequency of movement and deployment of parents resulting in difficulties in social, emotional and psychological functioning.[4] This chapter adds to what we already know about the consequences of boarding by examining the specific challenges faced by that cadre of children who come from military backgrounds. It argues that the intersection of these two differing but overlapping institutional experiences may put the child at risk of an even poorer outcome, especially without the buffer that wealth and privilege may provide for the more traditional boarder. In particular, it argues that the lack of a continuous secure attachment figure, coupled with the lack of a secure physical base, means that military ex-boarders may have a lifelong struggle with finding 'home'. The chapter concludes with a clinical vignette and clinical reflections on working with this population.

DOI: 10.4324/9781003515517-11

The encouragement of military boarding

It is not difficult to find the availability of boarding school provision, financially supported – either wholly or significantly – by prospective parents' respective military institutions just by searching on the internet. A freedom of information (FOI) request to the Ministry of Defence on 16 August 2022 revealed that, in the year 2021–2022, 4,320 pupils (out of approximately 70,000 boarders in the UK) received support amounting to £83.25 million for their fees in private schools.[5] A parliamentary question to the Ministry of Defence, tabled the following year, revealed similar results, suggesting that this is not unusual for annual expenditure for such purposes.[6] While the FOI figures are not broken down into day schools and boarding schools, boarding costs considerably increase the fees in fee-paying schools. If we divide the overall FOI funding figure by the number of pupils receiving support, the average annual subsidy for each child works out at around £30,000. This figure is high enough to suggest that a considerable number of the pupils receiving government support will be boarders.

In addition to this direct funding from the government, the *2024 Service Parents' Guide to Boarding Schools*[7] lists 208 schools (comprising just under half of the approximately 500 such schools in the UK) that offer bursaries or some form of allowance to afford easier access to boarders from the armed forces.[8] Moreover, as mentioned above, there is a plethora of websites – for example the Armed Forces Education Trust,[9] the British Army,[10] the Royal Air Force,[11] the Royal Navy,[12] The Armed Forces Boarding School Service,[13] as well as a number of independent advisory services, such as the Citizens Advice Bureau[14], providing information and guidance on accessing subsidies and grants for children from military families to attend boarding school. It seems, therefore, that boarding is an option that is actively encouraged in respect of military families, and the availability of funding makes it accessible and attractive to parents who feel they are making the best decision for their children.

Not belonging and the absence of mitigating privilege

As mentioned, many military boarders will not come from privileged backgrounds, and so although boarding is an encouraged and attractive option, this may not be reflected in the actual experience of the child at the school. The military boarders will be set apart from their peers in both obvious and subtle ways, particularly in the wealth and privilege differential between them. The subsidised place and relative lack of parental funds may mean that the child is not able to participate in some of the in-school activities requiring extra funding, as well as the other holiday-related activities the school may organise, such as skiing trips, visits to other countries and so forth. Moreover, the child is less likely to be in a position to share with their peers their experiences of expensive family holidays in exotic parts of the world, because their parents will not have had the resources to support such holidays.

Perhaps of even greater impact is the fact that the family may not even be able to afford for the child to travel home at periodic weekends, or 'exeats', or for holidays – especially if the parents are overseas. This may result in the child staying at school or at friends' houses in the holidays, and consequently getting a glimpse into 'how the other half lives'. One military ex-boarder described visiting a friend's house in the country in the holidays, a 2,000-acre farm with a sprawling house, as 'the biggest place I have ever seen'. In our clinical experience, working with a number of ex-boarders from military backgrounds, it is their lived experience that they feel different, or 'other' than their peers, and this entrenches their feelings of not belonging.

This may continue after school, as the child may not have access to the connections and privilege enjoyed by traditional boarders once they have left the school.

The importance of a secure attachment figure

Alongside these feelings of not belonging, the military ex-boarder will experience the impact of not really having a home or secure attachment to person or place, either at school or at home. Attachment theory suggests that a child has a need to be loved and cherished in their home environment, wherever that might be, and by a consistent and secure attachment figure, often but not always, the child's parent or parents. This need for a secure attachment figure is especially important when children are particularly young, as John Bowlby explains:

> The more the social environment in which a human child is reared deviates from the environment of evolutionary adaptedness (which is probably father, mother, and siblings in a social environment comprising grandparents and a limited number of other families) the greater will be the risk of his developing maladaptive social behaviour.[15]

The love and cherishing care that comes with being parented is something that no institution can provide in more than a paid stewardship capacity. Although it varies from school to school quite considerably, 'housemasters' or their female equivalents, who are, in practice, the 'stewards' for the boarders' non-educational welfare, frequently have custody of anything up to 60 boarders, possibly even more, and often do not even live on site. It is, therefore, in practice, impossible for the school to provide a secure attachment figure for the child.

According to the now growing psychological literature on the problems of boarding, in the absence of secure attachments or the potential for developing and fostering them, children sent away to board face the emotional, psychological and traumatic social consequences of abandonment.[16] They are compelled to survive by mental mechanisms such as dissociation and the development of the 'strategic survival personality'.[17] The impact on the child's developing identity can be devastating. One military ex-boarder described his boarding school as 'grim and oppressive' leading him to evade and avoid all engagement with staff, students and learning. Instead, he was engaged in a daily battle to maintain a sense of self – 'if I give in to this, then I give up on being myself'. His very identity felt under continuous existential threat.

The impact of a lack of secure attachment figure is likely increased in the case of the military boarder. This is because there is no stable home or secure base to go back to and because, for the military ex-boarder, there may be instability of attachment figures at home as well as at school.

Twice abandoned

Children sent away to boarding school face and deal with the consequences of feeling abandoned. Drawing on the attachment theory work of Bowlby in *Attachment and Loss*, Duffell and Bassett have described this abandonment and its consequences in terms of developmental trauma.[18] Given that the nature of this trauma involves the breaking of attachments both with family members and with related environments and social conditions in which the child grows up, the consequences of being sent to boarding school may be more serious for children who come from military backgrounds, where their parents are subject to frequent transfers of location. Many of these children, when they do go home at intervals during term time and ultimately at the end of term, often return to a different dwelling from the one they left, possibly in a different town, county or indeed country.

We have come across clients who, as children, have been sent to boarding school as young as age 8, who have during their years at school experienced a change of their family's address on an annual basis, and sometimes this translates to every time they go home. This means that there is an absence of a secure base to go home to. Sometimes parents may be posted thousands of miles away. As one military ex-boarder said:

Nothing prepares you for your parents being 8,000 miles away.

The military boarder is therefore left feeling twice abandoned – once at the school, and again when they 'go home' to an unfamiliar place.

This double abandonment may be exacerbated further. First, when one or both parents are deployed or when senior officers are moved away months in advance of their families, the child loses one of their secure attachment figures at home, and possibly even their home itself. Second, because, as mentioned, many boarders from military backgrounds have parents who cannot afford to pay for their return visits at weekends or half-term, due to their parents being posted overseas. This means they likely experience a further level of abandonment, either remaining in the institution (and seeing their peers being collected from the school for a weekend or an entire week by their loving parents) or experiencing what it must look and feel like to be in a 'normal' family environment, where at least the home remains the same while the child is absent at boarding school. One military ex-boarder described the experience of staying at friends' houses in the holidays as 'glimpses into a life I never had'.

Military boarders are forced to detach frequently from both place and person, leaving little or no secure base anywhere. For most of these clients, this has led to a different relationship with home and what it means to them. Effectively, their concept of home and all that lies therein has been developmentally frozen at the age the child was when they were first sent to boarding school, as Duffell and Bassett point out:

> Ex-boarder adults often seem to show signs of a child inside them who has been frozen in time and never organically grown up and who tends to dominate some of their behaviours, especially in intimate relationships.[19]

With the military ex-boarder, the situation is even more dire, because there may *never* have been an experience of home, even before being sent to boarding school.

Finding home

All boarding school survivors in our practices experience difficulties from their boarding school experiences, including anxiety, depression, unhappiness, addiction, relationship breakdown and so on. However, a specific thread that tends to run through all the experiences of boarders from military backgrounds is a particular difficulty in 'finding home' or even defining what 'home' means.

One military ex-boarder said that the closest he could come to defining home was 'Christmas'. Clients often describe themselves as feeling more at home in a particular location but have no idea why that might be the case. Others have said they feel at home nowhere and cannot remember when they last felt at home. It is surprisingly common for military ex-boarders to lead itinerant lifestyles after leaving school, such as living on the road or moving around from one temporary accommodation to the next.

Such clients also describe never having been 'at home' for any of the many moves made by their parents and therefore having had no agency even over their own possessions. One military ex-boarder clearly remembers being 11 years old and being allowed for the first and only time to choose wallpaper and a piece of furniture for his bedroom, believing that *finally* he was getting a permanent home. However, this was short lived as, within a year, his parents had sold up and moved on. It was the only time that he experienced the promise of continuity, only for it to disappear as quickly as it arrived. The more traditional boarder may at least have somewhere familiar and homely to return to; they frequently describe the importance of coming home to their bedroom and all their 'stuff' still being there. This experience not only gives some sense of security and safety but also a definite experience of *home* that may be denied military ex-boarders.

Furthermore, in military families sometimes the word 'home' is sharply juxtaposed against a strange and threatening environment, meaning that 'home' is associated with hostility, danger and fear. For example, one military ex-boarder described his family being posted where there was regular violence and no freedom of movement, and another where there were regular bombings. These kinds of experiences, when lived through outside of the context of 'home', are likely not conducive to connecting with place and community and instead foster a feeling of alienation and fear.

Lack of a 'relational home'

This lack of an experience of home seems to be the case not just in geographical terms, but also in relational ones. Some military ex-boarders do not ever really feel 'at home' with their partners, or broader families, because of their feeling of not belonging there – or indeed anywhere. As children, they got used to their family not being there, seeing photos of family experiences that did not include them and experiences of family moving home that did not involve them. It is as if the family was all about other people and nothing to do with them. They were outsiders on the edge of other people's lives.

In our clinical experience, clients who are experiencing difficulties – either consciously or unconsciously – arising from their boarding school past rarely appear in therapy before their early 40s at the earliest: many presenting as late as in their 70s or even 80s. While working life, as well as the 'busy-ness' of raising children, can mitigate and often disguise or suppress feelings around a lack of a relational home, they emerge more readily once retirement approaches, when those former boarders start to reflect on their own life experiences. It is at this point that it can come as a shock to them how unconnected they feel with their families, friends and surroundings, and even begin to doubt who they are, or have been in their life thus far.

This can be directly felt by the military ex-boarder and thus they are led into therapy. But it can also be felt by their spouses, partners and families vicariously, because they may detect an absence of feelings, sensitivity, responsiveness or empathy in the survivor, who may often resort to cocooning themselves in independence. Duffell has called this 'the game of one', a term he adopted from an early client, because it best describes how many children manage to survive at boarding school in the first place.[20] The draw towards returning to this protective cocoon can be highly magnetic, because so often it has been a major part of their survival personality in boarding school.

A clinical vignette – 'John'

The following clinical vignette aims to illustrate some of the points made in this chapter and to highlight how the clinician can work with them. It is based on a composition that draws from both our client base and published case material; the pronoun 'I' is employed for the therapist to make for easier reading. No clients will be identifiable in it.

'John' first came to therapy when he was 62 because his partner of six years had said that she would end their relationship if he didn't 'sort himself out'.

His parents had been in the air force, and by the time John was 18 he had lived in 17 different locations across 4 countries. His parents sent him to boarding school at the age of 8 with the help of funding secured through the air force. John was not always able to go home for holidays and he found this extremely difficult, especially as many of his peers did go home.

John loathed school and despite being bright did not achieve academically. After school he drifted for a number of years, moving around, trying out different locations and jobs. He couldn't settle at anything and used alcohol and drugs to numb his feelings. Then he met his wife and they had children, but that relationship ended after 23 years when his wife became fed up with his emotional dependence on her.

When John first arrived in therapy, he found it difficult to say why he was there. He presented rather closed, with arms and legs firmly crossed, and eyes darting between me and the rest of the room. He was conflicted between wanting to get through life as best he could, without being seen or discovered, but also knowing that there was something deeply wrong. He was torn between leaving his current partner, by whom he felt unseen and unappreciated within the home, or finding a way to love her and feel loved back. Now that he was facing retirement, he was scared about the future. He found it difficult to talk to anyone about all this, because he thought he should know what to do. He disliked being at home, but also disliked being away from home and did not really feel comfortable anywhere.

I trod carefully with this client, as he appeared uncomfortable and found it hard to trust me with his story. The way he avoided eye contact and bowed his head gave non-verbal cues that he may have felt ashamed for even being there in therapy. Over time it emerged that he was scared of disclosing anything that might make him feel vulnerable, which he perceived as 'weak' and thus bad. I felt it important to explore his current feelings further but was also aware that this might be difficult if, as with many other military ex-boarders, he had suppressed his emotions. As predicted, on asking about feelings, John said he found it difficult to access anything.

During the first weeks and months of the therapy, I noticed that John looked ready to run from the room at any moment. If we ever got close to a new realisation that triggered an emotional reaction, he looked like leaving the session; and on one or two occasions actually did, returning the following week without explanation.

I explored these moments with him so that he could become more aware of what was happening for him. There began to be other moments when he was able to express his feelings, and gradually through this painstaking work he started to re-accustom himself to having and tolerating difficult feelings.

Then, like many other military ex-boarders, he realised that he did not really know who he was or had been: this was a disturbing realisation for him. He felt a yawning vacuum inside. I reassured him that I understood and could hold this vacuum of uncertainty for him, while we explored his identity.

John failed to arrive for the following session, but returned the week after. It is not unusual for ex-boarders to interrupt their therapy, sometimes uncannily at those times that are meaningful in respect of school experience, or because something too painful has been touched upon, or because they do not want to keep talking about boarding school and cannot see where the work is heading.

John had lost the experience of home at a young age and did not feel properly at home anywhere. However, gradually, by noticing and expressing his feelings there was a sense of him being able to rediscover the child whose childhood had been so abruptly interrupted. Helping him to come home involved an internal process of finding a secure base within himself.

While John had forgotten about much of his childhood, I was able gradually to tease out some details through simple questions about the physical features in any one of the houses where he grew up. Sometimes this work was better achieved with his eyes closed, so external visual stimuli were removed. While this required great care and preparation, by now the therapeutic relationship had been going for over a year and John was becoming more open to exploring ways to unlock his past. Gradually recalling his closed-off memories in this way, his memory was stimulated during the week between sessions, and he would often return to the next session eager to relate what else he had recalled during the week. In that way we could piece together his past, and see warmth, joy and love, as well as the traumatic impact their sudden removal had brought. It was important to recall not only whatever he could about what home had been for him, but also the process of being taken to boarding school – and especially the first weeks and months, when he had to accustom himself to a new life without home comforts or the safety he had known, albeit briefly.

When describing his current home and work life, John felt equally disconnected in both spheres. Life was something to survive, preferably unnoticed, even though his lack of being noticed was also a source of frustration for him. When faced with a dilemma, he tended to solve it without reference to anyone else. However, more and more, he felt like a failure, finding his efforts falling increasingly short of his own expectations. Glowing reports from his managers and warm, supportive words from his family stood in stark contrast to his own self-reflections. I asked him what people had to gain in lying to him about his qualities? He tried to find sound arguments to qualify or negate the reports to prove his own inherent inadequacies, sometimes even resorting to a childlike insistence that they were simply wrong. At this point, I knew I was close to helping him to break down his personal wall of denial, start to accept that he was a good person and, most importantly, worthy of being loved.

Over time, John was able to acknowledge that, although he had never had a permanent home as a child and therefore was unable to recognise or trust what home might be, he could find comfort and solace in his family and current environment. He started to feel safer – both within himself and in the family. He learned to anticipate his visceral reaction towards daily challenges of work and home life and allow others 'in' to help him overcome them, rather than getting overwhelmed.

He grew to accept that he was not alone, and that, in that 'not-aloneness', he had found his home.

Clinical implications

As argued in this chapter and illustrated in the clinical vignette above, the military ex-boarder will likely have experienced being twice abandoned both at home and at school; having never really experienced a stable consistent home, they will have difficulty in finding such, in both a physical and relational sense. This double abandonment can be devastating for the child's development of identity and sense of security; it may result in a fragile and fragmented self that is used to hiding from others.

Such clients may arrive in the consulting room late in life, ashamed of needing help and having grave difficulty in describing the problem. Having never described it before, they may not have access to any appropriate language to do so. It may even seem to the clinician that there is no problem. However, the clinician should trust that if the client is seeking help there is something seriously wrong and should be committed to helping the client find out what it is.

Because of the client's difficulty in describing the problem, and history of hiding, the clinician needs to be extra sensitive and attuned to what is *not* being said and what may emerge in time, and should avoid meeting the client only at an explicit level. At the same time, the therapist should not be too intrusive or make assumptions. The client is used to hiding and their need for privacy must be respected. The clinician therefore needs to keep a delicate balance between not telling the client what the problem is, but also not waiting for the client to be able to articulate the problem.

Once a therapeutic alliance has been established, an important part of developing a secure attachment, the clinician need not shy away from making connections between the client's history and their current status, or indeed gently exploring the details of their early life and subsequent schooling. The clinician should not assume that they know what the client's experiences have been or how these have shaped them, but they should listen carefully to help the client piece it together.

The client is used to moving on, and the therapy may be no different. It is not uncommon for ex-boarding school clients to suddenly leave therapy, so it may be worth talking about endings right from the start of the therapy and also carefully planning for and exploring the meaning of breaks.

Most importantly, because military ex-boarders may have never developed a full sense of home and belonging, their relationship with home should be explored in the therapy. This may involve a slow and careful piecing together of fragments from the past, as illustrated in the vignette, together with a grieving for what never was. However, it is difficult to explore the absence of something, and so the clinician may choose to take the approach of exploring current home life, in the absence of a solid experience of home from childhood.

Sometimes military ex-boarders have a particular need to be noticed, rewarded or acknowledged for normal activities around the home: 'I cooked dinner last night and no one even noticed or said thank you!' The child in them needs to be noticed and valued and this is likely linked to the way they were completely absent from family life as children. Exploring these things fully provides the backdrop for an opportunity for the client to reimagine their own vision of home and belonging, with the establishment of an identity that is more rooted in the client's feelings and values.

Through developing a secure attachment relationship with the therapist, such clients can find a new kind of home within themselves, involving full connection and articulation with their own inner experiencing and with others and with place.

Notes

1 At the time of writing, up to £50,000 per annum.
2 Schaverien, J. (2015) *Boarding School Syndrome: The Psychological Trauma of the 'Privileged' Child*. London & New York: Routledge.
3 Duffell, N, (2000), *The Making of Them: The British Attitude to Children and the Boarding School System*. London: Lone Arrow Press.
4 Lester, P., Aralis, H., Sinclair, M., et al. (2016) 'The Impact of Deployment on Parental, Family and Child Adjustment in Military Families', *Child Psychiatry & Human Development*, 47: 938–949.
5 Roberts, J. (2022) Freedom of Information Request to the Ministry of Defence for Information. Retrieved from https://www.whatdotheyknow.com/request/subsidies_pai d_to_military_perso.
6 Luke Pollard MP (2023) Parliamentary Question answered by Rt Hon Dr Andrew Murrison MP on 20 April 2023, UIN 181072. Retrieved from https://questions-stateme nts.parliament.uk/written-questions/detail/2023-04-17/181072.
7 Available online at https://serviceschools.co.uk/the-guide/.
8 *The Service Parents' Guide to Boarding School*. Retrieved from www.serviceschools. co.uk, 30 April 2024.
9 The Armed Forces Education Trust. Retrieved from https://armedforceseducation.org, 30 April 2024.
10 The British Army. Retrieved from https://www.army.mod.uk/people/live-well/family-support/childcare-and-education/, 30 April 2024.
11 The Royal Air Force. Retrieved from https://www.raf.mod.uk/community-support/serv ing-families/schooling/, 30 April 2024.
12 The Royal Navy. Retrieved from https://forum.royalnavy.mod.uk/, 30 April 2024.
13 The Armed Forces Boarding School Service. Retrieved from https://www.facebook. com/armedforcesboardingschoolservice/, 30 April 2024.
14 The Citizens Advice Bureau. Retrieved from https://www.citizensadvice.org.uk/benef its/armed-forces-and-veterans/benefits-and-concessions-for-the-armed-forces-veterans-and-their-families/, 30 April 2024.
15 Bowlby, J. (1969), *Attachment and Loss. Vol. 1: Attachment*. London: Pelican, pp. 208–209.
16 Schaverien, J. (2015) *Boarding School Syndrome: The Psychological Trauma of the 'Privileged' Child*. London & New York: Routledge.
17 Duffell, N. and Bassett, T. (2016) *Trauma, Abandonment and Privilege: A Guide to Therapeutic Work with Boarding School Survivors*. Abingdon & New York: Routledge.

18 Duffell, N. and Bassett, T. (2016) *Trauma, Abandonment and Privilege: A Guide to Therapeutic Work with Boarding School Survivors*. Abingdon & New York: Routledge.
19 Duffell, N. and Bassett, T. (2016) *Trauma, Abandonment and Privilege: A Guide to Therapeutic Work with Boarding School Survivors*. Abingdon & New York: Routledge, p. 25.
20 Duffell, N. (2000). *The Making of Them: The British Attitude to Children and the Boarding School System*. London: Lone Arrow Press, p. 177.

Chapter 12

The Female Ex-Boarder Therapist

Collaborator or Ally?

Karen Macmillan

Introduction

The material in this chapter is gathered from my experience as a therapist and trainer. It represents some of what I have learned from working with ex-boarder clients, as well as from delivering training, from individual and peer supervision, and from conversations with colleagues. Within the specialism of working with 'boarding school survivors', most therapists are women, and many of us ourselves are ex-boarders or have some link to the boarding world. This brings challenges that I explore here and frame as either being a 'collaborator' – in the sense of colluding with an enemy – or being an 'ally'.

Sharing the same essential wound of being sent away to school with our clients is a double-edged sword. Our own experience, fully explored and digested, can provide a rich resource for our therapeutic work. Unprocessed material, on the other hand, can lead to avoidance, mutual blind spots and maintenance of the status quo, reinforcing those survival behaviours that cause so much damage to self and others. Although some of my observations may have a broader reach and be relevant to male and non-boarder clients, my focus here will be on working with female ex-boarders.

My hope is that, in sharing what I have learned, we can all be better allies to our clients.

Some personal background

I went to a well-known all-girls boarding school in England from the ages of 11 to 18 while my parents lived abroad. After an early childhood in tropical Malaysia, the culture shock was severe, with little shared experience to connect me to my fellow boarders. I did not enjoy my time at this school and quickly learned to have a sharp tongue, sarcasm being a useful currency at the time. I kept this part of my life largely hidden as an adult in a way I now recognise is common for ex-boarders. I was keenly aware that, after living in a strange and isolated institution for so many of my formative years, I was unprepared for a world that included relating comfortably with men and normal society. I felt unrooted and

DOI: 10.4324/9781003515517-12

was embarrassed by the assumptions made about me whenever my public school education became known.

After a first career as an accountant, in middle age I trained in transactional analysis (TA) counselling. I was not always an easy therapy client or counselling student. Questions like 'How did you survive that?' sounded dramatic and made little sense to me. Similarly, I was surprised that fellow students were able to answer the 'How old do you feel?' question and name the ways that they could self-soothe.

I found my therapy during training particularly challenging, resenting the restrictions of the counselling contract and feeling that all the power unfairly rested with the therapist. Whenever we got close to a deeper feeling, I did something I now recognise as dissociation. I also reacted with frustration to my therapist's interpretations. I resisted any kind of intimacy and delighted in her holidays.

Occasionally, I would look up and see a softness in her face that I did not know what to do with. When she got angry on my behalf at an incident I described, I felt buoyed up for days by the unfamiliar feeling of someone having my back. Those readers familiar with Joy Schaverien's ABCD of boarding (abandonment, bereavement, captivity and dissociation)[1] and Nick Duffell's 'strategic survival personality'[2] concepts, will recognise them at play in my description above.

Occasionally, when we were having a difficult session, my therapist would say: 'Remember this. You will have a client one day in front of you who is feeling this.' This advice proved profoundly helpful, and I pass it on now.

I did not speak about my own boarding school years in my personal therapy or during my training until the fourth and final year when I heard Schaverien talking about boarding school syndrome on the radio.[3] I was amazed to hear someone put words to my experience in a way I had never heard before and I remember being rooted to the spot.

While working as a trainee counsellor within a drug and alcohol service, I remember a client carefully 'outing' themselves as an ex-boarder and watching my reaction closely to see how I would respond. I was aware that something important had passed between us but could not fully make sense of it at the time.

I offer these examples as reminders of just how disconnected ex-boarders can be and how hard it can be to understand our own internal processes and engage in the therapeutic relationship. This is typical, as the boarding wound remains hidden and a source of shame until someone helps us understand what happened to us, how we survived it, and gives us the language to be able to talk about it. The dissociated, or split-off, parts are so deeply buried that it can be shocking to come into contact with them.

Finding allies

After first hearing about boarding school syndrome, I entered a period of discovery and immersion, reading Schaverien and Duffell's work, attending group workshops for ex-boarder women,[4] completing the 'Un-Making of Them' specialist training,[5] and attending Boarding School Survivors Support conferences.[6] All this amounted to a challenging, painful but energising process.

My second therapist was pivotal in helping me work through previously submerged material and the deeper task of attachment repair. My first therapist, who laid the foundations, retired when I completed my counselling training and I owe her, too, a debt of gratitude. Finding further allies in the boarding school survivors movement and among friends and peers has also been crucially important. Developing deeper connectedness with women, including women ex-boarders and therapists (especially those who work with ex-boarders), has provided much needed support and resource.

Integrating my TA therapy training with the insights and theory of Duffell and Schaverien's work has been an interesting process that has deepened my appreciation of both bodies of theory. I began working with ex-boarder clients very gradually, starting with one, then two: initially I did not advertise that I was offering this specialism. I sought out specialist supervision to support my work with ex boarders alongside regular supervision for my other client work. This pacing was important in growing my capacity to work well with ex-boarders when it inevitably also meant touching on my own material as an ex-boarder.

As my practice developed, the number of ex-boarder clients increased, and I now specialise in counselling ex-boarders, with a particular interest in working with women. Specialist supervision, wise colleagues and personal therapy continue to provide me with support and encouragement in this challenging work.

Transactional analysis in ex-boarder work

My original training in TA provided me with many concepts that I now use in an adapted form in my work with ex boarders. Eric Berne's 'ego states' model – parent, adult, child – has been particularly useful.[7]

Berne's ego states have a specific time dimension. The parent ego state includes thinking, feeling and behaving as others did in our past, whereas the child ego state includes thinking, feeling and behaving as we were in our past. The adult ego state involves responding in a healthy way to the present, the 'here and now'. Each of us have these three ego states and move between them frequently and sometimes they conflict with each other.

The parent ego state includes introjected parents, authority figures, older children and the culture of the school. Its function is regulatory and directive: it holds all the 'shoulds' and 'oughts'. I would locate Duffell's strategic survival personality in the parent ego state, because of its protective function. The parent ego state is not literally how others were in our past, but how we – in the past – interpreted and internalised them. A fierce inner and outer critic often resides here.

The child ego state includes developmentally stuck and split-off parts and unprocessed trauma. Paying attention to the age our clients were when sent to boarding school will give us a clue as to the most likely stuck part (4-year-old, 8-year-old, 15-year-old, etc.) and knowing the years they were away also helps us know what we can expect to encounter and whether a reparative experience and understanding of puberty and teenage years will be needed.[8]

When in our adult ego state, we are free to be autonomous and authentic. In ex-boarders, the parent and child ego states are generally the most active, and it is highly likely that, though hidden and disguised, the child will be running the show; however, what will be most present in the therapy room is the parent, doing its best to look like an adult ego state.

The goal of therapy is not to eliminate the parent and child ego states but to get to know them and recognise when they are activated, so that the adult can take care of the vulnerable child and recognise the parent messages as outdated survival strategies created in childhood to provide a degree of predictability and safety. Helping the client to strengthen their adult capacity for here-and-now awareness, self-compassion, problem-solving and boundary-setting is an important part of the work.

We can work with the ego state model quite explicitly. For example, we can address either the adult or parent: 'What do you think or feel about 8-year-old you?'. Or we can speak to the child: 'What does 8-year-old you feel about that?'. 'Little you' or 'Little Mary' or 'Little Paul', and so on, can be another way of talking about the child part. Working with ego states helps to frame what is happening psychologically and can provide enough structure for the parent ego state to get hold of, to support adult awareness of internal processes and to create safety for the child to express and be seen.

At the beginning of the therapeutic work, clients have often spontaneously said that they think they don't have much adult capacity and that they also hate their child part. Ultimately, the therapist is supporting the client to develop a nurturing relationship and partnership between their adult part with their often-disowned child part, so that the child part can be embraced, understood and integrated.

Other concepts from TA are also useful. One of these is the 'script' – the unconscious life plan and system of beliefs about ourselves, other people and the world.[9] A simple way of soliciting a client's underlying script is to ask them to complete the sentences 'I am ...', 'People are ...' or 'The world is ...'. Often this will reveal loneliness, lack of self-worth, distrust of others and life in general. At the core of many ex-boarders is an 'I am bad' belief. By making their underlying scripts more conscious, we can start to work with them.

Additionally, Claude Steiner's *The Stroke Economy* concept is especially helpful.[10] Strokes are units of attention; they can be either conditional or unconditional and positive or negative. Many ex-boarder clients were (and still are) stroke-deprived – particularly of positive strokes. They may have fierce stroke filters that allow in only the negative and they do not know how to ask for what they need.

Berne also introduced the concept of 'physis' – the impetus for healthy growth as a driver in human motivation.[11] Alongside the structure of models and theory, working through TA, therapists additionally provide a humanistic 'space' and supportive relationship for the client in which to grow and reflect, be validated and affirmed and allow space for their own physis to unfold.

Ex-boarder women working with ex-boarder women

As a female ex-boarder therapist working with female ex-boarder clients, I have in common with my clients an experience of being educated and living within an institution designed for boys, however different elements of our experience may have been. There is a risk to this communality of experience: with clients whose stories seem to parallel our own, we can make unfounded assumptions that we understand their experience.

In reverse, a client might assume the same, saying things such as, 'Well, you know what those awful Sundays were like'. They may want to befriend us or twin with us, and we too might really like and identify with our client. This can get in the way of our curiosity.

Clients also bring vulnerabilities and struggles that uncomfortably reflect our own. Possible shared areas of vulnerability include envy, competition, intimacy, internalised misogyny and homophobia, sex, sexuality, body image, relationship with food and being in groups of women. These are all areas that ex-boarder therapists need to get comfortable with in themselves in order to hold and work with them with female clients. Personal therapy and supervision are essential here.

With some female clients I become a stand-in for the housemistress, matron, teacher or headmistress. I might also stand in for the headgirl, a prefect or a bully. Here is an example in the case of client 'Jane'. Please note, this vignette is a composite created to provide a representative example and is not based on any individual client:

> From the moment I collected Jane from reception to sitting together in the therapy room, she was watchful, quiet and slightly hunched in her posture. Eye contact was often difficult, her gaze either full and direct or darting away. The beginnings of our sessions were slow, and moments of contact would come late in the session, once we had eased in. After several sessions she said, 'Gah! I feel like I'm coming and being inspected each week!'

Many clients have described the fawning behaviour they had to perform towards female staff to get basic needs met, coupled with the fear of judgement and punishment. At the same time, they harboured a contempt towards these figures whose hypocrisy and cruelty caused such moral injury to their child selves. This will inevitably play out in the therapeutic relationship and may not always be obvious. They may be very good at hiding or masking their feelings and may not be as direct as Jane in the above example. If the therapist does not enquire or guess, she may miss it.

It is also possible that the therapist's experience of having to mask her own feelings when she was at school can result her face being harder to read emotionally for the client. She may have to make what may be happening in the transference more explicit in words. On occasion, I am still surprised that what I am feeling has not been seen on my face, with comments such as: 'Well, you're paid to listen to me. I'm sure you forget about me the moment I leave.'

Equally, therapists must pay close attention to their client's words. We need to believe our clients when they describe their distress, especially when the words and their apparent affect may not match, due to masking. With two ex-boarders in the room there is a real risk of unconscious double-masking, as client and therapist keep their real selves and feelings hidden to each other.

I am also a stand-in for a mother, the needed and longed-for person who abandoned them. Clients watch me closely for any signs of rejection or disinterest, while at the same time craving my nurture and care. The reparative work of consistent presence, acceptance and nurture can be difficult if the therapist has not done their own attachment recovery.

For some ex-boarder clients, the idea of using of the relationship within the therapy can feel intrusive, terrifying, overly intimate and deeply unsafe. The risk for an ex-boarder therapist is that they may collude with the client in avoiding intimacy: this can play out in various ways, around breaks, endings, attachment and dependency.

Breaks

Breaks bring up a variety of reactions:

Did you miss me?
I felt really awful at our usual session time.
Whoo hoo! It's like having a holiday, not coming here.

A fear of being forgotten and not held in mind may be evoked, which repeats the fear of being forgotten while away at school, of not being loved and important and cherished. The fear of being erased in the mind of their mother is now transferred to the therapist. They may feel shame at missing the therapist during the break, feeling their dependence and unsure how to express this, or if it will be welcomed. They may be afraid that the therapist will die or become unwell during the break and so abandon them. When I once needed to take a few weeks off for a medical procedure, I was aware of the anxiety this provoked for some clients.

Not all of this will be conscious, and breaks can be responded to with anger and irritation or by withdrawal from the relationship, so that at the next meeting there can be a shyness or disconnect. A rebuilding of the relationship will be needed as well as the recognition of the impact of the break and what it brought up for the client. Issues of control, authority and lack of choice around the timing and length of breaks may echo the school experience. For others, who have not yet made an attachment, the breaks are a relief from the pain and difficulty of therapy and a repeat of the release from school into an exeat or half-term break.

Here are many pitfalls for ex-boarder therapists, given our own experience of repeated breaks and transitions from school to home and back again. We may discount the significance of breaks and not pay full attention to the impact on our clients; we may forget to enquire how the break was or fully account for our client missing us, or that we missed them. In this way we collude with either the client's avoidance or their experience of their parents' discounting of the impact of separation, that it is wrong or weak to miss and be missed. Part of the work for ex-boarder therapists is getting comfortable with the natural and normal process of clients attaching to us and us to them, and this may not be fully possible until we have had this experience in our own therapy and internalised a sense of healthy dependency and attachment.

Endings

Endings can be challenging for ex-boarders since they have experienced so many endings and will have found ways to avoid the pain of these repeated losses.

> I want to go now, I've had enough.
> Are you trying to get rid of me?
> I don't know how to leave therapy.

Even the *idea* of leaving therapy can be frightening for some clients, who may not have experienced a good ending that has been of their own choice: it is likely to bring up fears of being abandoned. Allowing enough time to work through the feelings that come up around the loss of the relationship and account for the work done together is important, so that the process of saying goodbye feels complete and congruent.

It may be good for the client to know that they can come back if they want to. The intensity of the work means that some clients may leave and come back a number of times. Being available and willing to work in this way provides a constancy of relationship and allows clients to pace themselves. In my own therapy, it was helpful to be able to leave and then come back to the same therapist to do the deeper attachment work when I was ready.

A temptation for the ex-boarder therapist may be to end too quickly or to discount their own feelings of sadness and loss at the end of the relationship, colluding in avoiding sharing and hearing these tender feelings. A more general point is that we may be over-respectful of client's defences that look rather like our own.

Can you help me?

Many clients mention wanting support and guidance at their initial contact, keenly aware that this was lacking in their childhood. Some aspects of this might fall into the life-skills category rather than pure psychological work. I think of this as the supportive godmother role. A concept I like is the idea of 'thinking with' our clients. They did not have someone to think with them when they were children, to work things through as they came up. This can be in areas like making friends, managing money or how to be comfortable in the clothes they choose. We can normalise their struggle as they did not have the opportunity to learn these skills within their family and help them find ways to learn now as an adult. This is not to rescue, but to be really interested in problem-solving with them.

Many ex-boarder women struggle to know what clothes suit them, feel awkward and clumsy in what they wear, and anxious at the idea of having to dress up for an occasion. This is not surprising considering they lived at a boarding school, in uniform for much of the time, perhaps with strict clothes rules and without the opportunity to shop with mum and friends and play with fashion. Mixed and misogynist messages about the female body are inherent in many school uniforms with shirt and tie on top – like male adult business wear – and tweed skirt and sensible shoes below, hiding the natural shape of their bodies.

Discovering pleasure in choosing what to wear as an adult can be meaningful, and therapists can encourage and support this. When I notice a new top, haircut or colour that looks good on clients who have brought this as an issue, I explicitly appreciate and compliment them. Having a woman take pleasure in their appearance without competing or criticising can feel good and repair some of the damage they may have experienced in groups of girls at school. If they have not repaired their own relationship with their bodies, with how they present themselves or with their relationships with women, female ex-boarder therapists could well miss this opportunity.

General tips for therapists

One of the areas I personally had to learn to be comfortable with was praise and delight. Neglect, which is endemic at boarding school, breeds an absence of expectation for validation and recognition; and yet, to the child within the survivor, it can mean so much. If you have also come from a positive-stroke-deprived upbringing it is easy to forget the need for and the joy of giving and receiving praise.

It is not enough simply to notice progress, it needs to be welcomed, celebrated and delighted in.

   That's fantastic!

How few of us were delighted in and what a joy it is to celebrate successes with our clients.

Joining the dots is also useful: this helps clients to make connections between what they are experiencing now and to their boarding experiences. This often happens spontaneously when therapists allow space for clients' memories to bubble up in session or between sessions and be brought to the therapy room. In the early stages, however, therapists may have to solicit or suggest connections so that clients can start to make the links for themselves. This may go beyond the usual 'Does this feel familiar?' or 'Does this remind you of anything?'. Something more directive like 'I'm wondering what mealtimes were like at school' or 'What was it like travelling to school on your own?' may be needed. It can feel clunky or even punitive to make such suggestions, and yet the therapist's job is to be aware of and sensitive to such connections. These can be around travel, food, endings, choice, humiliation and criticism, for example.

Making connections can be especially delicate when clients are on the edge of dissociation and feeling vulnerable. Therapists need to be especially present and tender at these moments so that the big feelings held in the child part can unfreeze, be felt and expressed. The job is to find sufficient space to hear and respond to distress – often non-verbally – without leaving them alone so long that they feel abandoned or under scrutiny. And yet jumping too soon to making sense with a meaningful narrative could risk a collusive response or it might bypass the energy for change held in the child ego state.

Learning regulation

One of the things that therapists can do is to act as a regulated body in the room for clients to physically co-regulate with. As children they were surrounded by a lot of dysregulated children and without a safe attachment figure who could be this caring emotionally regulated person. I often go beyond the usual grounding techniques of feet on the floor, shoulders dropped and conscious breathing to something more. For me this is letting my stomach muscles relax, almost like allowing a pot belly. I may need to do this several times during a session if a client is dominated by their distressed child ego state.

Sometimes communicating through my body that I can be with their distress, rather than offering words when they cannot be taken in, is needed. I might also consciously sigh to release the tension I can feel in myself and the client as a way of communicating the heaviness and difficulty of what they are bringing. If I am tight in my body at the end of a session without having noticed or acknowledged it is happening, it could be a clue that I might be colluding.

I like to use Noel Burch's learning stages model for de-shaming emotional skills work.[12] This model plots the journey from unconscious incompetence, through conscious incompetence, to conscious competence and finally towards unconscious competence. The conscious incompetence stage is the most uncomfortable and cannot be bypassed: learning involves experimenting and practising and getting feedback. Framing it this way can help to satisfy the parent ego state's need for structure, aiding adult understanding and creating some safety for the child.

I often tell my clients 'You've discovered a limit', especially those who are overwhelmed and burned out. Ex-boarder therapists need to be keenly aware of the limits to their own capacity in order to hold and work with boarding school trauma. This is especially true for those who carry old scripts of carrying on, pushing through, disregarding their own needs or shame at not being able to manage impossible standards. Pacing and balance are necessary to avoid becoming collusively blasé to trauma or at risk of dropping into personal trauma, and thereby unable to effectively support the client.

I keep a close eye on the proportion of my clients who are ex-boarders: if I am managing something challenging in my private life, I switch off my advertising and don't take on new clients. Periodically, a new book or film will appear in popular culture that generates debate and discussion about boarding school. Enquiries from potential new clients increase when there is a lot of media noise around the subject; friends, colleagues and other contacts may also be interested in talking about it. This can feel quite intense and as if, to quote a colleague, it is coming at you from all sides.

When this happens, and occasionally out of the blue, the ex-boarder therapist's own material can be evoked. A new layer of memories and feelings bubble up. Allowing these to flow and pass through is healthy, as is the need to take extra steps for our own self-care. Knowing that this happens, however much therapeutic work we have done, is really useful. Giving ourselves and the child part of us the tender care needed helps us be an ally to ourselves and so to our clients. Resisting and avoiding is what our strategic survival personality would like us to do. That said, we are not always going to catch it in the moment: some reactions can be automatic, and the art is to catch it kindly on reflection. This is as true for our clients as for us.

Conclusion

Recovery from boarding school syndrome looks more like integration rather than cure. The movement is from understanding the past towards integrating it into the narrative of our life: becoming better at looking after the child part within, knowing when the parent survivor self is activated, and having more choice in how to respond in the present.

I don't have to hide any more.
I feel more comfortable in myself.
I know myself better now.

Since working with ex-boarders, I have developed a much keener eye for the impact of childhood neglect on all adult clients; I pay closer attention to developmental gaps and routinely ask about school years in my client assessments. Working with clients who share the same childhood wound is a personal choice. To do it well means being willing to do our own personal work, having good skilled support and knowing our limits.

The word 'collaborator' now yields a double meaning. It means either someone who cooperates, conspires and colludes with an enemy, or someone who works jointly on a project or activity. In other words, it can mean someone who is good to work with – an ally. I have found that being an ally is ongoing and a deeply rewarding endeavour.

Notes

1   Schaverien, J. (2021) 'Revisiting Boarding School Syndrome: The Anatomy of Psychological Traumas and Sexual Abuse', *British Journal of Psychotherapy*, 37(4): 606–622.
2   Duffell, N. (2000). *The Making of Them: The British Attitude to Children and the Boarding School System.* London: Lone Arrow Press.
3   Schaverien, J. (2015) *Boarding School Syndrome: The Psychological Trauma of the 'Privileged' Child.* London & New York: Routledge.
4   See https://www.boardingschoolsurvivors.co.uk/events-and-workshops/.
5   See https://www.boardingschoolsurvivors.co.uk/for-therapists/.
6   See https://www.bss-support.org.uk/.
7   Berne, E. (1972) *Games People Play: The Psychology of Human Relationships.* New York: Grove Press.
8   Duffell, N. and Basset, T. (2016) *Trauma, Abandonment and Privilege. A Guide to Therapeutic Work with Boarding School Survivors.* Abingdon & New York: Routledge.
9   Berne, E. (1964) *What Do You Say After You Say Hello?* New York: Grove Press.
10 Steiner, C.M. (1971) 'The Stroke Economy', *Transactional Analysis Bulletin*, 1(3): 9–15.
11 Berne, E. (1964) *What Do You Say After You Say Hello?* New York: Grove Press.
12 Retrieved from https://www.gordontraining.com/free-workplace-articles/learning-a-new-skill-is-easier-said-than-done/.

Chapter 13

Supervision and Clients Impacted by Boarding School

John Andrew Miller

An elephant in the supervision room

Ex-boarding school clients can be among the most challenging a psychotherapist may encounter, as Nick Duffell and Thurstine Bassett state in their preface to *Trauma, Abandonment and Privilege*.[1] Clients impacted by a boarding school survivor, say a partner or a parent, also frequently present for psychotherapy; they too can also be very challenging. Not surprisingly, their therapists bring these challenging clients to supervision, in the hope of understanding better what is happening in the therapeutic space. In consequence, the supervision relationship involving ex-boarders becomes a further challenging area, which this chapter will explore.

What happens when the therapist brings these clients to supervision? Most often, both supervisor and supervisee fail to see a boarding school factor and focus on other issues. Many might believe, as one colleague told me, they have 'next to zero' experience with this client population, even though statistically many more ex-boarders come to psychotherapy than imagined. Most probably, the supervisor does not ask or think to ask or recognise an adverse boarding school experience in the background.

I know this from my personal experience as a supervisee. In my 40-plus years of private psychotherapy practice, I have sought supervisory help for a good dozen or more clients who happened to be ex-boarders, yet I cannot recall any supervisor asking me if the client I was presenting was traumatised by being sent away or mention what we would now call boarding school syndrome. When I conferred with the senior practitioners in my attachment theory peer supervision group, not one member connected my client's sense of entitlement with his unhappy time at a very famous public school. These are but two examples.

I too had a blind spot: I tended to focus – as I had been taught – on much earlier, mostly pre-school trauma, current relational difficulties or recurrent psychosomatic illnesses. I perhaps naively expected that if schooling were an issue, it would surface in due course. Some things I heard seemed hard to believe, such as bullying by beating with coat hangers, and others seemed hard to know how to respond to – for example, sexual play that might be construed as pubescent exploration

DOI: 10.4324/9781003515517-13

rather than abuse. Stories of returning home to find one's bedroom gone, all signs of belonging erased, or having nowhere to go over exeats might have sparked too much pain in me. I can cite other examples, but more importantly, I am not sure that I knew enough to think of boarding school problems when I presented a client in supervision.

Today, the expanding literature on what Joy Schaverien named boarding school syndrome plus articles in professional journals and the press have made everyone more aware.[2] Although having said that, even today a supervisor would find virtually nothing in any professional literature on the dynamics of psychotherapy with an ex-boarder; even two literature searches in 2024 revealed very little.

Over time, what I have learned is that those supervising therapists engaged in work with ex-boarders face particular challenges, above and beyond those challenges that are part-and-parcel, the bread-and-butter, of every supervisory situation. Much of what I have learned has come from 19 years of supervising trainees on Duffell's postgraduate training course focusing on psychotherapy with boarding school survivors or those impacted by ex-boarders. At those times I was frequently working with ex-boarder therapists on their work with ex-boarder colleagues, so some of those relationships had multiple dimensions.

Because my experience of working with supervisees of ex-boarder clients is with a finite sample, I enlisted the help of ten professional colleagues to share their insights and reactions in compiling this chapter. They brought a range of backgrounds to this task: some are themselves ex-boarders, some not; most are English, but at least one grew up elsewhere; six are men and four are women; several work psychodynamically, two trained in transpersonal psychotherapy, one has a Gestalt background, another an existential orientation; a few also focused on the body. Almost unanimously, what they reported back corroborates what I am saying here.

Perhaps it is time to consider the elephant in the supervision room.

Similarities and differences

Discerning the nuance of supervising ex-boarder clients mirrors much of what I would say about most supervision situations, especially when the supervisee is presenting a severely traumatised client, a client burdened with several developmental adverse experiences. Whether an ex-boarding client or not, the basic concerns in supervision remain the same: safety, creating an environment where vulnerabilities and mistakes in the therapeutic session can be discussed and understood; maintaining a 'binocular vision' by keeping in mind that the supervisee is the focus, the person coming for help, while at the same time trying to understand and empathise with the client as well with the supervisee. The supervisor also needs to consider how supervisor, supervisee and client each reflect the culture, the ethos of their backgrounds and the time in which they are living.[3]

This last point about preconceived notions is particularly salient when talking about boarding schools. The supervisee and the supervisor who are themselves ex-boarders need to be aware of their biases and prejudices, plus the possibility of collusion. The supervisor or supervisee who did not go to boarding school may find it hard to understand fully what life was like away from home and its impact.

Both need to decipher the complex attachment issues re-enacted in the present, while guarding against over-identification with the supervisee or the client, and yet at the same time expressing appropriate empathy, concern and compassion. The supervisor needs to focus on feelings, or more likely the avoidance of feelings, in either the client or supervisee. Survival strategies learned at boarding school can come into the supervisory situation as well as projective identification. Attention to the impact of holiday breaks and endings is important. The supervisor needs to develop in the supervisee self-supervision and self-care, while fostering a spirit of cooperation.

Context

First of all, the supervisor must try to understand 'who' the client is – whether an 'early' ex-boarder who started at age 7 or 8, or a later ex-boarder; next, they should explore the 'why' of going to boarding school, be it family tradition or marital breakup or disciplinary problems or overseas postings or, less often acknowledged, a parenting failure, or something else. The same question of 'when' would apply if the client is the spouse, adult child, even colleague of an ex-boarder.

Similarly, the 'where' and 'when' are significant. It behoves the supervisor to discover what sort of boarding school: in the beginning, I did not know of the wide variety of residential schools that exist in the UK and elsewhere. I had never heard of state-funded boarding schools until a client started telling me of the bullying, poor relating and compulsive self-reliance – problems that she encountered there – problems that we also expect to hear about in traditional public schools. For sure, the issue of privilege will be more paramount when the school has a prestigious reputation or if fee-payment entails parental sacrifice in hopes of social aspiration. The conflict of fitting in and feeling out of place can be more acute for a working-class student on a bursary at a high-reputation school or for the ex-boarder whose family is thousands of miles away at some foreign outpost.

The 'when' becomes important, because boarding schools have changed. Nowadays, co-educational schools, weekly boarding options, the abolition of corporal punishment, plus easier communication with mobile phones, mean more recent ex-boarders experienced problems against a different background than those experienced by older, more traditional ex-boarders, isolated in single-sex, often remotely located sites. Such differing client populations reflect different times and circumstances and present with different psychologies.

In the same vein, supervisors also need to be mindful of their supervisee's own experience and their personal, possibly unresolved, conflicts around boarding school elitism and privilege, or their own boarding experiences, or that of family members. In addition to supervising people who themselves went to boarding school, I have had supervisees aware through their own therapy of the impact of one or both parents going to boarding school. One woman supervisee had worked in therapy on her ongoing anger and frustration about her brothers being privileged with boarding school while she stayed home to go to a local grammar school.

The supervisor also needs to be aware of their own background, especially if they have been bullied, or, for example, sent away to a children's home or incurred some family trauma. The supervisor or the supervisee who grew up outside the UK, as I did, may not be fully aware of the subtleties and the struggles and tensions around the class system and social mobility. Such supervisees may miss some of the acute and confused feelings that their survivor clients may be struggling to recognise, articulate and resolve. I also found I needed to learn a whole new vocabulary, such as the words 'exeat' or 'beak'.

Here the problem can be twofold: just as the supervisee can over-identify with the ex-boarder and get into a sort of 'isn't it awful' rescuing mode, so can the supervisor. And instead of challenging how the client is living his or her current life and the choices made, the supervisor, along with the supervisee and the client, loads endless blame and justification for current behaviour on the boarding school experience.

A second, perhaps obvious, point is relevant here: in the supervision environment, it is the *supervisee* who should be the focus and not the ex-boarder or other client being presented. I have noticed, as have several colleagues, the supervisee focusing on what happened to the ex-boarder and not on what is happening in the therapeutic space. Especially if I think I am starting to over-identify with the supervisee (or the client), or if the supervisee is engrossed in the client's boarding school hardship, I will try to bring the supervision target back into focus by asking 'What is the supervisory question?' or 'What is the encoded message the client is trying to convey and get you to feel?'.

Third, the supervision situation is *ripe for re-enactment*: it is like a mini tutorial where the supervisee (as student) comes to learn from the supervisor (as teacher, authority figure).

Sometimes, the client material or the supervisory experience triggers in the supervisee feelings and perhaps unresolved issues from school or university. If the supervision is part of a training programme, the supervisee has come both to learn but also be judged, evaluated by the supervisor. Everyone – whether supervisor or supervised – wants to show how strong and knowledgeable they are, not how vulnerable they are. Everyone brings to supervision the conundrum, the feeling that something is not working as effectively as possible in the therapy sessions. The potential for shame and humiliation, let alone posturing, needs to be forefront in the supervisor's mind. Not surprisingly, supervisees can revert unconsciously to a survival strategy, especially if they are ex-boarders, and that too needs to be held in the mind of the supervisor.

Another, perhaps more positive, way of looking at this is how the supervisor serves as mentor, as stand-in parent, for the supervisee needs good parenting. Ideally it is like growing up in a family, in that the younger supervisee needs good parenting/mentoring from the older supervisor. Duffell reminds us that most ex-boarder clients, away from parents at boarding schools, with older students, staff members being insufficient parents, need their therapist as a rent-a-dad or rent-a-mum, and above all need good parenting.[4] The same would be true in supervision. One colleague suggested a better image would be the supervisor as grandparent, helping the supervisee to be a better parent.

Survival strategies in supervision

Drawing on what Duffell calls the 'strategic survival personality', we can conceptualise the supervisee, if an ex-boarder, as one of three survival types: the rebel, who is against all authority, having experienced repressive authority figures at school; the complier, who survives by going along with boarding ethos; or even the crushed, who has been defeated by abuse or bullying. Sometimes, even, a combination of these survival strategies surface in the supervision session.[5] This is not surprising, since the supervision session has flavours of the school situation, and both supervisor and supervised are keen to show the best of their skills. Again, reflecting on this with the supervisee can be a valuable learning tool, both about the supervisee's school experience coming into the sessions and about the what the client may be awakening in the supervisee.

A problem can arise if the supervisor is surprised or frustrated when the supervisee unexpectedly re-enacts such a survival strategy. An example might be the rebel who brings a boarding school sense of privilege and superiority. My supervisees often report their survivor client exhibiting a sense of entitlement and superiority. I have picked up something similar when working with a supervisee who attended boarding school. Sometimes the superiority is not expressed subtly: one supervisee told me 'I am smarter than you are'.

I can give other examples: whereas almost all non-boarder supervisees have fitted into available session times or kept negotiating until we could agree on a time, several ex-boarders have dictated the day and hour for our fortnightly sessions. Two have demanded monthly sessions only, even though I state explicitly that I offer fortnightly or even weekly supervision. One supervisee may have left because I needed to reschedule a session so we started on the hour, whereas she wanted to start at half-past the hour. Sessions where a supervisee habitually turns up late, keeping me waiting, might also be an expression of entitlement and superiority, or a way of rebelling, or getting me to feel their anger and frustration about having to be in supervision. In the context of the child sent away to board, entitlement could be understood as a compensation for loss.[6]

More often, a complier survival strategy can be seen to be at work. The supervisee is anxious to please. He or she puts on a veneer of charm, even being slightly seductive. Sometimes the complier types seem outwardly compliant yet are inwardly defiant.

More difficult is the supervisee who resorts to the crushed survival strategy in the supervision session, even though he or she is very competent and shows both insight and potential for deeper exploration. Three supervisees spring to mind: with each, I have had to find ways to support and encourage while also finding ways of gently challenging questionable interventions or even the supervisee's 'one-down' mindset.

Good supervision is about creating a safe environment to explore feelings of uncertainty and vulnerability and, by doing so, enhance therapist awareness. I would maintain that working with ex-boarders and those clients coping with ex-boarders requires a high degree of safety and empathic containment . In such an environment, these demonstrations of a survival strategy can be explored together as a learning tool. This is not unlike how all therapists use intuition, transference and countertransference to better understand their client.

Parallel process

Parallel process is a classic tool for investigating unusual phenomena arising in the supervision process. Often what is re-enacted in the supervision can reflect what is happening between the supervisee and the client. A good example of this is a 'push me – pull me' dance: a dynamic that I and several other colleagues have found more prevalent in supervising people with ex-boarder clients. Here is one example.

The supervisee may find the client asking for closeness while also pushing the therapist away, or arriving at an important insight that becomes a heightened emotional shared moment, only to miss the next session or sessions. A variation of this is how the heightened insight is forgotten by the next session, the emotional shared moment seems to have vanished from the client's memory.

This push-pull can play out in supervision: very occasionally, when the supervisee reports the therapy to be at a crucial, acute point, I have offered an extra session or brief telephone support consultation between supervisions, only to have the offer ignored, forgotten or derided. When I listen carefully in the next presentation, I can hear echoes of this closeness-distance in the client's story or behaviour. Then I might share this observation with the supervisee, only to be surprised that the same duet gets replayed in the next supervision, the supervisee asking for help and insight with the same difficult client.

This push me-pull me dynamic happened with 'Oscar', whose father and mother were ex-boarders, and his client, an ex-boarder named 'Lucien'. In supervision session after supervision session, Oscar reported that Lucien said he was terminating, as he had reached a satisfactory end. More frequently, Lucien would text to say he was cancelling next week's session, only to reappear at a future date. Yet Lucien would also send texts and emails between sessions, describing great distress and his need for more therapy.

In supervision with me, Oscar came to realise these cancellations and entreaties occurred after a particularly meaningful session in which Lucien could see how he was treating his wife in the same way his parents had treated him. Arriving late for therapy or cancelling at the last minute or emailing about termination also happened in the weeks after Oscar had scheduled breaks for holidays or additional training.

Oscar brought his dilemma to supervision: on the one hand, wondering how he could manage to keep Lucien as a client; on the other, whether he should bring the therapy to a close. When I offered support, which in the supervisory relationship represented closeness, Oscar always ignored it. Once I pointed out how the dynamic between us reflected the interaction between him and his client Lucien, which in turn mirrored the interactions between Lucien and his wife, and even the history between Lucien and his parents, Oscar began to make connections. He was then able to find ways of introducing the idea of closeness and avoidance into his work Lucien, and Lucien could make better sense of his own behaviour.

What may be at work here is a survival strategy from boarding school: 'Don't get too close, don't rely too much on someone else.' This gets coupled with a perverse strategy: 'I need you, but I don't need you.' Another possible replay that could have been echoing here is the alternating over-closeness of term time at boarding school with enforced separations for exeats and holiday breaks. One colleague suggested how with ex-boarder clients and supervisees both assume the supervisor is included but can hardly imagine the supervisor is really there to help.

Supervisee and supervisor self-care

Working with traumatised clients is very demanding work, whether they went to boarding school or not, and therapists need to embrace self-care in order to work with this level of complexity and confusion. The same can be said for those supervising clients with ex-boarders. Therefore, the question of how the supervisee looks after themself needs to be in the room, and the same holds true for the supervisor.

From time to time, the supervisor needs to get supervision on the supervision. Sometimes ongoing supervision will suffice, especially if the supervisor's supervisor is familiar with ex-boarding clients. But sometimes it is worthwhile seeking another colleague for additional help.

I found myself in this situation recently, trying to make sense of why, with one individual only, I was constantly 'tripped up' by holiday dates or rearranged sessions. I could not make sense of why, despite my usually meticulous attention to timetable arrangements, I ended up feeling 'wrong-footed' by this one person who, for plausible reasons, had to change sessions but also 'forgot' when I was on holiday.

Finally, at a time when my ongoing supervisor was away, I shared what I was experiencing with a colleague well-versed in working with ex-boarders. He raised the possibility that my supervisee was exhibiting her rebel personality and, more significantly, projecting into me her feelings of incompetence so that she could feel both competent and in control. An added factor could be how, with the imminent agreed ending of therapy, my client had to demonstrate her competence and her ability to thrive without me. These insights immediately made sense, and I have found ways of exploring these issues in our sessions.

When I shared this vignette with colleagues, several of them said they too had experienced such a projection of incompetence through wrong-footing.

Another colleague reported at some length how he had to take on a therapeutic role with a very crushed-like supervisee who was compulsively overworking, ever fearful of not keeping clients if she took a holiday break, and fearful of not earning sufficient income. Much of their work, I am told, was looking at how a more confident stance and a more manageable schedule would result in being a better, more incisive therapist whose clients chose to stay in therapy until achieving a good-enough ending. As this supervisee became better at taking care of herself, so did her clients.

Holidays and breaks

Holidays, breaks and the eventual ending of therapy all play an important part in any therapeutic relationship, but they have an added salience with survivors of boarding school. How could they not, given the endless cadence of school terms, exeat weekends and summer holidays? Yet so many supervisees seem to overlook a connection between a break in the therapy and the material the boarding school survivor is discussing.

This insight, for me, was reinforced by Joy Schaverien's experience, as recounted in her book *Boarding School Syndrome*.[7] I noticed with one ex-boarder client that our holiday breaks triggered many memories of returning home at the end of each term at boarding school. Among the areas we explored was how he numbed any feelings of excitement about being at home, remembering instead a sense of lostness and, above all, a sense of disconnection with his parents. He had coped with taking a very 'administrative' attitude to breaks: this is what is scheduled and this is what will happen.

A more trying point came when I started talking about my forthcoming retirement. I had been advised by my own supervisor to let all clients and supervisees know some 18 months in advance in order to have plenty of time to work through feelings of loss, anger and uncertainty. This timeframe proved too long for one supervisee, who could only stay until the summer break. He closed down his nascent ability to share his feelings in our sessions, reverting to his previous linguistic gymnastics and his highly intellectual approach. He could agree he had to leave me before I left him, he could see how he was treating me like the father and brother (both also ex-boarders) by not talking, and he could not process what was happening between us.

Based partially on this experience, I now remind my supervisees that all transitions are challenging, especially holiday breaks and therapeutic endings. One colleague noted that in environments such as international schools, where students frequently move because their parents have been posted elsewhere, students make strong bonds knowing they will have to end them at the time of the next move. I believe this also happens with boarding school students, who know all along that friendships will at least change with the end of term and graduation and they thus prepare themselves. As with Alan Turing and his friendship with Christopher,[8] returning to school to find a close friend has not come back or has died, can be particularly devastating.[9] The skilled supervisor would have these issues and examples in mind when exploring changes in client behaviour even when the impending holiday break or therapeutic ending is somewhat in the future and even when they are wishes.

While it does not happen often, I have had some re-enactment with supervisees who suddenly decide to terminate or, more frequently, become less open and take fewer risks in supervision as a long holiday approaches.

Feelings

Of all the areas I am outlining in this chapter, the one that resonated time and again with my colleagues is the difficulty and necessity of encouraging the supervisee to address *feelings* – feelings between supervisor and supervisee, feelings between supervisee and client, feelings within the supervisor.

Feelings, especially feelings of confusion or vulnerability, get short shrift in boarding school, since they would expose the survivor to bullying and ostracism if openly expressed. In the same way, supervisees can fear and consequently avoid feelings in sessions and also in supervision. Yet for good supervision to happen, the supervisor must encourage the supervisee to talk about him- or herself: their feelings, perceptions and discomfort with the client, or with not knowing what is going on, or their connections between what is happening in the consulting room and what insights from theorists (for example, Donald Winnicott, Fritz Perls or Alexander Lowen) might help them understand the psychology of the client.

Frequently, and as with other types of clients, the supervisee would prefer to talk about the detail, the history, the unfairness the survivor has been recounting, and not talk about what is happening in the here-and-now between client and therapist, let alone what might be the feeling or feelings between therapist and client. The therapist may instead focus on how to fix it, on solutions, or how to offer comfort. In a way, as one supervisee said, she becomes the social worker and avoids being the therapist, modelling how to identify and utilise feelings, especially uncomfortable feelings and traumatic memories. Along with virtually all the colleagues I consulted, I find this recounting of the client's words in session, instead of the supervisee's interventions and internal dialogue, happens more in supervision of ex-boarders than with supervision of any other client group.

Conclusion

If this variety of potential dynamics seems daunting, be assured that supervising therapists with ex-boarder clients or people impacted by ex-boarders can be immensely rewarding. By providing ongoing support, guidance and knowledge, this sort of work helps a colleague navigate the complexities of a long-distant past so that a traumatised person can feel alive and relational in the present. The skills developed will help in other supervisory situations. For example, concurrently with supervising therapists presenting ex-boarder clients, I provided twice-weekly therapy for a second-generation Holocaust survivor. I found I was better able to identify many themes that are familiar with ex-boarders (such as having parents who are poorly equipped to relate, contain and identify feelings, or the hypervigilance that something terrible is about to happen) than I had been with a previous client who was also a second-generation Holocaust survivor. Similarly, an understanding of ex-boarder clients can also help the therapist working with those who were in children's homes or long-stay hospitals when children, and especially those coping with non-Holocaust transgenerational transmission of trauma.

Supervising and being supervised on ex-boarder clients has helped me deepen my understanding and sharpen my skill set in working with a panoply of traumatised adults. I have become better at making targeted interventions and exploring difficult past and current internal states. I feel I have become better placed to heal and promote healthier choices in life along the chain of client-therapist-supervisor.

Getting to healthier choices to live better in the present is, of course, what psychotherapy is all about.

Notes

1 Duffell, N. and Basset, T. (2016) *Trauma, Abandonment and Privilege. A Guide to Therapeutic Work with Boarding School Survivors*. Abingdon & New York: Routledge.
2 Schaverien, J. (2015) *Boarding School Syndrome: The Psychological Trauma of the 'Privileged' Child*. London & New York: Routledge.
3 A helpful visual presentation of Robin Shohet's 'Seven eyed model of supervision' is available online at https://terapia.co.uk/wp-content/uploads/2022/11/7-eyed-SV-Mod-1.pdf.
4 Duffell, N. and Bassett, T. (2016) *Trauma, Abandonment and Privilege. A Guide to Therapeutic Work with Boarding School Survivors*. Abingdon & New York: Routledge.
5 Duffell, N. and Basset, T. (2016) *Trauma, Abandonment and Privilege. A Guide to Therapeutic Work with Boarding School Survivors*. Abingdon & New York: Routledge.
6 Duffell, N. (2014) *Wounded Leaders: British Elitism and the Entitlement Illusion – A Psychohistory*. London: Lone Arrow Press.
7 Schaverien, J. (2015) *Boarding School Syndrome: The Psychological Trauma of the 'Privileged' Child*. London & New York: Routledge.
8 *The Imitation Game* (2014) film, written by Graham Moore and directed by Morton Tlydum. The film gives a dramatic, if fictional, perspective of Alan Turing's difficult time at boarding school.
9 Bowlby, J. (2005) *The Making and Breaking of Affectional Bonds*. London & New York: Routledge.

Chapter 14

Epilogue

Boarding Recovery

Nick Duffell

Un-making them

At the end of this collection of essays the general reader will have an idea of the damage boarding can do to interpersonal relationships, families and even nations. He or she will have followed the discussions about various routes to treatment of the syndrome within group and individual modalities. The practitioner may be heartened to know that therapeutic pathways are being discovered to treat this difficult client group. However, all roads to boarding recovery depend on one crucial step: that the ex-boarder himself recognises that the very solution to his problem in childhood – surviving boarding school – has now become *the problem*. I could equally say 'herself' and 'her', but here I shall use the masculine pronoun for simplicity and because I have worked with many more men than women in this area.

If, at some point, something provokes an ex-boarder to look inside – let us imagine some disaster prompts him to turn to therapy – he may start to recognise how surviving boarding has affected him and those around him. He may now find he experiences himself as several different selves. Perhaps there is one self who is outwardly confident, justifying the demanded investment in his future alongside another self who is on the run, secretly afraid he will be found out and caught. Maybe one self thinks he knows better than the authorities, and yet another is quite unable to complete any project that reflects well on him. Alternatively, there may be one self who has several projects on the go, while another self cannot face getting up in the morning. He may discover he is subject to several internal voices: one saying, 'Don't show your real face, it is not safe!'. Another saying, 'Be whatever they want you to become'. Yet another saying, 'Your life is about achievement', while another whispers, 'It's all worthless and there is nothing underneath your pumped-up carapace'.

It is not surprising that he encounters these dilemmas when he begins to open up. He has been dumped in the institution at an early age, forced to put away his childish self and become a grown-up 'winner' as fast as he can. He has to repay the investment in him – not with his 'being' but with his 'doing'. He has had to betray his true self – whatever that was – multiple times to survive and satisfy his

DOI: 10.4324/9781003515517-14

investors; he has then to join a class of persons who do not wish his original child-self well. It is a repeated round of self-reinvention and self-betrayal.

No wonder the many novels of British ex-spy, ex-boarder and ex-teacher at Eton, John Le Carré, endlessly reworked these themes without fail over 60 years of writing spy novels, though he himself did not even quite get the connection.[1] Nor is it a surprise that the class of winners – those who have used the 'old school tie' network, which they usually reframe as merit or hard work, as a path to leadership – are bound to repeated self-reinvention. They have yet to find the motivation to deconstruct their strategic survival personalities and the courage to face the grief of self-betrayal.

We may imagine we can see such multiple selves in British political leaders – trying to look serious, concerned, competent, but rooted in strategic short-termism, unable to acknowledge their mistakes. Once we recognise how the psychology of ex-boarders works, we may construe that behind the competent, constructed false self – the strategic survival personality (SSP), which demands strategic action over the truth – there may lurk a terrifying fear of emptiness.

The treatment of clients who outwardly function well but are driven by unconscious chronic anxiety is not easy. Any psychotherapist's daily practice includes work around early deprivation, so the client with attachment problems is familiar – especially as attachment theory and trauma work are currently in vogue. Less understood is the sophistication of the ex-boarder's SSP and the widespread devastation it can bring to individuals, couples and families over generations. Besides, it can be difficult to identify in families because this personality style is well known and accepted in British life and not considered pathological, as Winnicott noted.

Happily, an expanding group of informed practitioners is now aware of boarding school syndrome. It is still difficult to treat, however, especially by therapists from less privileged backgrounds, who may be in awe of the ex-boarder's functioning false self. But chiefly because, psycho-dynamically, it relies on psychic defence's nuclear arsenal – dissociation and compartmentalisation.

Habitual dissociation

At a boarding school, where pupils are encouraged to disown their feelings of missing their parents and also dare not disappoint their parents, dissociation can become a way of life. Young children who board must cope with their initial feelings of sadness and loss by denying them. The reality of living as a youngster in a rule-bound militaristic institution is frightening: there are hundreds of other children, it is uncomfortable and they miss home. But they must desperately shut these feelings away and pretend they do not exist. This often means that, when they are adults, they are not in touch with their emotions in quite a shocking way.

Dissociation is commonplace; it begins as a self-saving mental trick that any of us may instinctively perform when we are ashamed or embarrassed to make something known or to accept or integrate something. We put it to one side, we think of something else. We use forgetting, compartmentalising, denial or not referring to in order to assist us in maintaining our internal composure. Dissociation is a useful evolutionary survival tool – until it becomes habitual. Then it exhibits its more pathological features, which consist of running socially acceptable identity propositions, rigid compartmentalisation and exploiting other individuals or groups to reinforce the 'good' but false self.

Dissociation also involves projection. Most psychotherapists understand that disowned feelings of vulnerability are bound to end up somewhere else, mixed with disgust or idealisation. An ex-boarder's therapist must understand this, whether their original training had a model of 'transference' or not. At school the disowned vulnerable identifications are projected onto other children; later on, domestically onto wives, children or pets; in the political realm, onto politicians or immigrants. Clinically, they end up inside the therapist.

Here's how it works at school. The imperative to not fail means that someone else had better be the vulnerable one, the one who gets it wrong. Someone has to be 'the stupid child', 'the pathetic one', 'the one who gets into trouble'. The boarder knows this in his bones: 'It had better not be me', runs the inevitable internal logic. Hence the boarder, who learns to live a solitary life in a 24/7 total institution with barely any privacy – sometimes not even in bed or in the toilets – *needs others* around him, not to rely on – he has given that up – but *psycho-dynamically*, so that they can embody the roles or qualities he wants to avoid. Over time, he becomes skilled at making this happen, and the habit can become ingrained, causing widespread damage later on, in his adult life, within families.

There is a violence to this habitual self-protective mental trick; but there is also a violence in the conditions that engender it, as attachment researcher Simon Partridge explains:

> At the prep school threshold, a terrible violence, disguised by privilege, is done to children and parents – ordained by a powerful and unquestionable Establishment.[2]

Habitual dissociation has serious long-term effects and can become structural. Today, the effects can be measured in fMRI scanners. Dr Dan Siegel from the Mindful Awareness Research Center reports:

> Looking at some of the studies of the brain in dissociation, we can see that the brain literally becomes fragmented – it is no longer linking its differentiated parts.[3]

Using 'functional localisation', brain specialists can now see that if a particular cognitive problem is found after an injury to a specific area of the brain, then the likelihood arises that this part of the brain is involved in its processing. Portuguese medical brain specialist, Professor Antonio Damasio, a leading light in cognitive neuropsychology, has regularly observed such phenomena. Damasio is famous for proposing that there is a neurological substrate to emotion that is critical to our optimal functioning. It works as a mediator for what we used to think were the purely mechanistic rational processes: emotional input is needed to create values and context. Damasio concludes:

> You cannot make good decisions without emotional information.[4]

It is a crucial insight and may explain why ex-boarders in power – 'wounded leaders' as I have called them – frequently make poor decisions that seem bereft of empathy.[5]

Survival and duplicity in leadership

If the encouragement of dissociation and compartmentalisation as prime survival mechanisms and the resulting unconscious traumatic hypervigilance is indelibly linked to boarding, then Britain has a problem. Our traditionally socially valued form of raising elites does not automatically produce individuals fit for today's world; neither in the domestic sphere where relationship, exchange and sharing are needed, nor a macro world that requires cooperative, communal solutions. In its extremes, boarding could be said to foster sociopathy and duplicity. Such traits require exposing for the collective dangers they risk, including the accompanying entitlement complexes that elite institutions encourage. For, as the Jungian analyst James Grotstein said:

> When innocence has been deprived of its entitlement, it becomes a diabolical spirit.[6]

In layman's terms, Grotstein means that if you withhold someone's in-built expectations of a good start – say, growing up in a warm family – and declare this to be OK, or even good for them, then you can expect them to behave rather badly when they grow up. And this issue seriously affects British life, I believe, at many levels – in particular in leadership, where ex-boarders abound. Below is an observation from the *International Journal of Press/Politics*, entitled 'Strategic Lying' (2021) that illustrates the leadership problem when dissociation has been trained into youngsters at an early age:

> Using the UK Brexit referendum and the 2019 general election as its case study, this conceptual paper argues that strategic political lying has been designed as a priming device to set the news agenda. As an effective campaigning tactic 'strategic lying' represents a development of political spin … intensified by the increasing professionalization of political communications and the rise of social media.[7]

'Strategic lying' seems to be dissociation in action for the purpose of power. Many Anglophone leaders, for example David Cameron and Boris Johnson, when very young, went to single-sex elite boarding institutions; Donald Trump went to one renowned for its vicious 'hazing'[8] rituals.[9] We should not be surprised then, knowing what we have been focusing on here, that such leaders were forced as children to develop SSPs, based on dissociation, that would equip them to be skilled in the art of 'strategic lying'. They might practise it seamlessly, probably without being aware of it, since they have been perfectly trained from a tender age.

Getting trained *out* of such habits – submitting to an un-making of one's personality – involves a major qualitative shift in anyone's life. Often it necessitates a serious fall before an inclination that there may be anything wrong occurs. Most ex-boarders enter therapy when some catastrophe in their life, such as divorce or unemployment, looms, and not because they have identified as survivors. Sometimes, there may be a light-bulb moment when they recognise how tender and innocent their own son or daughter is and remember that they had to leave their own homes at a similar age.

Otherwise, they continue to rely on their SSPs and the entitlement complex that gets hard-wired into our elites. Entitled attitudes do not inspire much compassion in others when they are deeply ingrained. As a clinician, the only way I can overcome my own feelings is to remember that the entitlement is likely to be a compensation for *irredeemable loss* in childhood. Here is Dr Bob Johnson again:

> The broken attachments of the early days in boarding school amount to a significant but unrecognised form of bereavement.[10]

Such a 'significant but unrecognised form of bereavement' requires significant attention to redeem. Unless Britain stops normalising the boarding habit, however, raising up unwittingly traumatised alumni to positions of power and influence, the necessary attention seems unlikely to be given. Beginning in 2015, some initial small steps towards recognising the widespread abuses in British institutions were taken with the establishment of the Independent Inquiry into Child Sexual Abuse (IICSA). But there is still a long way to go towards acknowledging the normalised neglect that is the breeding ground for mistreatment of children.

In conclusion

This book has, I imagine, demonstrated some of the effects of normalised neglect to readers who may have been in any doubt and also, hopefully, provided some signposts for clinicians. My own conclusion, after over three- and-a-half decades of studying the psychological fall-out from boarding, is that the cumulative cost of this expensive education is considerable. It is paid by individuals, families and the nation. And, given its spread in the Anglosphere, one could argue that it extends into the wider world – certainly to those parts of the world historically affected by the British Imperial project. I suggest that we, as a nation, have to embrace recovery from boarding.

Readers may have found this book challenging at times because of the distress exposed in these pages, or because of challenges to prior assumptions. But I think it also brings good news: in these chapters we have heard from a growing body of practitioners who understand how boarding school affects children and how survival compromises the adults they subsequently become; we have heard, too, how boarding has heavily impacted those *not* sent away, such as siblings and adult partners. This expanded knowledge base may help survivors in feeling more justified to question their own 'privileged abandonment'. On a wider scale, it could also become a guide for those parents who are considering sending their children away to board as well as for legislators working on national education policy for the future.

This enlarged view of the psychological fall-out from boarding comes from insiders who themselves boarded as children – and we have learned how this inside view can be a double-edged sword; we also heard from those from completely different backgrounds, who had sufficient curiosity to enquire and to develop ways of working with ex-boarder adults. We have heard of treatments varying from therapeutic group-work to pioneering ways of working with trauma.

What all these methods have in common is an agreement that ex-boarders need to feel safe first before they embark on boarding recovery – this safety is crucial, despite any outward veneer of confidence that may have learned in their hot-housed schooling. And we have also heard how some boarders were not compensated by social privilege. It is no good 'outing' people as 'boarding school survivors': only self-protection expressed as defence (which can often turn hostile) will be elicited. It's safety first for boarding recovery.

The ex-boarder has to recognise and *feel* that boarding has impacted them and their family relationships, as we have seen. Next, they will have to try to recover some of the emotions that had to be disowned in childhood; they certainly will have had to betray themselves in surviving. Then some personal responsibility is required: their survival personality has probably harmed others, particularly those who have tried to love them.

Boarding recovery means acknowledging these things; it works better when it involves making amends rather than demanding apology for the original abandonment, even if that seems unfair. The practitioners writing here understand this and have the patience to wait alongside their clients for this to happen. Their chapters demonstrate this informed patience and also that this field of study may be only at the beginning: it may have to become more widely recognised before it has the power to influence social and educational policy.

The link-up between attachment therapy, trauma studies and neuroscience has already accelerated our understanding of boarding school syndrome; it is possible that new advances in these areas may continue. I was for a time involved in a university research project to explore whether broken attachments could be repaired using emerging virtual reality (VR) technology, and these new sciences may prove helpful in the future.

Meanwhile, these chapters show that we now have a growing body of reflective clinicians who understand the true cost of boarding and whose testimonies of work at the 'coalface' of these issues may help guide families, legislators and educators to choose different and healthier routes for raising children in the future.

Notes

1 I learned this through private correspondence with the late David Cornwell, aka John Le Carré, who was kind enough to endorse *The Making of Them*, in the mid 1990s.
2 Partridge, S. (2007) 'Trauma at the Threshold: An Eight-Year-Old Goes to Boarding School', *Attachment: New Directions in Psychotherapy and Relational Psychoanalysis*, 3, November, pp. 310–312.
3 Siegel, D. (2014) 'The Neurobiology of Trauma Treatment: How Brain Science Can Lead to More Targeted Interventions for Patients Healing from Trauma', webinar transcript broadcast 14 November, National Institute for the Clinical Application of Behavioral Medicine, p. 16.
4 Damasio, A.R. (1994) *Descartes' Error: Emotion, Reason, and the Human Brain*, New York: Avon Books.
5 Duffell, N. (2014) *Wounded Leaders: British Elitism and the Entitlement Illusion – a Psychohistory*, London: Lone Arrow Press.
6 Grotstein, J. (1984) *Forgery of the Soul*, in Nelson, C. and Eigen, M. (eds), *Evil, Self and Culture*, New York: Human Sciences Press.
7 Gaber, I., & Fisher, C. (2022) 'Strategic Lying: The Case of Brexit and the 2019 U.K. Election', *The International Journal of Press/Politics*, 27(2), 460–477, retrieved from https://doi.org/10.1177/1940161221994100 22 March 2024.
8 The term 'hazing' means bullying as part of an initiation ritual.
9 Duffell, N. (2016) 'Boarding Schools are a National Security Threat', in 'Argument', *Foreign Policy Magazine*, July 6, New York.
10 Edwards, R. (2021) *Inside the Mind: Freddie Mercury*, TV documentary, Bristol: Honey Bee TV.

Index

For Product Safety Concerns and Information please contact our EU
representative GPSR@taylorandfrancis.com
Taylor & Francis Verlag GmbH, Kaufingerstraße 24, 80331 München, Germany

www.ingramcontent.com/pod-product-compliance
Lightning Source LLC
Chambersburg PA
CBHW050607280326
41932CB00016B/2947